VOLUME 5

THE FAR EAST AND A NEW EUROPE

THE ILLUSTRATED
HISTORY OF THE WORLD

VOLUME 5

THE FAR EAST AND A NEW EUROPE

J. M. ROBERTS

DUNCAN BAIRD PUBLISHERS
LONDON

The Illustrated History of the World

This edition first published in Great Britain in 1999

Duncan Baird Publishers
Sixth Floor
Castle House
75–76 Wells Street
London W1P 3RE

Art Direction by Duncan Baird Publishers
Produced by Duncan Baird Publishers, London, England,
and Editorial Debate, Madrid, Spain

British Library Cataloguing-in-Publication Data:
A catalogue record for this book is available from the British Library.

ISBN 1-900131-28-5

DBP team:
Senior editor: Joanne Levêque
Assistant editor: Georgina Harris
Senior designer: Steven Painter
Assistant designer: Anita Schnable
Picture research: Julia Ruxton
Sales fulfilment: Ian Smalley
Map artwork: Russell Bell
Decorative borders: Lorraine Harrison

Editorial Debate team:
Editors and picture researchers:
Isabel Belmonte Martínez, Feliciano Novoa Portela,
Ruth Betegón Díez, Dolores Redondo
Editorial coordination: Ana Lucía Vila

Typeset in Sabon 11/15 pt
Colour reproduction by Trescan, Madrid, Spain
Printed in Singapore by Imago Limited

NOTE
The abbreviations CE and BCE are used throughout this book:
CE Common Era (the equivalent of AD)
BCE Before Common Era (the equivalent of BC)

10 9 8 7 6 5 4 3 2 1

CONTENTS

THE FAR EAST AND A NEW EUROPE

PATTERNS OF BEHAVIOUR still vigorously alive when the twentieth century began had been established in China and the Chinese sphere of civilization long before what Europeans think of as their Middle Ages. This was also true for the Indian subcontinent, whose first civilizations collapsed in circumstances still mysterious, but whose only slightly later and less remote Aryan cultures provide patterns and influences there and over much of South Asia and Indonesia which have set frameworks for the lives of hundreds of millions of people. In Asia, societies (some of considerable complexity, some until recently almost barbaric) were long to live within traditions deriving from these sources which were to remain largely unchanged for thousands of years until the coming of others vigorous enough first to threaten, sometimes to overturn and, occasionally, to invigorate them. Europe, by contrast is a late-comer to the ranks of distinctive civilizations. For a long time after the "Dark Ages", she was, indeed, hardly discernible at all as a cultural entity; rooted as she was in the larger reality of Christendom. By the end of the first millennium of the Common Era, though, there are observable at least the beginnings of the construction of a distinctive European tradition. Based on Christianity and a selection from the classical past, the role of religion in it was of overwhelming importance (but so was that of more material forces, geographical position, for instance, or of circumstance, such as the threat perceived in the alien world of Islam). Somehow, in a huge and complex process, an idea of Europe and of what it might mean to be a European, was evolving, though very slowly, and it was to emerge in the end as a dominant fact of nearly three centuries of world history.

The Eastern world was hardly aware of western Europe as a coherent force before the First Crusade at the end of the 11th century, when stories of Muslim attacks on Christian pilgrims visiting the Holy Places of the Near East were used to justify Pope Urban II's call to liberate the Holy Sepulchre in Jerusalem. This manuscript illustration depicts equestrian knights from the Spanish Order of Santiago, who fought, alongside knights from other military orders, in the crusades.

Ffernãt G. de goyas alcalde de bur-
gos guarda de nro señor el Rey.
Ffernãt de avelcea.
Johan G. de avelcea.
Alffon Gr. de camargo el moço.

1 INDIA

THOUGH ACCOMPANIED and advised by scholars and savants, Alexander the Great had only hazy ideas of what he would find in India; he seems to have thought the Indus part of the Nile and that beyond it lay more of Ethiopia. A fair amount had long been known by the Greeks about the Indian northwest, the seat of the Persian satrapy of Gandhara. But beyond that all was darkness. So far as political geography is concerned, the obscurity has remained; the relations between and, for that matter, the nature of the states of the Ganges valley at the time of Alexander's invasion are still hard to get at. A kingdom of Magadha, based on the lower river and exercising some sort of hegemony over the rest of the valley, had been the most important political unit in the subcontinent for two centuries or more, but not much is known about its institutions or history. Indian sources say nothing of Alexander's arrival in India and, as the great conqueror never penetrated beyond

Hindu art flourished in India's Gupta Empire. This detail is from a 6th-century cave painting in Ajanta representing a woman from the court of Prince Gautama.

Megasthenes on India

"To prove the Indians' artistic abilities, he recounts that they imitated the sponges that the Macedonians had seen, sewing wool with hairs with fine twine and cords and, after having matted them together, they took out the threads and dyed the wool; that many of them also learnt how to make scrubbing brushes and little jars of salves. Moreover, he says, they write letters on thickly woven cotton material, although others say that they do not know how to write at all; he also says that they use smelted bronze, but they do not decorate it. Another item in the report about India says that it is customary to stand upright to petition kings and everyone who has power and majesty, instead of throwing oneself at their feet. What is more, the country also produces precious gems as well as crystals and all types of carbuncles and pearls."

An extract from Book XV of *Geographica* by Strabo (c.60 BCE–20 CE), in which the author writes about Megasthenes' report.

Alexander the Great (356–323 BCE), who is portrayed on this 4th-century BCE silver coin, invested considerable energy in his attempt to conquer India. Although Alexander was to leave India without achieving his goal, Hellenistic culture penetrated a few settlements in the country's northwestern borderlands.

the Punjab, we can learn from Greek accounts of his day only of his disruption of the petty kingdoms of the northwest, not about the heartland of Indian power.

THE MAURYA EMPIRE AND MEGASTHENES

UNDER THE SELEUCID DYNASTY more reliable information became available in the West about what lay beyond the Punjab. This new knowledge roughly coincides with the rise of a new Indian power, the Maurya Empire, and here the India of historical record really begins. One of our informants is a Greek ambassador, Megasthenes, sent to India by the Seleucid king in about 300 BCE. Fragments of his account of what he saw were preserved long enough for later writers to quote him at length. As he travelled as far as Bengal and Orissa and was respected both as a diplomat and as a scholar, he met and interrogated many Indians. Some later writers found him a credulous and unreliable reporter; they dwelt upon his tales of people who subsisted on odours instead of food and drink, of others who were Cyclopean or whose feet were so large that they used them to shelter from the sun, of pygmies and creatures without mouths. Such tales were, of course, nonsense. But they were not necessarily without foundation. They may well represent only the highly developed awareness shown by Aryan Indians of the physical differences which marked them off from neighbours or remote acquaintances from central Asia or the jungles of Burma. Some of these must have looked very strange indeed, and some of their behaviour was, no doubt, also very strange in Indian eyes. Others among these tales may dimly reflect the curious ascetic practices of Indian religion

Time chart (c.563 BCE–1605 CE)

c.563–c.483 BCE
The life of the Buddha

327–325 BCE
Alexander the Great's expedition to India

268–232 BCE
The reign of Asoka

0

c.78–c.101 CE
The reign of King Kanishka, the greatest of the Kushana rulers

320–c.335 CE
The reign of Chandra Gupta, founder of the Gupta Dynasty

1000 CE

1206 CE
Foundation of the Delhi Sultanate

1500 CE

1526–1530 CE
The reign of Babur

1526–1858 CE
The Moghul Empire in India

1556–1605 CE
The reign of Akbar

which have never ceased to impress outsiders and usually improve in the telling. Such tales need not discredit the teller; therefore they do not mean that other things he reports must be wholly untrue. They may even have a positive value if they suggest something of the way in which Megasthenes' Indian informants saw the outside world.

CHANDRAGUPTA

Megasthenes describes the India of a great ruler, Chandragupta, founder of the Maurya line. Something is known about him from other sources. The ancients believed that he had been inspired to conquest by having as a youth seen Alexander the Great during his invasion of India. However this may be, Chandragupta usurped the Magadha throne in 321 BCE and on the ruins of that kingdom built a state which encompassed not only the two great valleys of the Indus and Ganges, but most of Afghanistan (taken from the Seleucids) and Baluchistan. His capital was at Patna, where Chandragupta inhabited a magnificent palace. It was made of wood; archaeology still cannot help us much at this stage of Indian history. From Megasthenes' account it might be inferred that Chandragupta exercised a sort of monarchical presidency but Indian sources seem to reveal a bureaucratic state, or at least something that aspired to be one. What it was like in practice is hard to see. It had been built from political units formed in earlier times, many of which had been republican or popular in organization, and many of these were connected to the emperor through great men who were his officers; some of these, nominally subjects, must often have been very independent in practice.

About the empire's inhabitants, too, Megasthenes is informative. Besides providing a long list of different peoples, he distinguished two religious traditions (one the Brahmanical and the other apparently Buddhist), mentioned the rice-eating habits of Indians and their abstention from wine except for ritual purposes, said much about

Muslim India

The Muslim conquest of India started in the Punjab in the 11th century. It was led by various Islamic dynasties, some of which were known as the "northern" (Pala, Sena, Lohara, etc.) or "southern" (Rasthrakuta, Chola, etc.) dynasties. Other ruling powers included the Ghaznavids, the Guries, the Delhi Sultanate, the Turkish dynasties and, finally, the Moghul Empire.

the domestication of elephants, and remarked on the fact (surprising to Greek eyes) that in India there were no slaves. He was wrong, but excusably so. Though Indians were not bought and sold in absolute servitude, there were those bound to labour for their masters and legally incapable of removal. Megasthenes also reported that the king diverted himself by hunting, which was done from raised platforms, or from the backs of elephants – much as tigers still are shot today.

Chandragupta is said to have spent his last days in retirement with Jains, ritually starving himself to death in a retreat near Mysore. His son and successor turned the expansive course of empire already shown by his father to the south. Maurya power began to penetrate the dense rain-forests east of Patna, and to push down the eastern coast. Finally, under the third Maurya, the conquest of Orissa gave the empire control of the land and sea routes to the south and the subcontinent acquired a measure of political unity not matched in extent for over two thousand years. The conqueror who achieved this was Asoka, the ruler under whom a documented history of India at last begins to be possible.

ASOKA

From Asoka's era survive many inscriptions bearing decrees and injunctions to his subjects. The use of this means of propagating official messages and the individual style of the inscriptions both suggest Persian and Hellenistic influence, and India under the Mauryas was certainly more continually in touch with the civilizations to the West than ever before. At Kandahar, Asoka left inscriptions in both Greek and Aramaic.

Such evidence reveals a government capable of much more than that sketched by Megasthenes. A royal council ruled over a society based on caste. There was a royal army and a bureaucracy; as elsewhere, the coming of literacy was an epoch in government as well as in culture. There seems also to have been a large secret police, or internal intelligence service. Besides raising taxes and maintaining communication and irrigation services, this machine, under Asoka, undertook the promotion of an official ideology. Asoka had himself been converted to Buddhism early in his reign. Unlike Constantine's conversion, his did not precede but followed a battle whose cost in suffering appalled Asoka. Be that as it may, the result of his conversion was the abandonment of the pattern of conquest which had marked Asoka's career until then. Perhaps this is why he felt no temptation to campaign outside the subcontinent – a limitation which, however, he shared with most Indian rulers, who never aspired to rule over barbarians, and one which, of course, was only evident when he had completed the conquest of India.

Asoka's precepts reflected a moral code of behaviour greatly influenced by Buddhism, the religion to which the emperor had converted in 260 BCE. The precept that is inscribed on this rock pillar, which is from the Buddhist site at Sarnath in northern India, refers to the expulsion of dissenting monks.

The 16th-century Adinatha temple at Ranakpur in Rajasthan is the biggest Jain temple in India. Founded by Mahavira (c.599–527 BCE), Jainism was the product of attempts to reform the Brahmanical system. It enjoyed offical patronage from the time of the 4th-century BCE emperor Chandragupta and is still an important religious force in India today.

DHAMMA

The philosophy of Asoka's Buddhism is expressed in the recommendations he made to his subjects in the rock inscriptions and pillars dating from this part of his reign (roughly after 260 BCE). The consequences are remarkable – they amounted to a complete new social philosophy. Asoka's precepts have the overall name of *Dhamma*, a variant of a Sanskrit word meaning "Universal Law", and their novelty led to much anachronistic admiration of Asoka's modernity by twentieth-century Indian politicians. Asoka's ideas are, none the less, striking. He enjoined respect for the dignity of all people, and, above all, religious toleration and non-violence. His precepts were general rather than precise and they were not laws. But their central themes are unmistakable and they were intended to provide principles of action. While Asoka's own bent and thinking undoubtedly made such ideas agreeable to him, they suggest less a wish to advance the ideas of Buddhism (this is something Asoka did in other ways) than a wish to allay differences; they look very much like a device of government for a huge, heterogeneous and religiously divided empire. Asoka was seeking to establish some focus for a measure of political and social unity spanning all India, which would be based on its people's interests as well as upon force and spying. "All men", said one of his inscriptions, "are my children."

This may also explain his pride in what might be called his "social services", which sometimes took forms appropriate to the climate: "on the roads I have had banyan trees planted," he proclaimed, "which will give shade to beasts and men." The value of this apparently simple device would have been readily apparent to those who toiled and travelled in the great Indian plains. Almost incidentally, improvements also smoothed the path of trade, but like the wells he dug and the rest-houses he set up at nine-mile intervals, the banyan trees were an expression of *Dhamma*. Yet *Dhamma* does not appear to have succeeded, for we hear of sectarian struggles and the resentment of priests.

THE SPREAD OF BUDDHISM

Asoka did better in promoting simple Buddhist evangelization. His reign brought the first great expansion of Buddhism, which had prospered, but had remained hitherto confined to northeastern India. Now Asoka sent missionaries to Burma who did well; in Ceylon others did better still, and from his day the island was predominantly Buddhist. Those sent, more optimistically, to Macedonia and Egypt were less successful, though Buddhist teaching left its mark on some of the philosophies of the Hellenistic world and some Greeks were converted.

The vitality of Buddhism under Asoka may in part explain signs of reaction in the Brahmanical religion. It has been suggested that a new popularization of certain cults which dates from about this time may have been a conscious Brahman response to challenge. Notably, the third and second centuries BCE brought a new prominence to the cults of two of the most popular avatars of Vishnu. One is the proteiform Krishna, whose legend offers vast possibilities of psychological identification to the worshipper, and the other Rama, the embodiment of the benevolent king, good husband and son, a family god. It was in the second century BCE, too, that the two great Indian epics, the *Mahabharata* and the *Ramayana*, began to take their final form. The first of these was extended by a long passage which is now the most famous work of Indian literature and its greatest poem, the *Bhagavad Gita*, or "Song of the lord". It was to become the central testament of Hinduism, weaving around the figure of Vishnu/Krishna the ethical doctrine of duty in the performance of the obligations laid upon one by membership of one's class (*dharma*) and the recommendation that works of devotion, however meritorious, might be less efficacious than love of Krishna as a means to release into eternal happiness.

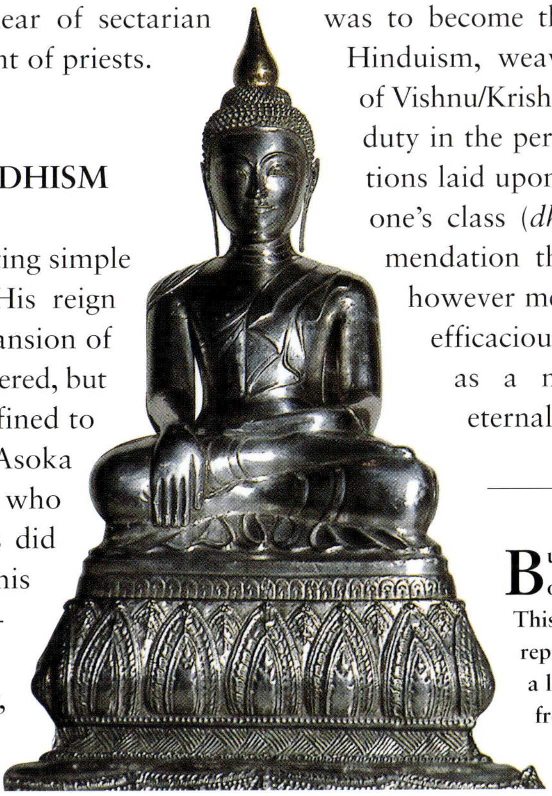

Buddhism eventually spread over almost the whole of Asia. This 19th-century statue, which represents the Buddha seated on a lotus-flower throne, comes from Burma, where Buddhism is still the most popular religion today.

MAURYA DECLINE

Mounted archers were the shock troops of the Parthian Empire, which harassed the western border of the Punjab region. Above are the obverse and reverse of a Parthian coin dating from the 2nd century BCE.

These were important facts for the future of Hinduism, but were to develop fully only over a period which ran on far past the crumbling of the Maurya Empire, and this began soon after Asoka's death. Such a disappearance is so dramatically impressive – and the Maurya Empire had been so remarkable a thing – that, though we are tempted to look for some special explanation, yet perhaps there is only a cumulative one. In all ancient empires except the Chinese, the demands made on government eventually outgrew the technical resources available to meet them: when this happened, they broke up. The Mauryas had done great things. They conscripted labour to exploit large areas of wasteland, thereby both feeding a growing population and increasing the tax base of the empire. They undertook great irrigation works which survived them for centuries. Trade prospered under Maurya rule, if we may judge from the way northern pottery spread throughout India in the third century BCE. They kept up a huge army and a diplomacy which ranged as far afield as Epirus. The cost, however, was great. The government and army were parasitical upon an agricultural economy which could not be limitlessly expanded. There was a limit to what it could pay for. Nor, though bureaucracy seems at this distance to have been centralized in principle, was it likely to have been very effective, let alone flawless. Without a system of control and recruitment to render it independent of society, it fell at one end into the control of the favourites of the monarch on whom all else depended and at the other into the gift of local élites who knew how to seize and retain power.

One political weakness was rooted deep in pre-Maurya times. Indian society had already sunk its anchors in the family and the institutions of caste. Here, in social institutions rather than in a dynasty or an abstract notion of a continuing state (let alone a nation) was the focus of Indian loyalties. When an Indian empire began to crumble under economic, external or technical pressures, it had no unthinking popular support to fall back upon. This is a striking indication of the lack of success of Asoka's attempts to provide ideological integument for his empire. What is more, India's social institutions, and especially caste, in its elaborated forms, imposed economic costs. Where functions were inalterably allocated by birth, economic aptitude was held back. So was ambition. India had a social system which was bound to cramp the possibilities of economic growth.

POLITICAL DISUNITY RETURNS

The assassination of the last Maurya was followed by a Ganges dynasty of Brahmanical origin and thereafter the story of India for five hundred years is once more one of political disunity. References in Chinese sources become available from the end of the second century BCE, but it cannot be said that they have made agreement between scholars about what was happening in India any easier:

even the chronology is still largely conjectural. Only the general processes stand out.

The most important of these is a new succession of invasions of India from the historic northwestern routes. First came Bactrians, descendants of the Greeks left behind by Alexander's empire on the upper Oxus, where by 239 BCE they had formed an independent kingdom standing between India and Seleucid Persia. Our knowledge of this mysterious realm is largely drawn from its coins and has grave gaps in it, but it is known that a hundred years later the Bactrians were pushing into the Indus valley. They were the foremost in a current which was to flow for four centuries. A complex series of movements was in train whose origins lay deep in the nomadic societies of Asia. Among those who followed the Indo-Greeks of Bactria and established themselves at different times in the Punjab were Parthians and Scythians. One Scythian king, according to legend, received St Thomas the apostle at his court.

THE KUSHANAS

One important people came all the way from the borders of China and left behind them the memory of another big Indian empire, stretching from Benares beyond the mountains to the caravan routes of the steppes. These were the Kushanas. Historians still argue about how they are related to other nomadic peoples, but two things about them seem clear enough. The first is that they (or their rulers) were both enthusiastically Buddhist and also patronized some Hindu sects. The second was that their political interests were focused in central Asia, where their greatest king died fighting.

The Kushana period brought strong foreign influences once more into Indian culture, often from the West, as the Hellenistic flavour of its sculpture, particularly of the Buddha, shows. It marks an epoch in another way, for the depicting of the Buddha was something of an innovation in Kushana times. The Kushanas carried it very far and the Greek models gradually gave way to the forms of Buddha familiar today. This was one expression of a new complicating and developing of Buddhist religion. One thing which was

This stucco head of the Buddha dates from the Kushana period (c.50–240 CE). Although the Buddha's face is clearly influenced by the Hellenistic style of earlier sculpture, the Indian features are quite pronounced.

happening was that Buddhism was being popularized and materialized; Buddha was turning into a god. But this was only one among many changes. Millenarianism, more emotional expressions of religion and more sophisticated philosophical systems were all interplaying with one another. To distinguish Hindu or Buddhist "orthodoxy" in this is somewhat artificial.

THE ASSIMILATION OF INVADERS

In the end the Kushanas succumbed to a greater power: Bactria and the Kabul valley were taken by Artaxerxes early in the third century CE. Soon after, another Sassanid king took the Kushana capital of Peshawar – and such statements make it easy to feel impatient with the narrative they provide. Contemplating them, the reader may well feel with Voltaire: "What is it to me if one king replaces another on the banks of the Oxus and Jakartes?" It is like the fratricidal struggles of Frankish kings, or of the Anglo-Saxon kingdoms of the Heptarchy, on a slightly larger scale. It is indeed difficult to see much significance in this ebb and flow beyond its registration of two great constants of Indian history, the importance of the northwestern frontier as a cultural conduit and the digestive power of Hindu civilization. None of the invading peoples could in the end resist the assimilative power India always showed. New rulers were before long ruling Hindu kingdoms (whose roots went back possibly beyond Maurya times to political units of the fourth and fifth centuries BCE), and adopting Indian ways.

Invaders never penetrated far to the south. After the Maurya break-up, the Deccan long remained separate and under its own Dravidian rulers. Its cultural distinction persists even today. Though Aryan influence was stronger there after the Maurya era and Hinduism and Buddhism were never to disappear, the south was not again truly integrated politically with the north until the coming of the British Raj.

TRADE

In this confusing period not all India's contacts with outsiders were violent. Trade with Roman merchants grew so visibly that Pliny blamed it (wrongly) for draining gold out of the empire. We have little hard information, it is true, except about the arrival of embassies from India to negotiate over trade but the remark suggests that one feature of India's trade with the West was already established; what Mediterranean markets sought were luxuries which only India could supply and there was little they could offer in return except bullion. This pattern held until the nineteenth century. There are also other interesting signs of intercontinental contacts arising from trade. The sea is a uniter of the cultures of trading communities; Tamil words for commodities turn up in Greek, and Indians from the south had traded

A 6th-century bronze statue of the Buddha, made during the Gupta period. Many of the Gupta emperors were known as patrons of the arts and numerous Indian artistic styles still common today were established during that era.

Gupta-period stone temples, with their smooth and supple carvings, profoundly influenced the development of Indian art for hundreds of years. This 5th-century stone bas-relief, which depicts lovers enjoying a dance performance, was found among the ruins of a Gupta temple in Deogarh in Rajasthan.

with Egypt since Hellenistic times. Later, Roman merchants lived in southern ports where Tamil kings kept Roman bodyguards. Finally, it seems likely that whatever the truth may be about the holy apostle Thomas, Christianity appeared in India first in the western trading ports, possibly as early as the first century CE.

THE GUPTA EMPIRE

POLITICAL UNITY DID NOT APPEAR again even in the north until hundreds of years had passed. A new Ganges valley state, the Gupta Empire, was then the legatee of five centuries of confusion. Its centre was at Patna, where a dynasty of Gupta emperors established itself. The first of these, another Chandra Gupta, began to reign in 320 CE, and within a hundred years north India was once more for a time united and relieved of external pressure and incursion. It was not so big an empire as Asoka's, but the Guptas preserved theirs longer. For some two centuries north India enjoyed under them a sort of Antonine age, later to be imagined with nostalgia as India's classical period.

ART IN THE GUPTA ERA

The Gupta age brought the first great consolidation of an Indian artistic heritage. From the earlier times little has survived from before the perfection of stone-carving under the Mauryas. The columns which are its major monuments were the culmination of a native tradition of stonework. For a long time stone-carving and building still showed traces of styles evolved in an age of wood construction, but techniques were well advanced before the arrival of Greek influence, once thought to be the origin of Indian stone sculpture. What the Greeks brought were new artistic motifs and techniques from the West. If we are to judge by what survives, the major deployment of these influences was found in Buddhist sculpture until well into the Common Era. But before the Gupta era, a rich and indigenous tradition of Hindu sculpture, too, had been established, and from this time India's artistic life is mature and self-sustaining. In Gupta times there began to be built the great numbers of stone temples (as distinct from excavated and embellished caves) which are the great glories of both Indian art and architecture before the Muslim era.

LITERATURE

Gupta civilization was also remarkable for its literary achievement. Again, the roots are deep. The standardization and systematization of Sanskrit grammar just before Maurya times opened the path to a literature which could be shared by the élite of the whole subcontinent. Sanskrit was a tie uniting north and south in spite of their cultural differences. The great epics were given their classical form in Sanskrit (though they were also available in translations into local languages) and in it wrote the greatest of Indian poets, Kalidasa. He was also a dramatist, and in the Gupta era there emerges from the shadowy past the Indian theatre whose traditions have been maintained and carried into the popular Indian film of the present day.

Intellectually, too, the Gupta era was a great one. It was in the fifth century that Indian arithmeticians invented the decimal system. A layman can perhaps glimpse the importance of this more readily than he can that of the Indian philosophical resurgence of the same period. The resurgence was not confined to religious thought, but what can be gathered from it about general attitudes or the direction of culture seems highly debatable. In a literary text such as the *Kama Sutra* a western observer may be most struck by the prominence given in it to the acquisition of techniques whose use, however stimulating to the individual, can at most have absorbed only a small fraction of the interest and time of a tiny élite. A negative point is perhaps safest: neither the emphasis on *dharma* of the Brahmanical tradition, nor the ascetic severities of some Indian teachers, nor the frank acceptance of sensual pleasure suggested by many texts beside the *Kama Sutra* have anything in common with the striving, militant puritanism so strong in both the Christian and Islamic traditions. Indian civilization moved to very different rhythms from those further west; here, perhaps, lay its deepest strength and the explanation of its powers of resistance to alien cultures.

These fragments of manuscripts form part of a collection of more than 100 similar pieces, all of which are thought to have belonged to the Buddhist school of Mahasangika-Lokottaravadin. Although some of the texts have been dated to as early as the 2nd century, most of the fragments found date from the Gupta period (4th and 5th centuries).

Kalidasa's poetry

"You are not the only one to feel sad when you leave the village;
even the trees are touched by the sadness
that your separation produces.
You only have to look: the deer
they can hardly eat the grass,
the cherry trees stop their dance
and the reeds drop their pale leaves on the earth
as if they were tears."

An extract from *Sakuntala* by the Indian poet Kalidasa.

HINDU SOCIETY

In the Gupta era Indian civilization came to its mature, classical form. Chronology derived from politics is a hindrance here; important developments flow across the

The caste system

Although the term caste comes from the Latin *castus*, meaning "pure", the Indians use the word *varna*, which means "colour", demonstrating the system's racial origins. The caste system has been present in many cultures throughout history, but nowhere has it taken root to the same extent as in India. Most researchers believe that it emerged after the conquest of India by the Aryans in around 1500 BCE. The Aryans probably imposed their strongly hierarchical social structure – consisting of a religious and judicial body, a military class and a merchant class – on the rest of Hindu society. This social structure was then consolidated during the Brahman period.

Theoretical concepts, taken from the *Rig-Veda*, suggest that there were originally four Indian castes: the Brahmans (priests), the Kshatriyas (warriors), the Vaishyas (farmers and merchants) and the Shudras (labourers). Each of the main castes has been gradually subdivided into innumerable layers, which are known as *jatis*. A further group, the Untouchables, are considered so impure that they are outside the caste system. Despite modern legislation outlawing discrimination against them, Untouchables are still often treated as less than human and are obliged to carry out "unclean" tasks such as those of "sweepers": cleaning lavatories and collecting manure.

The castes to which individuals belong govern every facet of their lives, including the job they do, the food they eat and whom they are permitted to marry. Caste should not, however, be confused with social class, since paradoxes abound: poverty-stricken Brahmans and wealthy Untouchables are not uncommon.

Between the 3rd and 2nd centuries BCE, the Brahman priests reacted against the threat to Hinduism posed by the arrival of Buddhism, making their own rituals ever more elaborate and exclusive. As a result, ordinary Hindus increasingly turned to the more open bhakti *(devotion) movement, which was at its height between the 6th and 16th centuries.* Bhakti *cults emphasized the worshipper's personal relationship with a deity and often rejected the intermediary role of the priest, proclaiming that direct contact with the divine was available to men and women of every caste. In this 19th-century painting, Krishna's love for Rada is represented, symbolizing* bhakti *devotion.*

boundaries of any arbitrary period. Nevertheless, in Gupta culture we can sense the presence of the fully evolved Hindu society. Its outstanding expression was a caste system which by then had come to overlay and complicate the original four-class division of Vedic society. Within castes which locked them into well-defined groups for marriage and, usually, into their occupations, most Indians lived a life close to the land. The cities were for the most part great markets or great centres of pilgrimage. Most Indians were, as they are now, peasants, whose lives were lived within the assumptions of a religious culture already set in its fundamental form in pre-Maurya times. Some of its later developments have been mentioned already; others run on past the Gupta period and will have to be discussed elsewhere. Of their vigour and power there can be no doubt; with centuries of further elaboration ahead, they were already expressed in Gupta times in a huge development of carving and sculpture which manifest the power of popular religion and

Hinduism and the Ganges river

The Ganges river rises on the southern slopes of the Himalayas and after flowing for a total of 1,680 miles (2,700 km) enters the Bay of Bengal. The great river passes across the plains of northeastern India and into Bangladesh, where it is joined by the waters of the Brahmaputra.

For Hindus, the Ganges has been a sacred river from time immemorial – they believe that the goddess Ganga was born in Mount Meru, where the gods reside. The god Shiva's hair served as a pathway down from the holy mountain to the earth.

The banks of the Ganges are lined with countless temples, sanctuaries and Hindu holy places. These include Hardwar, one of the seven sacred cities and home every 12 years to the important Kumba Mela religious festival. During the festival thousands of Hindu pilgrims immerse themselves in the Ganges' waters, which they believe will purify their *karma* from their former and current lives, with the hope of achieving a perfect reincarnation.

Another important pilgrimage centre is the city of Allahabad (also known as Prayag, meaning "Place of Sacrifice"), where, legend has it, the invisible Sarasvati river joins the Ganges and the Yamuna.

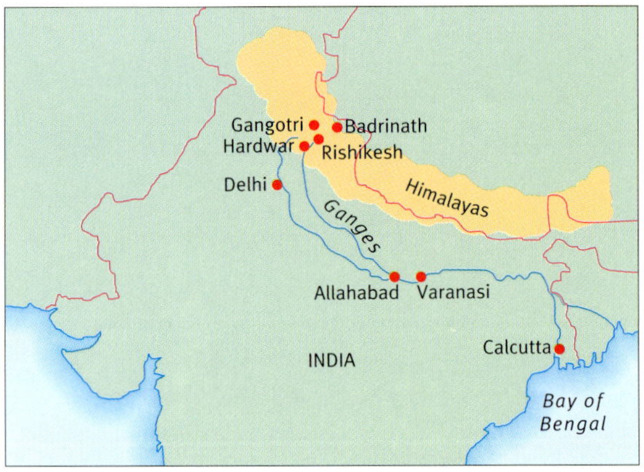

This map shows the route of the Ganges, from its source in the Himalayas to its estuary in the Bay of Bengal.

Varanasi, another of the sacred cities, is a place of pilgrimage not only for Hindus, but also for Buddhists and Jains. According to tradition, the Buddha, Siddhartha Gautama, gave his first sermon (on "The Foundation of Righteousness") in Sarnath, near Varanasi, and Mahavira, the founder of Jainism, lived in the historic city.

take their place alongside the *stupa*s and Buddhas of pre-Gupta times as enduring features of the Indian landscape. Paradoxically, India, largely because of its religious art, is a country where we have perhaps more evidence about the minds of the people of the past than we have about their material lives. We may know little about the precise way in which Gupta taxation actually weighed on the peasant (though we can guess), but in the contemplation of the endless dance of the gods and demons, the forming and dissolving patterns of animals and symbols, we can touch a world still alive and to be found in the village shrines and juggernauts of our own day. In India as nowhere else, there is some chance of access to the life of the uncounted millions whose history should be recounted in such books as this, but which usually escapes us.

RELIGIOUS CHANGES

In the climax of Hindu civilization, between Gupta times and the coming of Islam, the fertility of Indian religion, the soil of Indian culture, was hardly troubled by political events. One symptom was the appearance by 600 or thereabouts of an important new cult which quickly took a place it was never to lose in the Hindu worship, that of the mother-goddess Devi. Some have seen in her an expression of a new sexual emphasis which marked both Hinduism and Buddhism. Her cult was part of a general effervescence of religious life, lasting a couple of centuries or more, for a new popular emotionalism is associated with the cults of Shiva and Vishnu at about the same time. Dates are not very helpful here; we have to think of continuing change during the whole of the centuries corresponding to those of the early Common Era whose result was the final evolution of the old Brahmanical religion into Hinduism.

From it there emerged a spectrum of practice and belief offering something for all needs. The philosophic system of the *Vedanta* (which stressed the unreality of the factual and material and the desirability of the winning of disengagement in true knowledge of reality, *brahma*) was at one end of a spectrum which ran at the other into the village superstitions which worshipped local deities long assimilated into one of the many cults of Shiva or Vishnu. Religious effervescence thus found expression antithetically in the simultaneous growth of image worship and the rise of new austerity. Animal sacrifice had never stopped. It was one of the things now endorsed by a new strictness of conservative religious practice. So was a new rigidity of attitudes towards women and their intensified subordination. The religious expression of this was an upsurge of child marriage and the practice called *suttee*, or self-immolation of Indian widows on their husbands' funeral pyres.

MAHAYANA BUDDHISM

The richness of Indian culture is such that this coarsening of religion was accompanied also by the development to their highest pitch of the philosophical tradition of the *Vedanta*, the culmination of Vedic tradition, and the new development of *Mahayana* Buddhism, which asserted the divinity of the Buddha. The roots of the latter went back to early deviations from the Buddha's teaching on contemplation, purity and non-attachment. These deviations had favoured a more ritualistic and popular religious approach and also stressed a new interpretation of the Buddha's role. Instead of merely being understood as a teacher and an example, Buddha was now seen as the greatest of *bodhisattvas*, saviours who, entitled to the bliss of self-annihilation themselves, nevertheless rejected it to remain in the world and teach people the way to salvation.

To become a *bodhisattva* gradually became the aim of many Buddhists. In part, the efforts of a Buddhist council summoned by the Kushan ruler Kanishka had been directed towards re-integrating two tendencies in Buddhism which were increasingly divergent. This had not been successful. *Mahayana* Buddhism (the word means "great vehicle") focused upon a Buddha who was effectively a divine saviour who might be worshipped and followed in faith, one manifestation of a great, single heavenly Buddha who begins to look somewhat like the undifferentiated soul behind all things found in Hinduism. The disciplines of austerity and contemplation Gautama had taught were now increasingly confined to a minority of orthodox Buddhists, the followers of *Mahayana* winning conversions among the masses. One sign of this was the proliferation in the first and second centuries CE of statues and representations of the

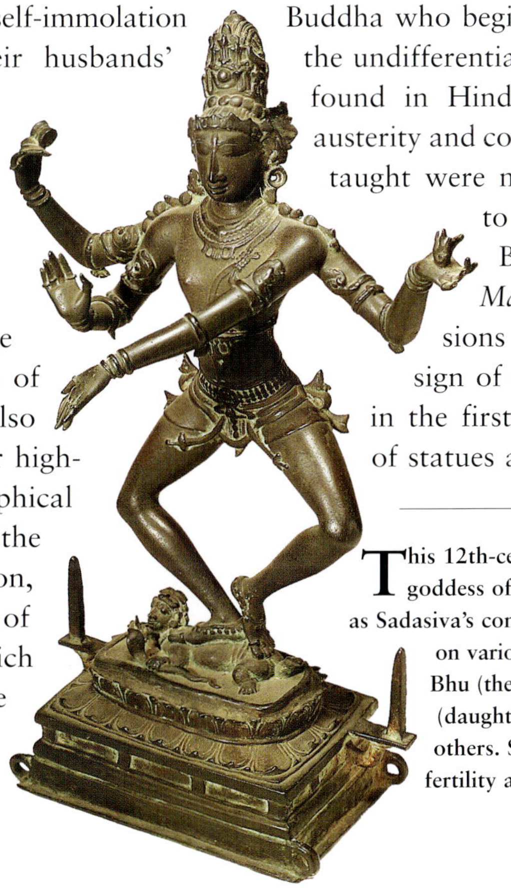

This 12th-century statue represents Devi, the goddess of the Hindu pantheon, portrayed as Sadasiva's consort, with four arms. Devi takes on various forms, sometimes appearing as Bhu (the ancient earth goddess) or Parvati (daughter of the Himalayas), among others. She is generally associated with fertility and with the earth.

Buddha, a practice which had been hitherto restrained by the Buddha's prohibition of idol-worship. *Mahayana* Buddhism eventually replaced earlier forms in India, and spread also along the central Asian trade routes through Central Asia to China and Japan. The more orthodox tradition did better in Southeast Asia and Indonesia.

INDIAN PHILOSOPHY

Hinduism and Buddhism were thus both marked by changes which broadened their appeal. The Hindu religion prospered better, though there is a regional factor at work here; since Kushan times, the centre of Indian Buddhism had been the northwest, the region most exposed to the devastations of the Hun raiders. Hinduism prospered most in the south. Both the northwest and the south, of course, were zones where cultural currents intermingled most easily with those from the classical Mediterranean world, in the one across land and in the other by sea.

These changes provoke a sense of culmination and climax. They matured only shortly before Islam arrived in the subcontinent, but early enough for a philosophical outlook to have solidified which has marked India

Buddhist *bodhisattvas*, such as the one portrayed in this *Mahayana* stone bas-relief, were masters of the "six perfections": energy, generosity, meditation, morality, patience and wisdom.

ever since and has shown astonishing invulnerability to competing views. At its heart was a vision of endless cycles of creation and reabsorption into the divine, a picture of the cosmos which predicated a cyclic and not a linear history. What difference this made to the way Indians have actually behaved – right down to the present day – is a huge subject, and almost impossible to grasp. It might be expected to lead to passivity and scepticism about the value of practical action, yet this is very debatable. Few Christians live lives that are logically wholly coherent with their beliefs and there is no reason to expect Hindus to be more consistent. The practical activity of sacrifice and propitiation in Indian temples survives still. Yet the direction of a whole culture may none the less be determined by the emphasis of its distinctive modes of thought, and it is difficult not to feel that much of India's history has been determined by a world outlook which stressed the limits rather than the potential of human action.

THE IMPACT OF ISLAM ON INDIA

FOR THE BACKGROUND to Islam in India we must return to 500 CE or so. From about that time, northern India was once again divided in obedience both to the centrifugal tendencies which afflicted early empires and to the appearance of a mysterious invasion of "Hunas". Were they perhaps Huns? Certainly they behaved like them, devastating much of the northwest, sweeping away many of the established ruling families. Across the mountains, in Afghanistan, they mortally wounded Buddhism, which had been strongly established there. In the subcontinent itself, this anarchic period did less fundamental damage. Though the northern plains had broken up again into warring kingdoms, Indian cities do not seem to have been much disturbed and peasant life recovers quickly from all but the worst blows. Indian warfare appears rapidly to have acquired important and effective conventional limits on its potential for destructiveness. The state of affairs over much of the north at this time seems in some ways rather like that of some European countries during the more anarchic periods of the Middle Ages, when feudal relationships more or less kept the peace between potentially competitive grandees but could not completely contain outbreaks of violence which were essentially about different forms of tribute.

Mahayana Buddhism created a new anthropomorphic configuration of the Buddha in the Kushana period: the upright posture and monastic wrap became the defining characteristics of the statuary of the Buddha, as is demonstrated by this 8th- or 9th-century bronze.

Meanwhile, Islam had come to India. It did so first through Arab traders on the western coasts. Then, in 712 or thereabouts, Arab armies conquered Sind. They got no further, gradually settled down and ceased to trouble the Indian peoples. A period of calm followed which lasted until a Ghaznavid ruler broke deep into India early in the eleventh century with raids which were destructive, but again did not produce radical change. Indian religious life for another two centuries moved still to its own rhythms, the most striking changes being the decline of Buddhism and the rise of Tantrism, a semi-magical and superstitious growth of practices promising access to holiness by charms and ritual. Cults centred

In 1192 the Turkish leader Muhammad Ghur defeated the Hindu alliance. His successor, a slave and loyal general, Qutb ud-Din Aibvak, built the Qutb-Minar in Delhi. This victory tower, 240 ft (73 m) high, was erected to proclaim the victory of Islam over the infidel and became a potent symbol of the Muslim domination of India.

on popular festivals at temples also prospered, no doubt in the absence of a strong political focus in post-Gupta times. Then came a new invasion of central Asians.

MUSLIM INVADERS

The new invaders were Muslims and were drawn from the complex of Turkish peoples. Theirs was a different sort of Islamic onslaught from earlier ones, for they came to stay, not just to raid. They first established themselves in the Punjab in the eleventh century and then launched a second wave of invasions at the end of the twelfth century which led within a few decades to the establishment of Turkish sultans at Delhi who ruled the whole of the Ganges valley. Their empire was not monolithic. Hindu kingdoms survived within it on a tributary basis, as Christian kingdoms survived to be tributaries of Mongols in the West. The Muslim rulers, perhaps careful of their material interests, did not always support their co-religionists of the *Ulema* who sought to proselytize and were willing to persecute (as the destruction of Hindu temples shows).

The heartland of the first Muslim empire in India was the Ganges valley. The invaders rapidly overran Bengal and later established themselves on the west coast of India and the tableland of the Deccan. Further south they did not penetrate and Hindu society survived there largely unchanged. In any case, their rule was not to last long even in the north. In 1398 Timur Lang's army sacked Delhi after a devastating approach march which was made all the speedier, said one chronicler, because of the Mongols' desire to escape from the stench of decay arising from the piles of corpses they left in their wake. In the troubled waters after this disaster, generals and local potentates struck out for themselves and Islamic India fragmented again. None the less, Islam was by now established in the subcontinent, the greatest challenge yet seen to India's assimilative powers, for its active, prophetic, revelatory style was wholly antithetical both to Hinduism and to Buddhism (though Islam, too, was to be subtly changed by them).

THE DELHI SULTANATE: BABUR

New sultans emerged at Delhi but long showed no power to restore the former Islamic empire. Only in the sixteenth century was it revived by a prince from outside, Babur of Kabul. On his father's side he descended from Timur and on his mother's from Chinghis, formidable advantages and a source of inspiration to a young man schooled in adversity. He quickly discovered he had to fight for his inheritance and there can have been few monarchs who, like Babur, conquered a city of the importance of Samarkand at the age of fourteen (albeit to lose it again almost at once). Even when legend and anecdote are separated, he remains, in spite of cruelty and duplicity, one of the most attractive figures among great rulers: munificent, hardy, courageous, intelligent and sensitive. He left a remarkable autobiography, written from notes made throughout his life, which was to be treasured by his descendants as a source of inspiration and guidance. It displays a ruler who did not think of himself as Mongol in culture, but Turkish in the tradition of those peoples long settled in the former eastern provinces of the Abbasid caliphate. His taste and culture were formed by the inheritance of the Timurid princes of Persia; his love of gardening and poetry came from that country and fitted easily into the setting of an Islamic India whose court cultures were already much influenced by Persian models. Babur was a bibliophile, another Timurid trait; it is reported that when he took Lahore he went at once to his defeated adversary's library to choose texts from it to send as gifts to his sons. He himself wrote, among other things, a forty-page account of his conquests in Hindustan, noting its customs and caste structure and, even more minutely, its wildlife and flowers.

This 16th-century illustration depicts the troops of Timur Lang, one of Babur of Kabul's ancestors, sacking the city of Isfahan.

THE MOGHUL EMPIRE

BABUR WAS CALLED IN TO INDIA by Afghan chiefs, but had his own claims to make to the inheritance of the Timurid line in Hindustan. This was to prove the beginning of Moghul India; Moghul was the Persian word for Mongol, though it was not a word Babur applied to himself. Originally, those whose discontent and intrigue called him forward had only aroused in him the ambition of

In his famous memoirs Babur expresses his great love of gardening and natural history. This 16th-century painting depicts Babur in a palace garden.

conquering the Punjab, but he was soon drawn further. In 1526 he took Delhi after the sultan had fallen in battle. Soon Babur was subduing those who had invited him to come to India while at the same time conquering the infidel Hindu princes who had seized an opportunity to renew their own independence. The result was an empire which in 1530, the year of his death, stretched from Kabul to the borders of Bihar. Babur's body, significantly, was taken, as he had directed to Kabul, where it was buried in his favourite garden with no roof over his tomb, in the place he had always thought of as home.

The reign of Babur's son, troubled by his own instability and inadequacy and by the presence of half-brothers anxious to exploit the Timurid tradition which, like the Frankish, prescribed the division of a royal inheritance, showed that the security and consolidation of Babur's realm could not be taken for granted. For five years of his reign he was driven from Delhi, though he returned there to die in 1555. His heir, Akbar, born during his father's distressed wanderings (but enjoying the advantages of a very auspicious horoscope and the absence of rival brothers), thus came to the throne as a boy. He inherited at first only a small part of his grandfather's domains, but was to build from them an empire recalling that of Asoka, winning the awed respect of Europeans, who called him "the Great Moghul".

AKBAR

AKBAR HAD MANY kingly qualities. He was brave to the point of folly – his most obvious weakness was that he was headstrong – enjoying as a boy riding his own fighting elephants and preferring hunting and hawking to lessons (one consequence was that, uniquely in Babur's line, he was almost illiterate). He once killed a tiger with his sword in single combat and was proud of his marksmanship with a gun (Babur had introduced firearms to the Moghul army). Yet he was also, like his predecessors, an admirer of learning and all things beautiful. He collected books, and in his reign Moghul architecture

From "The Life of Akbar", this 16th-century illustration depicts the celebrations that followed the birth in 1569 of Salim, son of Akbar and Mariam Uz-Zamani Begum, who can be seen in the top left of the picture. Prince Salim would eventually inherit his father's throne as Emperor Jahangir (1605–1627).

Akbar was a skilled and experienced military leader. At the age of 15 he had conquered Ajmer and a large part of central India. In 1567–1568 the emperor brought most of present-day Rajasthan under his control when his armies took Chittoor and Ranthambor; Akbar is shown leading the siege of the latter in this illustration.

and painting came to their peak, a department of court painters being maintained at his expense. Above all, he was statesmanlike in his handling of the problems posed by religious difference among his subjects.

Akbar reigned for almost half a century, until 1605, thus just overlapping at each end the reign of his contemporary, Queen Elizabeth I of England. Among his first acts on reaching maturity was to marry a Rajput princess who was, of course, a Hindu. Marriage always played an important part in Akbar's diplomacy and strategy, and this lady (the mother of the next emperor) was the daughter of the greatest of the Rajput kings and therefore an important catch. None the less, something more than policy may be seen in the marriage. Akbar had already permitted the Hindu ladies of his harem to practise the rites of their own religion within it, an unprecedented act for a Muslim ruler. Before long, he abolished the poll tax on non-Muslims; he was going to be the emperor of all religions, not a Muslim fanatic. Akbar even went on to listen to Christian teachers; he invited the Portuguese who had appeared on the west coast to send missionaries learned in their faith to his court and three Jesuits duly arrived there in 1580. They disputed vigorously with Muslim divines before the emperor and received many marks of his favour, though they were disappointed in their long-indulged hope of his conversion. He seems, in fact, to have been a man of genuine religious feeling and eclectic mind; he went so far as to try to institute a new religion of his own, a sort of mishmash of Zoroastrianism, Islam and Hinduism. It had little success except among prudent courtiers and offended some.

IMPERIAL EXPANSION

However Akbar's religious tolerance is interpreted, it is evident that the appeasement of non-Muslims would ease the problems of government in India. Babur's advice in his memoirs to conciliate defeated enemies pointed in this direction too, for Akbar launched himself on a career of conquest and added many new Hindu territories to his empire. He rebuilt the unity of northern India from Gujarat to Bengal and began the conquest of the Deccan. The empire was governed by a system of administration much of which lasted well into the era of the British Raj, though Akbar was less an innovator in government than the confirmer and establisher of institutions he inherited. Officials ruled in the emperor's name and at his pleasure; they had the primary function of providing soldiers as needed and raising the land tax, now reassessed on an empire-wide

India's Moghul Empire was at its most splendid under Akbar. This miniature from "The Life of Akbar" gives an impression of the elegance of the imperial court. The emperor, seated on his throne, is depicted receiving Prince Abdur Rahin in the city of Agra in 1562.

and more flexible system devised by a Hindu finance minister and which seems to have had an almost unmatched success in that it actually led to increases in production which raised the standard of living in Hindustan. Among other reforms which were notable in intention if not in effect was the discouragement of *suttee*.

Moghul India

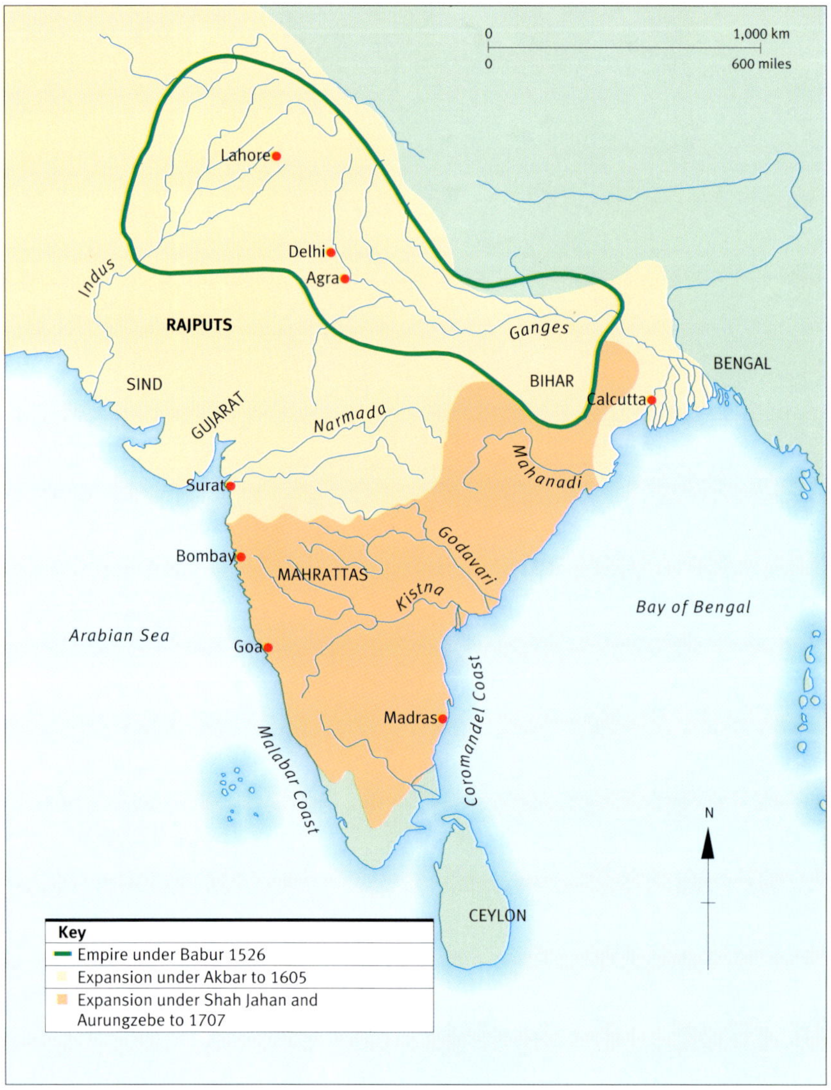

During the reign of Akbar, the Moghul Empire conquered all of northern India and a large part of the Deccan States, which were later totally annexed by Emperor Aurungzebe (1658–1707). By the late 17th century, however, the days of imperial expansion were over and the empire began to decline.

RELIGIOUS ASSIMILATION

Above all, Akbar stabilized the régime. He was disappointed in his sons and quarrelled with them, yet the dynasty was solidly based when he died. There were revolts nevertheless. Some of them seem to have been encouraged by Muslim anger at Akbar's apparent falling-away from the faith. Even in the "Turkish" era the sharpness of the religious distinction between Muslim and non-Muslim had somewhat softened as invaders settled down in their new country and took up Indian ways. One earlier sign of assimilation was the appearance of a new language, Urdu, the tongue of the camp. It was the *lingua franca* of rulers and ruled, with a Hindi structure and a Persian and Turkish vocabulary. Soon there were signs that the omnivorous power of Hinduism would perhaps even incorporate Islam; a new devotionalism in the fourteenth and fifteenth centuries had spread through popular hymns an abstract, almost monotheistic, cult, of a God whose name might be Rama or Allah, but who offered love, justice and mercy to all. Correspondingly, some Muslims even before Akbar's reign had shown interest in and respect for Hindu ideas. There was some absorption of Hindu ritual practice. Soon it was noticeable that converts to Islam tended to revere the tombs of holy men: these became places of resort and pilgrimage which satisfied the scheme of a subordinate focus of devotion in a monotheistic religion and thus carried out the functions of the minor and local deities who had always found a place in Hinduism.

RELATIONS WITH EUROPE

An important development before the end of Akbar's reign was the consolidation of India's

Akbar is described by a Western visitor

"Akbar was imbued with a spirit which enabled him to perceive and judge things rapidly, as well as a strict sense of duty. He was intelligent, pleasant and generous; to these characteristics were added the courage of a brave and very enterprising person. He could be friendly and be in a good mood, without losing any of his dignity as king. He recognized virtue and was well-disposed to foreigners, particularly towards Christians, some of whom he always wanted near him. Impressed and eager to learn, he had a profound knowledge not only of political and military matters, but also of technical things."

An extract from the *History of memorable things that happened in the East Indies and in the countries discovered by the Portuguese* by Jarric.

first direct relations with Atlantic Europe. Links with Mediterranean Europe may already have been made slightly easier by the coming of Islam; from the Levant to Delhi a common religion provided continuous, if distant, contact. European travellers had turned up from time to time in India and its rulers had been able to attract the occasional technical expert to their service, though they were few after the Ottoman conquests. But what was now about to happen was to go much further and would change India for ever. The Europeans who now arrived would be followed by others in increasing numbers and they would not go away.

The process had begun when a Portuguese admiral reached Malabar at the end of the fifteenth century. Within a few years his countrymen had installed themselves as traders – and behaved sometimes as pirates at Bombay and on the coast of Gujarat. Attempts to dislodge them failed in the troubled years following Babur's death, and in the second half of the century the Portuguese moved round to found new posts in the Bay of Bengal. They made the running for Europeans in India for a long time. They were liable, none the less, to attract the hostility of good Muslims because they brought with them pictures and images of Christ, His mother and the saints, which smacked of idolatry. Protestants were to prove less irritating to religious feeling when they arrived. The British age in India was still a long way off, but with rare historical neatness the first British East India Company was founded on 31 December 1600, the last day of the sixteenth century. Three years later the Company's first emissary arrived at Akbar's court at Agra and by then Elizabeth I, who had given the

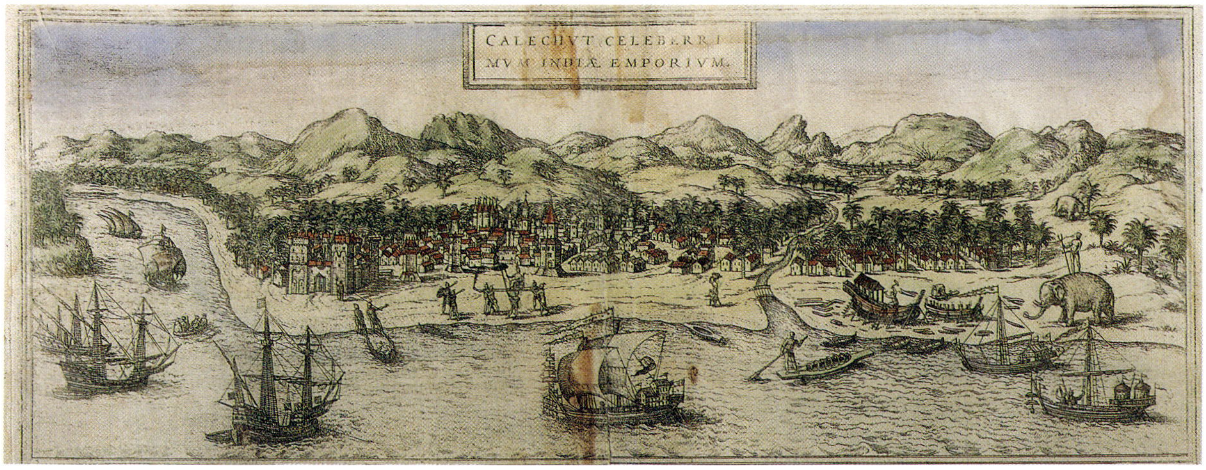

Calicut (Kozhikode) was the first place where the Portuguese landed on the Indian mainland (on 21 May 1498). They were eventually given trading rights and allowed to build a fort at the site. The Calicut trading station, depicted in this engraving, was a centre of Portuguese commerce for more than 100 years.

merchants their charter of incorporation, was dead. Thus at the end of the reigns of two great rulers came the first contact between two countries whose historical destinies were to be entwined so long and with such enormous effect for them both and for the world. At that moment no hint of such a future could have been sensed. The English then regarded trade in India as less interesting than that with other parts of Asia. The contrast between the two realms, too, is fascinating: Akbar's empire was one of the most powerful in the world, his court one of the most sumptuous, and he and his successors ruled over a civilization more glorious and spectacular than anything India had known since the Guptas, while Queen Elizabeth's kingdom, barely a great power, even in European terms, was crippled by debt and contained fewer people than modern Calcutta. Akbar's successor was contemptuous of the presents sent to him by James I a few years later. Yet the future of India lay with the subjects of the queen.

SHAH JAHAN

The moghul emperors continued in Babur's line in direct descent, though not without interruption, until the middle of the nineteenth century. After Akbar, so great was the dynasty's prestige that it became fashionable in India to claim Mongol descent. Only the three rulers who followed Akbar matter here, for it was under Jahangir and Shah Jahan that the empire grew to its greatest extent in the first half of the seventeenth century and under Aurungzebe that it began to decay in the second. The reign of Jahangir was not so glorious as his father's, but the empire survived his cruelty and alcoholism, a considerable test of its administrative structure. The religious toleration established by Akbar also survived intact. For all his faults, too, Jahangir was a notable promoter of the arts, above all of painting. During his reign there becomes visible for the first time the impact of European culture in Asia, through artistic motifs drawn from imported pictures and prints. One of these motifs was the halo or nimbus given to Christian saints and, in Byzantium, to emperors. After Jahangir all Moghul emperors were painted with it.

COURT LIFE

Shah Jahan began the piecemeal acquisition of the Deccan sultanates though he had little success in campaigns in the northwest and failed to drive the Persians from Kandahar. In domestic administration there was a weakening of the principle of religious toleration, though not sufficiently to place Hindus at a disadvantage in government service; administration remained multi-religious. Although the emperor decreed that all newly built Hindu temples should be pulled down, he patronized Hindu poets and musicians. At Agra, Shah Jahan maintained a lavish and exquisite court life. It was there, too, that he built the most celebrated and the best-known of all Islamic buildings, the Taj Mahal, a tomb for his favourite wife; it is the only possible rival to the mosque of Córdoba for the title of the most beautiful building in the world. She had died soon after Shah Jahan's accession and for over twenty years his builders were at work. It is the culmination of the work with arch and dome which is one of the most conspicuous Islamic legacies to Indian art and the greatest monument of Islam in India. The waning of Indian representational sculpture after the Islamic invasions had its compensations. Shah Jahan's court also brought to its culmination a great tradition of miniature painting.

The reign of the Moghul emperor Shah Jahan, who is shown seated on his peacock throne in this 18th-century painting, lasted from 1628 until 1658.

TAXATION

Beneath the level of the court, the picture of life in Moghul India is far less attractive. Local officials had to raise more and more money to support not only the household expenses and campaigns of Shah Jahan but also the social and military élites who were

Emperor Aurungzebe built the Bibika Maqbara mausoleum in Aurangabad for his wife, Rabia Daurani. Modelled on the Taj Mahal, which had been completed 25 years earlier, the Bibika Maqbara was half the size of its predecessor. The construction of elaborate tombs in the Moghul period reflects the Islamic nature of the dynasty: unlike Hindus, who believe in cremation and reincarnation, Muslims believe in burial and eternal life.

essentially parasitic on the producing economy. Without regard for local need or natural disaster, a rapacious tax-gathering machine may at times have been taking from the peasant producers as much as half their incomes. Virtually none of this was productively invested. The flight of peasants from the land and rise of rural banditry are telling symptoms of the suffering and resistance these exactions provoked. Yet even Shah Jahan's demands probably did the empire less damage than the religious enthusiasm of his third son, Aurungzebe, who set aside three brothers and imprisoned his father to become emperor in 1658. He combined, disastrously, absolute power, distrust of his subordinates and a narrow religiosity. To have succeeded in reducing the expenses of his court is not much of an offsetting item in the account. New conquests were balanced by revolts against Moghul rule which were said to owe much to Aurungzebe's attempt to prohibit the Hindu religion and destroy its temples, and to his restoration of the poll tax on non-Muslims. The Hindu's advancement in the service of the state was less and less likely; conversion became necessary for success. A century of religious toleration was cancelled and one result was the alienation of many subjects' loyalties.

HINDU OPPOSITION

Among other results, the alienation of Hindus helped to make it impossible finally to conquer the Deccan, which has been termed the ulcer which ruined the Moghul Empire. As under Asoka, north and south India could not be united. The Mahrattas, the hillmen who were the core of Hindu opposition, constituted themselves under an independent ruler in 1674. They allied with the remains of the Muslim armies of the Deccan sultans to resist the Moghul armies in a long struggle which threw up a heroic figure who has become something of a paladin in the eyes of modern Hindu nationalists. This was Shivagi, who built from fragments a Mahratta political identity which soon enabled him to exploit the tax-payer as ruthlessly as the Moghuls had done. Aurungzebe was continuously campaigning against the Mahrattas down to his death in 1707. There followed a grave crisis for the régime, for his three sons disputed the succession. The empire almost at once began to break up and a much more formidable legatee than the Hindu or local prince was waiting in the wings – the European.

MOGHUL DECLINE

Perhaps the negative responsibility for the eventual success of the Europeans in India is Akbar's, for he did not scotch the serpent in the egg. Shah Jahan, on the other hand, destroyed the Portuguese station on the Hooghly, though Christians were later tolerated at Agra. Strikingly, Moghul policy never seems to have envisaged the building of a navy, a weapon used formidably against the Mediterranean Europeans by the Ottomans. One consequence was already felt under Aurungzebe, when coastal shipping and even the pilgrim trade to Mecca were in danger from the Europeans. On land, the Europeans had been allowed to establish their toeholds and bridgeheads. After beating a Portuguese squadron, the English won their first west-coast trading concession early in the seventeenth century. Then, in 1639, on the Bay of Bengal and with the permission of the local ruler, they founded at Madras the settlement which was the first territory of British India, Fort St George. The headstones over their graves in its little cemetery still commemorate the first English who lived and died in India. Thousands more would do the same in the next three centuries.

The English later fell foul of Aurungzebe, but got further stations at Bombay and Calcutta before the end of the century. Their ships had maintained the paramountcy in trade won from the Portuguese, but a new

Aurungzebe, the son of Shah Jahan and the last of the great Moghul emperors, is portrayed in this 17th-century painting.

European rival was also in sight by 1700. A French East India Company had been founded in 1664 and soon established its own settlements.

A century of conflict lay ahead, but not only between the newcomers. Europeans were already having to make nice political choices because of the uncertainties aroused when Moghul power was no longer as strong as it once had been. Relations had to be opened with his opponents as well as with the emperor, as the English in Bombay discovered, looking on helplessly while a Mahratta squadron occupied one island in Bombay harbour and a Moghul admiral the one next to it. In 1677 an official sent back a significant warning to his employers in London: "the times now require you to manage your general commerce with your sword in your hands." By 1700 the English were well aware that much was at stake.

After the arrival of the Portuguese, the Malabar coastal region became an important financial centre where several commercial routes converged. This French miniature shows the harvest of local pepper for export to Europe.

THE EUROPEAN LEGACY

By 1700 we are into the era in which India is increasingly caught up in events not of her own making, the era of world history, in fact. Little things show it as well as great; in the sixteenth century the Portuguese had brought with them chillies, potatoes and tobacco from America. Indian diet and agriculture were already changing. Soon maize, pawpaws and pineapple were to follow. The story of Indian civilizations and rulers can be broken once this new connexion with the larger world is achieved. Yet it was not the coming of the European which ended the great period of Moghul Empire; that was merely coincidental, though it was important that newcomers were there to reap the advantages. No Indian empire had ever been able to maintain itself for long. The diversity of the subcontinent and the failure of its rulers to find ways to tap indigenous popular loyalty are probably the main explanations. India remained a continent of exploiting ruling élites and producing peasants upon whom they battered. The "states", if the term can be used, were only machinery for transferring resources from producers to parasites. The means by which they did this destroyed the incentive to save – to invest productively.

India was, by the end of the seventeenth century, ready for another set of conquerors. They were awaiting their cue, already on stage, but as yet playing hardly more than bit parts. Yet in the long run the European tide, too, would recede. Unlike early conquerors, though Europeans were to stay a long time, they were not to be overcome by India's assimilative power as their predecessors had been. They would go away defeated, but would not be swallowed. And when they went they would leave a deeper imprint than any of their predecessors because they would leave true state structures behind.

The Taj Mahal is one of the most enchanting buildings in the world. It was constructed by the grief-stricken Shah Jahan as a tomb for his wife Mumtaz Mahal (which means "Jewel of the Palace"), who died in 1631 while giving birth to her 14th child. The Moghul Empire, which was already in decline, could hardly afford such an extravagant project; the shah almost bankrupted the state to create his monument to love. It is said that 1,000 elephants were used to carry white marble the 185 miles (300 km) from the quarry at Makrana. Precious stones for the inlays were brought from as far away as Russia and China.

2 IMPERIAL CHINA

The lettering (top left) on this Ch'ing-era painting of Chinese nobles means "Chart of the ancestors of the Honourable Madame Wu".

One explanation of the striking continuity and independence of Chinese civilization is obvious: China was remote, inaccessible to alien influence, far from sources of disturbance in other great civilizations. Empires came and went in both countries, but Islamic rule made more difference to India than any dynasty's rise or fall made to China. It was also endowed with an even greater capacity to assimilate alien influence, probably because the tradition of civilization rested on different foundations in each country. In India the great stabilizers were provided by religion and a caste system inseparable from it. In China stability rested on the culture of an administrative élite which survived dynasties and empires and kept China on the same course.

OFFICIAL RECORDS

One thing we owe to this élite is the maintenance of written records from very early times. Thanks to them, Chinese historical accounts provide an incomparable documentation, crammed with often reliable facts, though the selection of them was dominated by the assumptions of a minority, whose preoccupations they reflect, and they still leave us uninformed about many things. The Confucian scholars who kept up the historical records had a utilitarian and didactic aim: they wanted to provide a body of examples and data which would make easier the maintenance of traditional ways and values. Their histories emphasize continuity and the smooth flow of events. Given the needs of administration in so huge a country this is perfectly understandable; uniformity and regularity were clearly to be desired. Yet such a record leaves much out. It remains very difficult even in historical times – and much more difficult than in the classical Mediterranean world – to recover the concerns and life of the vast majority of Chinese. Moreover, official history may well give a false impression both of the unchanging nature of Chinese administration and of the permeation of society by Confucian values. For a long time, the assumptions behind the Chinese administrative machine can only have been those of a minority, even if they came in the end to be shared by many Chinese and accepted, unthinkingly and even unknowingly, by most.

With the Ch'in Dynasty (221–206 BCE), all China's feudal kingdoms were united for the first time. Shih-Huang-ti, who designated himself First Emperor in 221 BCE, was the best-known of the Ch'in rulers. These infantry men are part of the famous terracotta army that guarded his tomb.

GEOGRAPHICAL ISOLATION

Chinese official culture was extraordinarily self-sufficient. Such outside influences as played upon it did so with little effect and this remains impressive. The fundamental explanation, again, is geographic isolation. China was much further removed from the classical West than the Maurya and Gupta empires. She had little intercourse with it even indirectly, although until the beginning of the seventh century Persia, Byzantium and the Mediterranean depended upon Chinese silk and valued her porcelain. Always, too, China had complicated and close relations with the people of Central Asia; yet, once unified, she had for many centuries on her borders no great states with whom relations had to be carried on. This isolation was, if anything, to increase as the centre of gravity of Western civilization moved west and north and as the Mediterranean was more and more cut off from East Asia first by the inheritors of the Hellenistic legacy (the last and most important of which was Sassanid Persia), and then by Islam.

DYNASTIC RULE

China's history between the end of the period of Warring States and the beginning of the T'ang in 618 has a backbone of sorts in the waxing and waning of dynasties. Dates can be attached to these, but there is an element of the artificial, or at least a danger of being over-emphatic, in using them. It could take decades for a dynasty to make its power a reality over the whole empire and

Time chart (c.1523 BCE–1912 CE)

1000 BCE — 0 — 500 CE — 1000 CE — 1500 CE — 2000 CE

- c.1523–1027 BCE The Shang Dynasty
- 551–479 BCE The life of Confucius
- 221–206 BCE The unification of China by the Ch'in Emperor Shih-Huang-ti
- c.110 BCE The Silk Route opens up
- c.150 CE Buddhism is introduced to China
- 618–907 CE The T'ang Dynasty
- 1206–1227 CE Chinghis Khan is Mongol emperor
- 1368–1644 CE The Ming Dynasty
- 1557 CE The Portuguese settle in Macao
- 1644–1912 CE The Manchu Ch'ing Dynasty

This bas-relief, on the flagstone of a sarcophagus from the Han era, depicts typical scenes from palace life.

even longer to lose it. With this reservation, the dynastic reckoning can still be useful. It gives us major divisions of Chinese history down to this century which are called after the dynasties which reached their peaks during them. The first three which concern us are the Ch'in, the Han and the Later Han.

THE CH'IN

The Ch'in ended the disunity of the period of Warring States. They came from a western state still looked upon by some as barbarous as late as the fourth century BCE. Nevertheless, the Ch'in prospered, perhaps in part because of a radical reorganization carried out by a legalist-minded minister in about 356 BCE; perhaps also because of their soldiers' use of a new long iron sword. After swallowing Szechwan, the Ch'in claimed the status of a kingdom in 325 BCE. The climax of Ch'in success was the defeat of their last opponent in 221 BCE and the unification of China for the first time in one empire under the dynasty which gives the country its name.

This was a great achievement. China from this time may be considered the seat of a single, self-conscious civilization. There had been earlier signs that such an outcome was likely. Given the potential of their own Neolithic cultures, the stimuli of cultural diffusion and some migration from the north, the first shoots of civilization had appeared in several parts of China before 500 BCE. By the end of the Warring States period some of them showed marked similarities which offset the differences between them. The political unity achieved by Ch'in conquest over a century was in a sense the logical corollary of a cultural unification already well under way. Some have even claimed that a sense of Chinese nationality can be discerned before 221 BCE; if so, it must have made conquest itself somewhat easier.

THE TWO HAN DYNASTIES

Fundamental administrative innovations by the Ch'in were to survive that dynasty's displacement after less than twenty years by the Han, who ruled for two hundred years (206 BCE–9 CE), to be followed after a brief

The principal Chinese dynasties

Shang ?1523–?1027 BCE
Chou ?1027–?256 BCE
Ch'in 21–206 BCE (*having annihilated Chou in 256 BCE and other rival states afterwards*)

Former Han 206 BCE–9 CE
Hsin 9–23
Later Han 25–220
Wei 220–265
Shu 221–263
Wu 222–280
Western Chin 265–316
Sixteen Kingdoms 304–439

Eastern Chin 317–420
Liu Sung 420–479
Southern Ch'i 479–502
Liang 502–557
Ch'en 557–589

Northern Wei 386–581
Western Wei 535–557
Eastern Wei 534–550

Northern Chou 557–581
Northern Ch'i 550–577

Sui 581–618
T'ang 618–907

Five Dynasties 906–960
Ten Kingdoms 907–979
Northern Han 951–979 (*reckoned as one of the Ten Kingdoms*)

Sung 960–1126
(*the extreme north of China being ruled by the Liao 947–1125*)

Chin 1126–1234
Southern Sung 1127–1279
Yuan 1279–1368 (*having succeeded the Chin in North China in 1234*)
Ming 1368–1644
Ch'ing 1644–1912

interlude by the almost equally creative Later Han dynasty (25–220 CE). Though they had their ups and downs, the Han emperors showed unprecedented strength. Their sway extended over almost the whole of modern China, including southern Manchuria and the southeastern province of Yueh. The Later Han went on to create an empire as big as that of their Roman contemporaries. They faced an old threat from Mongolia and a great opportunity towards the south. They handled both with skill aided by the tactical superiority given their armies by the new crossbow. This weapon was probably invented soon after 200 BCE and was both more powerful and more accurate than the bows of the barbarians, who did not for a long time have the ability to cast the bronze locks required. It was the last major achievement of Chinese military technology before the coming of gunpowder.

EXPANSION

In Mongolia at the beginning of Han times lived the Hsiung-Nu, whom we have already met as the forerunners of the Huns. The Han emperors drove them north of the Gobi desert and then seized control of the caravan routes of Central Asia, sending armies far west into Kashgaria in the first century BCE. They even won tribute from the Kusharas, whose own power straddled the Pamirs. To the south, they occupied the coasts as far as the Gulf of Tonkin; Annam accepted their suzerainty and Indo-China has been regarded by Chinese statesmen as part of their proper sphere ever since. To the north-east they penetrated Korea. All this was the work of the Later, or "Eastern", Han whose capital was at Loyang. From there they continued to press forward in Turkestan and raised tribute from the oases of Central Asia.

One general in 97 CE may have got as far as the Caspian.

Tentative diplomatic encounters with Rome in Han times suggest that expansion gave China much more contact with the rest of the world. Before the nineteenth century this was in the main by land, and besides the silk trade which linked her regularly with the Near East (caravans were leaving for the West with silk from about 100 BCE), China also developed more elaborate exchanges with her nomadic neighbours. Sometimes this was within the fictional framework of tribute acknowledged in turn by gifts, sometimes within official monopolies which were the foundation of great merchant families. Nomadic contacts may explain one of the most astonishing works of Chinese art, the great series of bronze horses found in tombs at Wu-Wei. These were only one among many fine works of Han bronze-workers; they evidently broke more readily with tradition than the Han potters, who showed more antiquarian respect for past forms. At a different level, though, Han pottery provides evidence of some of the very few exploitations in art of the subject-matter of the daily life of most Chinese, in the form of collections of tiny figures of peasant families and their livestock.

During the excavations of a tomb thought to be that of a general from the Later Han period, a series of artifacts were found. Among them was this famous figure of a flying horse. One of the horse's hooves rests on a swallow, instilling the figure with a sense of speed and dynamism.

CHINESE CIVILIZATION

A brilliant culture flourished in Han China, centred on a court with huge, rich palaces built in the main of timber – unhappily, for the result is that they have disappeared, like the bulk of the Han collections of paintings on silk. Much of this cultural capital was dissipated or destroyed during the fourth and fifth centuries, when the barbarians returned to the frontiers. Failing at last to provide China's defence from her own manpower, the Han emperors fell back on a policy tried elsewhere, that of bringing within the Wall some of the tribes who pressed on it from outside and then deploying them in its defence. This raised problems of relations between the newcomers and the native Chinese. The Han emperors could not prolong for ever their empire, and after four hundred years China once more dissolved into a congeries of kingdoms.

Some of these had barbarian dynasties, but in this crisis there is observable for the first time China's striking powers of cultural digestion. Gradually the barbarians were swallowed by Chinese society, losing their own identity and becoming only another kind of Chinese. The prestige which Chinese civilization enjoyed among the peoples of Central Asia was already very great. There was a disposition among the uncivilized to see China as the centre of the world, a cultural pinnacle, somewhat in the way in which the Germanic peoples of the West had seen Rome. One Tatar ruler actually imposed Chinese customs and dress on his people by decree in 500. The Central Asian threat was not over; far from it, there appeared in Mongolia in the fifth

Under the T'ang Dynasty emperors became increasingly powerful. This painting on silk, which dates from the later Ming era, shows the lavish procession that accompanied an emperor and his entourage leaving the palace.

century the first Mongol Empire. Nonetheless, when the T'ang, a northern dynasty, came to receive the mandate of heaven in 618 China's essential unity was in no greater danger than it had been at any time in the preceding two or three centuries.

THE T'ANG DYNASTY

Political disunity and barbarian invasion had not damaged the foundations of Chinese civilization, which entered its classical phase under the T'ang. Among those foundations, the deepest continued to lie in kinship. Throughout historical times the clan retained its importance because it was the mobilized power of many linked families, enjoying common institutions of a religious and sometimes of an economic kind. The diffusion and ramification of family influence were all the easier because China did not have primogeniture; the paternal inheritance was usually divided at death. Over a social ocean in which families were the fish that mattered presided one Leviathan, the state. To it and to the family the Confucians looked for authority; those institutions were unchallenged by others, for in China there were no entities such as Church or communes which confused questions of right and government so fruitfully in Europe.

The state's essential characteristics were all in place by T'ang times. They were to last until this century and the attitudes they built up linger on still. In their making, the consolidating work of the Han had been especially important, but the office of the emperor, holder of the mandate of heaven, could be taken for granted even in Ch'in times. The comings and goings of dynasties did not compromise the standing of the office since they could always be ascribed to the withdrawal of the heavenly mandate. The emperor's liturgical importance was, if anything, enhanced by the inauguration under the Han of a sacrifice only he could make. Yet his position also changed in a positive sense. Gradually, a ruler who was essentially a great feudal magnate, his power an extension of that of the family or

Chinese civil servants, such as the two portrayed in these drawings, wore special clothes to denote their rank.

the manor, was replaced by one who presided over a centralized and bureaucratic state.

THE GREAT CHINESE STATE

Centralization had begun a long way back. Already in Chou times a big effort was made to build canals for transport. Great competence in organization and large human resources were required for this and only a potent state could have deployed them. A few centuries later the first Ch'in emperor was able to link together the existing sections of the Great Wall in 1,400 miles of continuous barrier against the barbarians (legendarily, his achievement cost a million lives and that story, too, is revealing of the way the empire was seen). His dynasty went on to standardize weights and measures and impose a degree of disarmament on its subjects while itself putting in the field perhaps a million soldiers. The Han were able to impose a monopoly of coining and standardized the currency. Under them, too, entry to the civil service by competitive examination began; though it was to fade out again, not to be resumed until T'ang times, it was very important. Territorial expansion had required more administrators. The resulting bureaucracy was to survive many periods of disunion (a proof of its vigour) and remained to the end one of the most striking and characteristic institutions of imperial China. It was probably the key to China's successful emergence from the era when collapsing dynasties were followed by competing petty and local states which broke up the unity already achieved. It linked China together by an ideology as well as by administration. The civil servants were trained and examined in the Confucian classics; under the Han, legalism finally lost its grip after a lively ideological struggle. Literacy and political culture were thus wedded in China as nowhere else.

SCHOLARSHIP AND THE BUREAUCRACY

Chinese scholars had been deeply offended by the Ch'in. Though a few of them had been favoured and gave the dynasty advice, there had been a nasty moment in 213 BCE when the emperor turned on scholars who had criticized the despotic and militaristic character of his régime. Books were burned and only "useful" works on divination, medicine or agriculture were spared; more than four hundred scholars perished. What was really at stake is not clear; some historians have seen this attack as an offensive aimed at "feudal" tendencies opposed to Ch'in centralization. If so, it was far from the end of the confusion of cultural and political struggle with which China has gone on mystifying foreign observers even in the last one hundred years. Whatever the sources of this policy, the Han took a different tack and sought to conciliate the intellectuals.

This led first to the formalization of Confucian doctrine into what quickly became an orthodoxy. The canonical texts were established soon after 200 BCE. True, Han Confucianism was a syncretic matter; it had absorbed much of legalism. But the important fact was that Confucianism had been the absorbing force. Its ethical precepts remained dominant in the philosophy which formed China's future rulers. In 58 CE sacrifices to Confucius were ordered in all government schools. Eventually, under the T'ang, administrative posts were confirmed to those trained in this orthodoxy. For over a thousand years it provided China's governors with a set of moral principles and a literary culture doggedly acquired by rote-learning. The

Confucianism

Confucianism represents a way of life that has been followed by the Chinese and other neighbouring peoples for more than 2,000 years. The doctrine systematized by Confucius in the 6th century BCE, which was designed with the aim of creating an ideal society led by an élite, states that:

Each individual has a duty to behave with virtue (*te*), integrity (*yi*) and benevolence (*jen*).

The family is the basis of society and the state represents "the Great Family" – the emperor is mother and father to his people.

The clearly defined relationships between "superiors and inferiors" (sovereign and subject, father and son, husband and wife, older and younger brothers, etc.) must be respected.

These hierarchical principles and the organized structures of the state should be preserved through the observance of a minutely detailed set of ceremonies and rituals known as *li*.

This stone rubbing portraying Confucius (551–479 BCE) is a somewhat idealized representation of the great teacher.

examinations they underwent were designed to show which candidates had the best grasp of the moral tradition discernible in the classical texts as well as to test mechanical abilities and the capacity to excel under pressure. It made them one of the most effective and ideologically homogeneous bureaucracies the world has ever seen and also offered great rewards to those who successfully made the values of Confucian orthodoxy their own.

The official class was in principle distinguished only by educational qualification (the possession of a degree, as it were) from the rest of society. Most civil servants came from the land-owning gentry, but they were set apart from them. Their office once achieved by success in the test of examination, they enjoyed a status only lower than that of the imperial family, and great material and social privileges besides. Officials' duties were general rather than specific, but they had two crucial annual tasks, the compilation of the census returns and the land registers on which Chinese taxation rested. Their other main work was judicial and supervisory, for local affairs were very much left to local gentlemen acting under the oversight of about two thousand or so district magistrates from the official class. Each of these lived in an official compound, the *yamen*, with his clerks, runners and household staff about him.

The gentry undertook a wide range of quasi-governmental and public-service activities which were both an obligation of the privileged class and also an insurance of much of its income. Local justice, education, public works were all part of this. The gentry also often organized military forces to meet local emergencies and even collected the taxes, from which it might recoup its own expenses. Over the whole of these arrangements and the official class itself, there watched a state apparatus of control, checking and reporting on a bureaucracy bigger by far than that of the Roman Empire and, at its greatest extent, ruling a much larger area.

SOCIAL ORGANIZATION

The structure of imperial China had huge conservative power. Crisis only threatened legal authority, rarely the social order. The permeation of governmental practice by the agreed ideals of Confucian society was rendered almost complete by the examination system. Moreover, though it was very hard for anyone not assured of some wealth to support himself during the long studies necessary for the examination – writing in the traditional literary forms itself took years to master – the principle of competition ensured that a continuing search for talent was not quite confined to the wealthier and established gentry families; China was a meritocracy in which learning always provided some social mobility. From time to time there were corruption and examples of the buying of places, but such signs of decline usually appear towards the end of a dynastic period. For the most part, the imperial officials showed remarkable independence of their background. They were not supposed to act on such assumptions of obligation to family and connexion as characterized the public servants drawn from the eighteenth-century English gentry. The civil servants were the emperor's men; they were not allowed to own land in the province where they served, serve in their own provinces, or have relatives in the same branch of government. They were not the representatives of a class, but a selection from it, an independently recruited élite, renewed and promoted by competition. They made the state a reality.

Imperial China was thus not an aristocratic polity; political power did not pass by descent within a group of noble families, though noble birth was socially important. Only in the small closed circle of the court was hereditary access to office possible, and there it was a matter of prestige, titles and standing, rather than of power. To the imperial counsellors who had risen through the official hierarchy to its highest levels and had become more than officials, the only rivals of importance were the court eunuchs. These creatures were often trusted with great authority by the emperors because, by definition, they could not found families. They were thus the only political force escaping the restraints of the official world.

Two young noblewomen are depicted with their tutor in this detail from a 4th-century hand scroll (red and black ink on silk). Chinese society was divided into two clearly differentiated groups: the ruling classes, made up of the nobility and the civil servants, and the peasants, who made up 90 per cent of the population.

Buddhism first arrived in China during the Later Han period and gradually spread all over the country, becoming the dominant religion. The Ch'an school of Chinese Buddhism emerged in the late 6th century and was linked to a period of great artistic creativity during the T'ang Dynasty. This gigantic Ch'an sculpture of the Buddha of Leshan, in Szechwan, dates from 713–722.

The ideas which inspired it were profoundly conservative; the predominant administrative task was seen to be the maintenance of the established order; the aim of Chinese government was to oversee, conserve and consolidate, and occasionally to innovate in practical matters by carrying out large public works. Its overriding goals were regularity and the maintenance of common standards in a huge and diverse empire, where many district magistrates were divided from the people in their charge even by language. In achieving its conservative aims, the bureaucracy was spectacularly successful and its ethos survived intact across all the crises of the dynasties.

CONFUCIAN VALUES AND RIVAL CREEDS

Clearly, in the Chinese state there was little sense of the European distinction between government and society. Official, scholar and gentleman were usually the same man, combining many roles which in Europe were increasingly to be divided between governmental specialists and the informal authorities of society. He combined them, too, within the framework of an ideology which was much more obviously central to society than any to be found elsewhere than perhaps in Islam. The preservation of Confucian values was not a light matter, nor satisfiable by lip-service. The bureaucracy maintained those values by exercising a moral supremacy somewhat like that long exercised by the clergy in the West – and in China there was no Church to rival the state.

The best-known figures of popular Taoist mythology are the Eight Immortals, who are depicted in this painting.

Below the Confucian orthodoxy of the officials and gentry, it is true, other creeds were important. Even some who were high in the social scale turned to Taoism or Buddhism. The latter was to be very successful after the Han collapse, when disunity gave it an opportunity to penetrate China. In its *Mahayana* variety it posed more of a threat to China than any other ideological force before Christianity, for, unlike Confucianism, it posited the rejection of worldly values. It was never to be eradicated altogether, in spite of persecution under the T'ang; attacks on it were, in any case, probably mounted for financial rather than ideological reasons. Unlike the persecuting Roman Empire, the Chinese state was more interested in property than in the correction of individual religious eccentricity. Under the fiercest of the persecuting emperors (who is said to have been a Taoist) over four thousand monasteries were dissolved, and over a quarter of a million monks and nuns dispersed from them. Nevertheless, in spite of such material damage to Buddhism, Confucianism had to come to terms with it. No other foreign religion influenced China's rulers so strongly until Marxism in the twentieth century; even some emperors were Buddhists.

PEASANT REVOLTS

Taoism developed into a mystical cult (borrowing something from Buddhism in the process) appealing both to those who sought personal immortality and to those who felt the appeal of a quietistic movement as an outlet from the growing complexity of Chinese life. As such it would have enduring significance. Its recognition of the subjectivity of human thought gives it an appearance of humility which some people in different cultures with more self-confident intellectual traditions find attractive today. Such religious and philosophical traditions, important as they were, touched the lives of the peasants directly only a little more than Confucianism, except in debased forms. A prey to the insecurities of war and famine, a peasant's outlet lay in magic or superstition. What little can be discerned of peasant life suggests that it was often intolerable, sometimes terrible. A significant symptom is the appearance under the Han of peasant rebellion, a phenomenon which became a major theme of Chinese history, punctuating it almost as rhythmically as the passing of dynasties. Oppressed by officials acting either on behalf of an imperial government seeking taxes for its campaigns abroad or in their own interest as grain speculators, the peasants turned to secret societies, another recurrent theme. Their revolts often took religious forms. A millenarian, Manichaean strain has run through Chinese revolution, bursting out in many guises, but always positing a world dualistically divided into good and evil, the righteous and the demons. Sometimes this threatened the social fabric, but the peasants were rarely successful for long.

Chinese society changed very slowly. In spite of some important cultural and administrative innovations, the lives of most Chinese were for centuries little altered in style or appearance. The comings and goings of the dynasties were accounted for by the notion of the mandate of heaven and although great intellectual achievements were possible, China's civilization already seemed self-contained, self-sufficient, stable to the point of immobility. No innovation compromised the fundamentals of a society more closely woven into a particular governmental structure than anything in the West. This structure proved quite competent to contain such changes as did take place and to regulate them so as not to disturb the traditional forms.

URBANIZATION AND TAXATION

One visibly important change was a continuing growth of commerce and towns which made it easier to replace labour service by taxation. Such new resources could be tapped by government both to rule larger areas effectively and to provide a series of great material monuments. They had already permitted the Ch'in to complete the Great Wall, which later dynasties were further to extend, sometimes rebuilding portions of it. It still astonishes the observer and far outranks the walls of Hadrian and Antoninus. Just before the inauguration of the T'ang, too, at the other end of this historical epoch, a great system of canals was completed which linked the Yangtze valley with the Yellow river valley to the north, and Hangchow to the south. Millions of labourers were employed on this and on other great irrigation schemes. Such works are comparable in scale with the Pyramids and surpass the great cathedrals of medieval Europe. They imposed equally heavy social costs, too, and there were revolts against conscription for building and guard duties.

POPULATION PRESSURE

It was a state with great potential and a civilization with impressive achievements already to its credit which entered its mature phase in 618. For the next thousand years, as for the previous eight hundred, its formal development can be linked to the comings and goings of the dynasties which provide a chronological structure (T'ang, 618–907; Sung, 960–1126; Mongol ascendancy, 1234–1368; Ming, 1368–1644; Manchu or

This illustration from a Ch'ing-era scroll shows workmen building a dyke.

Ch'ing, 1644–1912). Many historical themes overrun these divisions. One is the history of population. There was an important shift of the demographic centre of gravity towards the south during the T'ang period; henceforth most Chinese were to live in the Yangtze valley rather than the old Yellow river plain. The devastation of the southern forests and exploitation of new lands to grow rice fed them, but new crops became available, too. Together they made possible an overall growth of population which accelerated under the Mongols and the Ming. Estimates have been made that a population of perhaps eighty million in the fourteenth century more than doubled in the next two hundred years, so that in 1600 there were about 160 million subjects of the empire. This was a huge number, given populations elsewhere, but there was still great increase to come.

In this detail from an illustration on a Ming-Dynasty vase, tea workers are shown in the process of drying tea leaves in order to preserve them.

The weight of this fact is great. Apart from the enormous importance it gives to China in world population history, it puts in perspective the great manifestations of Chinese culture and imperial power, which rested on the huge mass of desperately poor peasants utterly unconcerned with such things. For the most part their lives were confined to their villages; only a few could hope to escape from this, or can have envisaged doing so. Most could have dreamed only of obtaining the precarious, but best, security available to them: the possession of a little land. Yet this became more and more difficult as numbers grew and, gradually, all available land was occupied. It was farmed more and more intensively in smaller and smaller plots. The one way out of the trap of famine was rebellion. At a certain level of intensity and success this might win support from the gentry and officials, whether from prudence or sympathy. When that happened, the end of a dynasty was probably approaching, for Confucian principles taught that, though rebellion was wrong if a true king reigned, a government which provoked rebellion and could not control it ought to be replaced for it was *ipso facto* illegitimate. At the *very* end of this road lay the success of a twentieth-century Chinese revolution based on the peasants.

AN OVERLONG FRONTIER

For many centuries population pressure, a major fact of modern China's history, made itself felt to the authorities only in indirect and obscured ways, when, for instance, famine or hunger drove people to rebellion. A much more obvious threat came from the outside. Essentially the problem was rather like that of Rome, an overlong frontier beyond which lay barbarians. T'ang influence over them was weakened when Central Asia succumbed to Islam. Like their Roman predecessors, too, the later T'ang emperors found that reliance on soldiers could be dangerous. There were hundreds of military rebellions by local warlords under the T'ang and any rebellion's success, even if short-lived, had a multiplier effect, tending to disrupt administration and damage the irrigation arrangements on which food (and therefore internal peace) depended. A régime thought of as a possible ally by Byzantium, which had sent armies to fight the Arabs and received ambassadors from Haroun-al-Raschid, was a great world power. In the end, though, unable to police their frontier effectively, the T'ang went under in the tenth century, and China collapsed again into political chaos. The Sung who emerged from it had to face an even graver external threat, the Mongols, and were in due course swallowed after the barbarian dynasty which had evicted them from north China had itself been engulfed by the warriors of Chinghis Khan.

SOCIAL STABILITY AND DYNASTIC CHANGE

During the whole of this time, the continuity and recuperative power of the bureaucracy and the fundamental institutions of society kept China going. After each dynastic change, the inheritors of power, even if from outside, turned to the relatively smaller number of officials (an estimate for the eighteenth century gives less than 30,000 civil and military officers actually in post). They thus drew into

Li Po (701–762), who is portrayed in this drawing, was one of the most important poets of the T'ang era, often considered to be the golden age of classical Chinese poetry. His poems, the central themes of which were always wine, music or women, were renowned for their beauty.

the service of each new government the unchanging values of the Confucian system, which were strengthened, if narrowed, by disaster. Only a small number of especially crucial matters were ever expected to be the reserved province of the imperial government. Confucian teaching supported this distinction of spheres of action and made it easy for the dynasty to change without compromising the fundamental values and structure of society. A new dynasty would have to turn to the officials for its administration and to the gentry for most of its officials who, in their turn, could get some things done only on the gentry's terms.

T'ANG CULTURE

Recurrent disunity did not prevent China's rulers, sages and craftsmen from bringing Chinese civilization to its peak in the thousand years after the T'ang inauguration. Some have placed the classical age as early as the seventh and eighth centuries, under the T'ang themselves, while others discern it under the Sung. Such judgments usually rest on the art-form considered, but even Sung artistic achievement was in any case a culmination of development begun under the T'ang, between whom and the Han much more of a break in style is apparent. It was in fact the last important break in the continuity of Chinese art until the twentieth century.

T'ang culture reflects the stimulus of contacts with the outside world, but especially with Central Asia, unprecedentedly close under this dynasty. The capital was then at Ch'ang-an, in Shensi, a western province. Its name means "long-lasting peace" and to this city at the end of the Silk Route came Persians, Arabs and Central Asians who made it one of the most cosmopolitan cities in the world. It contained Nestorian churches, Zoroastrian temples, Muslim mosques, and was probably the most splendid and luxurious capital of its day, as the objects which remain to us show. Many of them reflect Chinese recognition of styles other than their own – the imitation of Iranian silverware, for example – while the flavour of a trading entrepôt is preserved in the pottery figures of horsemen and loaded camels which reveal the life of Central Asia swirling in the streets of Ch'ang-an. These figures were often finished with the new polychromatic glazes achieved by T'ang potters; their style was imitated in places as far away as Japan and Mesopotamia. The presence of the court was as important in stimulating such craftsmanship as the visits of merchants from abroad, and from tomb paintings something of the life of the court aristocracy can be seen. The men relax in hunting, attended by Central Asian retainers; the women, vacuous in expression, are luxuriously dressed and, if servants, elaborately equipped with fans, cosmetic boxes, back-scratchers and other paraphernalia of the boudoir. Great ladies, too, favour Central Asian fashions borrowed from their domestic staff.

UNOFFICIAL CULTURE

The history of women, though, is the history of one of those other Chinas always obscured by the bias of the documentation towards the official culture. We hear little of them, even in literature, except in sad little poems and love stories. Yet presumably they must have made up about half of the population, or perhaps slightly less, for in hard times girl babies were exposed by poor families to die. That fact, perhaps, characterizes women's place in China until very recent times even better than the more familiar and superficially striking practice of foot-binding, which produced grotesque deformations and could leave a

From "The Thirteen Emperors", this illustration depicts the 7th-century T'ang emperor Yen Li-Pen.

The building of the Great Wall

"In olden times, the Chou ordered Nan Zhong to build a wall in that northern region and Prince Ling Wu and Ch'in Shih-Huang-ti built the Great Wall and the emperor Han Wu Ti eagerly imitated those ancient feats ... . The reason why the heroic sovereigns took on these difficult tasks was not a lack of tactical capacity or political intelligence, nor a military weakness, but rather it was inspired by the principle that it is extremely important to take measures against the barbarians. This is why they had to build, then, a Great Wall ... as a protection against the barbarians from the north. Although a great effort had to be made and hard work undertaken for some time, afterwards we will be able to enjoy the advantage of a long period of peace."

An extract from the *History of the Northern Dynasties*.

high-born lady almost incapable of walking. Another China still all but excluded from the historical evidence by the nature of the established tradition was that of the peasants. They become shadowly visible only as numbers in the census returns and as eruptions of revolt; after the Han pottery figures, there is little in Chinese art to reveal them, and certainly nothing to match the uninterrupted recording of the life of the common worker in the fields which runs from medieval European illumination, through the vernacular literature to the Romantics, and into the peasant subjects of the early Impressionists.

Official culture also excluded the tenth or so of the Chinese population who lived in the cities, some of which grew as time passed to become the biggest in the world. Ch'ang-an, when the T'ang capital, is said to have had two million inhabitants. No eighteenth-century European city was as big as contemporary Canton or Peking, which

Surviving classical Chinese documents tend to deal only with official culture, glossing over the aspects of daily life that could have given us an insight into women's lives. This wall painting, from the tomb of a T'ang princess called Yongtai, shows some ladies of her court.

were even larger. Such huge cities housed societies of growing complexity. Their development fostered a new commercial world; the first Chinese paper money was issued in 650. Prosperity created new demands, among other things for a literature which did not confine itself to the classical models and in colloquial style far less demanding than the elaborate classical Chinese. City life thus gradually secreted a literate alternative to the official culture, and because it was literate, it is the first part of unofficial China to which we have some access. Such popular demand could be satisfied because of two enormously important inventions: that of paper in the second century BCE, and of printing before 700 CE. The latter derived from the taking of rubbed impressions from stone under the Han. Printing from wood blocks was taking place under the T'ang and movable type appeared in the eleventh century CE. Soon after this, large numbers of books were published in China, long before they appeared anywhere else. In the cities, too, flourished popular poetry and music which abandoned the classical tradition.

The culture of Ch'ang-an never recovered from its disruption by rebellion in 756, only two years after the foundation of an Imperial Academy of Letters (about nine hundred years before any similar academy in Europe). After this the dynasty was in decline. The Sung ascendancy produced more great pottery; the earlier, northern phase of Sung history was marked by work still in the coloured, patterned tradition, while southern Sung craftsmen came to favour monochromatic, simple products. Significantly, they attached themselves to another tradition: that of the forms evolved by the great bronze-casters of earlier China. For all the beauty of its ceramics, though, Sung is more notable for some of the highest achievements of Chinese painting, their subject-matter being, above all, landscape. As a phase of Chinese development, though, the Sung era is more remarkable still for a dramatic improvement in the economy.

SUNG INDUSTRIALIZATION

In part this can be attributed to technological innovation – gunpowder, movable type and the sternpost all can be traced to the Sung

The origins of Chinese printing

At the beginning of the 8th century BCE the first bronze tablets appeared engraved with Chinese characters alongside drawings. However, archaeological research has indicated that the characters were placed in moulds separately.

Another printing system used by the Chinese during the 2nd century CE involved using carved stones stamped with ink. Later came stencilling, which consisted of punching very fine holes onto a piece of paper to create an image that was revealed when the paper was pressed onto a blank sheet and ink was applied to it. This system was widely used by the Buddhists.

The printing press first came into use in classical China in the 7th century, long before it was used in Europe. Text was reproduced by means of a polished wooden tablet, on which the words were written by cutting away the wood surrounding the characters, leaving the inscription in relief. The tablet was then covered in ink and pressed on to a sheet of rice-paper. The substitution, in the 11th century, of engraved tablets by independent movable characters was an enormous step forward.

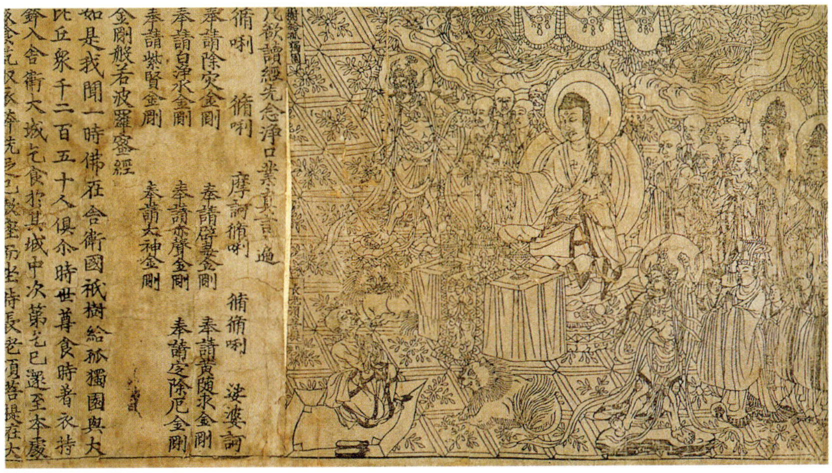

The earliest-known printed book is the Diamond Sutra, *which dates from 858. It comprises a scroll that is 16 ft (5 m) long and 11 in (27 cm) wide. The cover, shown here, is illustrated with a drawing of the Buddha talking to his disciple Subhuti.*

Technological advances are evident in many aspects of productive life in imperial China, such as in spinning. This illustration, which dates from the 12th or 13th century, shows various stages in the processes of spinning and weaving hemp.

era – but it was also linked to the exploitation of technology already long available. Technological innovation may indeed have been as much a symptom as a cause of a surge in economic activity between the tenth and thirteenth centuries which appears to have brought most Chinese a real rise in incomes in spite of continuing population growth. For once in the pre-modern world economic growth seems for a long period to have outstripped demographic trends. One change making this possible was certainly the discovery and adoption of a rice variety which permitted two crops a year to be taken from well-irrigated land and one from hilly ground only watered in the spring. The evidence of rising production in a different sector of the economy has been dramatically distilled into one scholar's calculation that within a few years of the battle of Hastings, China was producing nearly as much iron as the whole of Europe six centuries later. Textile production, too, underwent dramatic development (notably through the adoption of water-driven spinning machinery) and it is possible to speak of Sung "industrialization" as a recognizable phenomenon.

It is not easy (the evidence is still disputed) to say why this remarkable burst of growth took place. Undoubtedly there was a real input to the economy by public – that is, governmental – investment in public works, above all, communications. Prolonged periods of freedom from foreign invasion and domestic disorder also must have helped, though the second benefit may be explained as much by economic growth as the other way round. The main explanation, though, seems likely to be an expansion in markets and the rise of a money economy which owed something to factors already mentioned, but which rested fundamentally on the great expansion in agricultural productivity. So long as this kept ahead of population increase, all was well. Capital became available to utilize more labour, and to tap technology by investment in machines. Real incomes rose.

A RELATIVE LACK OF INNOVATION IN CHINA

It is hard to say why, after temporary and local regression at the end of the Sung era, and the resumption of economic growth, this intensive growth, which made possible rising consumption by greater numbers, came to an end. Nonetheless, it did, and was not resumed. Instead, average real incomes in China stabilized for something like five centuries, as production merely kept pace with population growth. (After that time, incomes began to fall, and continued to do so to a point at which the early twentieth-century Chinese peasant could be described as a man standing neck-deep in water, whom even ripples could drown.) But the economic relapse after Sung times is not the only factor to be taken into account in explaining why China did not go on to produce a dynamic, progressive society. In spite of printing, the mass of Chinese remained illiterate down to the twentieth century. China's great cities, for all their growth and commercial vitality, produced neither the freedom and immunities which sheltered people and ideas in Europe, nor the cultural and intellectual life which in the end revolutionized European civilization, nor effective questioning of the established order. Even in technology, where China achieved so much so soon, there is a similar strange gap between intellectual fertility and revolutionary change. The Chinese could invent (they had a far more efficient wheelbarrow than other civilizations), but once Chou times were over, it was the use of new land and the introduction of new crops rather than technical change which raised production. Other examples of a low rate of innovation are even more striking. Chinese sailors already had the magnetic compass in Sung times, but though naval expeditions were sent to Indonesia, the Persian Gulf, Aden and East Africa in the fifteenth century, their aim was to impress those places with the power of the Ming, not to accumulate information and experience for further voyages of exploration and discovery. Masterpieces had been cast in bronze in the second millennium BCE and the Chinese knew how to cast iron fifteen hundred years before Europeans, yet much of the engineering potential of this metallurgical tradition was unexplored even when iron production rose so strikingly. What he called "a sort of black stone" was burnt in China when Marco Polo was there; it was coal, but there was to be no Chinese steam engine.

This list could be much lengthened. Perhaps the explanation lies in the very success of Chinese civilization in pursuit of a different goal, the assurance of continuity and the prevention of fundamental change. Neither officialdom nor the social system favoured the innovator. Moreover, pride in the Confucian tradition and the confidence generated by great wealth and remoteness made it difficult to learn from the outside. This was not because the Chinese were intolerant. Jews, Nestorian Christians, Zoroastrian Persians, and Arab Muslims long practised their own religion freely, and the last even made some converts, creating an enduring Islamic minority. Contacts with the West multiplied, too, later under Mongol rule. But what has been called a "neo-Confucian" movement was by then already manifesting tendencies of defensive hostility, and formal tolerance had never led to much receptivity in Chinese culture.

MONGOL CHINA

INVASION BY THE MONGOLS showed China's continuing seductive power over its conquerors. By the end of the thirteenth century, all China had been overrun by them – and this may have cost the country something like thirty million lives, or well over a quarter of its whole population in 1200 – but the centre of gravity of the Mongol Empire had moved from the steppes to Peking, Kubilai's capital. This grandson of Chinghis was the last of the Great Khans and after his time Mongol China can be considered Chinese, not Mongol; Kubilai adopted a dynastic life in 1271 and the remainder of the Mongol era is recorded as that of the Yuan Dynasty. China changed Mongols more than Mongols changed China, and the result was the magnificence reported by the amazed Marco Polo. Kubilai made a break with the old conservatism of the steppes, the distrust of civilization and its works, and his followers slowly succumbed to Chinese culture in spite of their initial distrust of the scholar officials. They were, after all, a tiny minority of rulers in an ocean of Chinese subjects; they needed collaborators to survive. Kubilai spent nearly all his life in China, though his knowledge of Chinese was poor.

But the relationship of Mongol and Chinese was long ambiguous. Like the British in nineteenth-century India who set up social conventions to prevent their assimilation by their subjects, so the Mongols sought by positive prohibition to keep themselves apart. Chinese were forbidden to learn the Mongol language or marry Mongols. They were not allowed to carry arms. Foreigners, rather than Chinese, were employed in administration where possible, a device paralleled in the western khanates of the Mongol Empire: Marco Polo was for three years an official of the Great Khan; a Nestorian presided over the imperial bureau of astronomy; Muslims from Transoxiana administered Yunan. For some years, too, the traditional examination system was suspended. Some of the persistent Chinese hostility to the Mongols may be explained by such facts, especially in the south. When Mongol rule in China collapsed, seventy years after Kubilai's death, there appeared an, if possible, even more exaggerated respect for tradition and a

This portrait of the Mongol emperor Kubilai Khan (1259–1294) is from a collection entitled "Portraits of Famous Chinese Figures", which dates from the 18th century.

From the *Book of the Wonders of the World* by Marco Polo (1254–1324), this Italian illustration depicts Kubilai Khan's tax collectors at work. Some of the Mongols' heaviest taxes were imposed on salt, sugar and coal.

renewed distrust of foreigners among the Chinese ruling class.

THE ACHIEVEMENTS OF MONGOL RULE

The short-run achievement of the Mongols was very impressive. It was most obvious in the re-establishment of China's unity and the realization of its potential as a great military and diplomatic power. The conquest of the Sung south was not easy, but once it was achieved (in 1279) Kubilai's resources were more than doubled (they included an important fleet) and he began to rebuild the Chinese sphere of influence in Asia. Only in Japan was he totally unsuccessful. In the south, Vietnam was invaded (Hanoi was three times captured) and after Kubilai's death Burma was occupied for a time. These conquests were not, it is true, to prove long-lasting and they resulted in tribute rather than prolonged occupation. In Java, too, success was qualified; a landing was made there and the capital of the island taken in 1292, but it proved impossible to hold. There was also further development of the maritime trade with India, Arabia and the Persian Gulf which had been begun under the Sung.

Since it failed to survive, the Mongol régime cannot be considered wholly successful, but this does not take us far. Much that was positive was done in just over a century. Foreign trade flourished as never before. Marco Polo reports that the poor of Peking were fed by the largesse of the Great Khan, and it was a big city. A modern eye finds something attractive, too, about the Mongols' treatment of religion. Only Muslims were hindered in the preaching of their doctrine; Taoism and Buddhism were positively

The Forbidden City in Peking was founded by the Ming emperor Yung-lo (1403–1424).

encouraged, for example by relieving Buddhist monasteries of taxes (this, of course, meant heavier impositions on others, as any state support for religion must; the peasants paid for religious enlightenment).

REVOLT AND THE MING DYNASTY

In the fourteenth century natural disasters combined with Mongol exactions to produce a fresh wave of rural rebellions – the telling symptom of a dynasty in decline. They may have been made worse by Mongol concessions to the Chinese gentry. Giving landlords new rights over their peasants can hardly have won the régime popular support. Secret societies began to appear again and one of them, the "Red Turbans", attracted support from gentry and officials. One of its leaders, Chu Yan-chang, a monk, seized Nanking in 1356. Twelve years later he drove the Mongols from Peking and the Ming era began. Yet like many other Chinese revolutionary leaders Chu Yan-chang gradually became an upholder of the traditional order. The dynasty he founded, though it presided over a great cultural flowering and managed to maintain the political unity of China which was to last from Mongol times to the twentieth century, confirmed China's conservatism and isolation. In the early fifteenth century the maritime expeditions by great fleets came to an end. An imperial decree forbade Chinese ships to sail beyond coastal waters or individuals to travel abroad. Soon, Chinese shipyards lost the capacity to build the great ocean-going junks; they did not even retain their specifications. The great voyages of the eunuch Cheng Ho, a Chinese Vasco da Gama, were almost forgotten. At the same time, the merchants who had prospered under the Mongols were harassed.

In the end the Ming Dynasty ran to seed. A succession of emperors virtually confined to their palaces while favourites and imperial princes disputed around them the enjoyment of the imperial estates registered the decline. Except in Korea, where the Japanese were beaten off at the end of the sixteenth century, the Ming could not maintain the peripheral zones of Chinese empire. Indo-China fell away from the Chinese sphere, Tibet went more or less out of Chinese control and in 1544 the Mongols burnt the suburbs of Peking.

Under the Ming, too, came the first Europeans to seek more than a voyage of trade or discovery. In 1557 Portuguese established themselves at Macao. They had little to offer which China wanted, except silver; but missionaries followed and the official tolerance of Confucian tradition gave them opportunities they successfully exploited. They became very influential at the Ming court and in the early seventeenth century Chinese officials began to feel alarmed. The Portuguese were ordered back to Macao. By then, besides the mechanical toys and clocks which the missionaries added to the imperial collections, their scientific and cosmographical learning had begun to interest Chinese intellectuals. The correction of the Chinese calendar, which one Jesuit carried out, was of great importance, for the authenticity of the emperor's sacrifices depended on accurate dating. From the Jesuits the Chinese learnt also to cast heavy cannon, another useful art.

THE MANCHU CONQUEST

Early in the seventeenth century, the Ming needed any military advantages they could procure. They were threatened from the north by a people living in Manchuria, a province to which they later gave its name, but who were not known as Manchu until after their conquest of China. The way was opened to them in the 1640s by peasant revolt and an attempted usurpation of the Chinese throne. An imperial general asked the Manchu to help him and they came through the Wall, but only to place their own dynasty, the Ch'ing, on the throne in 1644 (and incidentally wipe out the general's own clan). Like other barbarians

This Ch'ing-era painting depicts a scene from Emperor K'ang-hsi's tour of Kiang-Han in 1699. The imperial troops are shown marching through the city gates, watched by the townspeople.

The Sui emperor Yang Kuang (1605–1617), who was canonized as Yang-ti, is shown on a boat on the Grand Canal in this 18th-century painting on silk. Yang Kuang was responsible for an ambitious construction programme that included reinforcing the Great Wall, dredging canals, and building huge palaces. Thousands of Chinese labourers died working on his extravagant projects.

and semi-barbarians, the Manchu had long been fascinated by the civilization they threatened and were already somewhat sinicized before their arrival. They were familiar with the Chinese administrative system, which they had imitated at their own capital of Mukden, and found it possible to cooperate with the Confucian gentry as they extended their grip on China. The attachment of Manchu inspectors stimulated the bureaucracy who needed to change little in their ways except to conform to the Manchu practice of wearing pigtails (thus was introduced what later struck Europeans as one of the oddest features of Chinese life).

THE EMPEROR K'ANG-HSI

The cost of Manchu conquest was high. Some twenty-five million people perished. Yet recovery was rapid. China's new power was already spectacularly apparent under the Emperor K'ang-hsi, who reigned from 1662 to 1722. This roughly corresponded to the reign of Louis XIV of France, whose own exercises in magnificence and aggrandizement took different forms but showed curious parallels on the other side of the world. K'ang-hsi was capable of a personal violence which the Sun King would never have permitted himself (he once attacked two of his sons with a dagger) but for all the difference in the historical backgrounds which formed them, there is a similarity in their style of rule. Jesuit observers speak of K'ang-hsi's "nobility of soul" and the description seems to have been prompted by more than the desire to flatter, and justified by more than his patronage. He was hard-working, scrutinizing with a close eye the details of business (and its manner, for he would painstakingly correct defective calligraphy in the memorials placed before him), and, like Louis, he refreshed himself by indulging his passion for hunting.

Characteristically, though K'ang-hsi was unusual among the Chinese emperors in admiring European skill (he patronized the Jesuits for their scientific knowledge), the merits of his reign were set firmly within accepted tradition; he identified himself with the enduring China. He rebuilt Peking, destroyed during the Manchu invasion, carefully restoring the work of the Ming architects and sculptors. It was as if Versailles had been put up in the Gothic style or London rebuilt in Perpendicular after the Great Fire. K'ang-hsi's principles were Confucian and he had classical works translated into Manchu. He sought to respect ancient tradition and assured his Chinese subjects their usual rights; they continued to rise to high office in the civil service in spite of its opening to Manchus, and K'ang-hsi appointed Chinese generals and viceroys. In the style of his personal life the emperor was, if not austere, at least moderate. He enjoyed the bracing life of the army and on campaigns lived simply; in Peking the pleasures of the palace were deliberately reduced and the emperor relaxed from the burdens of state with a harem of a mere three hundred girls.

RELATIONS WITH THE OUTSIDE WORLD

K'ang-hsi extended imperial control to Formosa, occupied Tibet, mastered the Mongols and made them quiescent vassals. This was something of a turning-point, as final as anything can be in history; from this time the nomadic peoples of Central Asia at last begin gradually to recede before the settler. Further north, in the Amur valley, another new historical chapter opened when, in 1685, a Chinese army attacked a Russian post at Albazin. Negotiations led to the withdrawal of the Russians and the razing of their fort. The treaty of Nershinsk which settled matters contained among its clauses one which prescribed that boundary posts should be set up with inscriptions not only in Russian, Manchu, Chinese and Mongolian, but also in Latin. The suggestion had been made by a French Jesuit who was a member of the Chinese delegation and, like the establishment of a frontier line at all, was a symptom of new Chinese relationships to the outside world, relationships developing faster, perhaps, than any Chinese knew. The treaty was far from being the final settlement of accounts between China and the only European power with which she shared a land frontier but it quietened things for a time. Elsewhere, Manchu conquest continued to unroll; later in the eighteenth century Tibet was again invaded and vassal status reimposed on Korea, Indo-China and Burma. These were major feats of arms.

This woodcut, which dates from 1696, is one of a series commissioned by the emperor K'ang-hsi. It depicts peasants involved in rice cultivation.

MANCHU CULTURE

AT HOME, PEACE AND PROSPERITY marked the last years of Manchu success. It was a silver age of the high classical civilization which some scholars believe to have reached its peak under the later Ming. If it did, it could still produce much beauty and scholarship under the Manchu. Great efforts of compilation and criticism, initiated and inspired by K'ang-hsi himself, opened a hundred years of transcription and publication which not only spawned such monsters as a five-thousand-volume encyclopedia, but also collections of classical editions now given canonical form. In K'ang-hsi's reign, too, the imperial kilns began a century of technical advance in enamelling which produced exquisite glazes.

Yet however admirable – and however the emphasis is distributed between its various expressions in different arts – Manchu China's civilization was still, like that of its predecessors, the civilization of an élite. Although there was at the same time a popular culture of great vigour, the Chinese civilization which Europeans were struck by was as much the property of the Chinese ruling class as it always had been, a fusion of artistic, scholarly and official activity. Its connexion with government still gave it a distinctive tone and colour. It remained profoundly conservative, not only in social and political matters but even in its aesthetic. The art it esteemed was based on a distrust of innovation and originality; it strove to imitate and emulate the best, but the best was always past. The traditional masterpieces pointed the way. Nor was art seen as the autonomous expression of aesthetic activity. Moral criteria were brought to the judgment of artistic work and these criteria were, of course, the embodiments of Confucian values. Restraint, discipline, refinement and respect for the great masters were the qualities admired by the scholar-civil servant who was also artist and patron.

ART

Whatever appearances might suggest at first sight, Chinese art was no more directed towards escape from conventional life and values than that of any other culture before the European nineteenth century. This was also paradoxically apparent in its traditional exaltation of the amateur and the disapprobation it showed towards professionals. The man most esteemed was the official or landowner who was able to execute with sureness and apparent lack of effort works of painting, calligraphy or literature. Brilliant amateurs were greatly admired and in their activities, Chinese art escapes from its anonymity; we often know such artists' names. Its beautiful ceramics and textiles, on the other hand, are the products of tradesmen whose names are lost, often working under the direction of civil servants. Artisans were not esteemed for originality; craftsmen were encouraged to develop their skills not to the point of innovation but towards technical perfection. Central direction of large bodies of craftsmen within the precincts of the imperial palace only imposed upon these arts all the more firmly the stamp of traditional style. Even a brilliant explosion of new technical masteries at the imperial kilns during the reign of K'ang-hsi still expressed itself within the traditional canons of restraint and simplicity.

This water buffalo, which dates from c.1400 CE, was carved from green jade during the early Ming Dynasty. The animal's shape means that as little of the stone as possible is wasted.

THE LIMITATIONS OF CHINESE SUCCESS

The final Chinese paradox is the most obvious and by the eighteenth century it seems starkly apparent. For all her early technological advances China never arrived at a mastery of nature which could enable her to resist Western intervention. Gunpowder is the most famous example; the Chinese had it before anyone else, but could not make guns as good as those of Europe, nor even employ effectively those made for them by European craftsmen. Chinese sailors had long had the use of the mariner's compass and a cartographical heritage which produced the first grid map, but they were only briefly exploring navigators. They neither pushed across the Pacific like the more primitive Melanesians, nor did they map it, as did later the Europeans. For six hundred years or so before Europe had them, the Chinese made mechanical clocks fitted with the escapement which is the key to successful time-keeping by machines, yet the Jesuits brought with them an horological technology far superior to the Chinese when they arrived in the sixteenth century. The list of unexploited intellectual triumphs could be much lengthened, by important Chinese innovations in hydraulics, for example, but there is no need to do so. The main point is clear. Somehow, a lack of interest in the utilization of invention was rooted in a Confucian social system which, unlike that of Europe, did not regard as respectable association between the gentleman and the technician.

NEW THREATS TO STABILITY

Pride in a great cultural tradition long continued to make it very hard to recognize

The *Atlas of China*, which was produced by the monk Martin Martini in 1655, was based on Chinese maps.

its inadequacies. This made learning from foreigners – all barbarians, in Chinese eyes – very difficult. To make things worse, Chinese morality prescribed contempt for the soldier and for military skills. In a period when external threats would multiply, China was, therefore, dangerously cramped in her possibilities of response. Even under K'ang-hsi there were signs of new challenges ahead. In his old age he had to restore Manchu power in Tibet, when Mongol tribes had usurped it. The Russians were by 1700 installed in Kamchatka, were expanding their trade on the caravan routes and were soon to press on into the Trans-Caspian region. Even peace and prosperity had a price, for they brought faster population growth. Here, unsolved because unrecognized and perhaps insoluble, was another problem to upset the stability of the order authorized by the mandate of heaven. By 1800 there were over three hundred, perhaps even four hundred, million Chinese, and already signs were appearing of what such an increase might portend.

During the Ming era (1368–1644), the first European traders appeared in China. The arrival of a Dutch vessel off the coast of China is represented in this detail from a 17th-century Coromandel screen.

3 JAPAN

There was a time when the English liked to think of Japan as the Great Britain of the Pacific. The parallel was developed at many levels; some were less plausible than others, but there was an indisputable hard nugget of reality in the facts of geography. Both are island kingdoms whose peoples' destinies have been shaped deeply by the sea. Both, too, live close to neighbouring land masses whose influence on them could not but be profound. The Straits of Tsushima which separate Korea from Japan are about five times as wide as the Straits of Dover, it is true, and Japan was able to maintain an isolation from the Asian *terra firma* far more complete than any England could hope for from Europe. Nevertheless, the parallel can be pressed a good way and its validity is shown by the excitement which the Japanese have always shown about the establishment of a strong power in Korea; it rivals that of the British over the danger that the Low Countries might fall into unfriendly hands.

AN EMERGING JAPANESE CIVILIZATION

Even before Japan emerges in her own historical records, in the eighth century CE, there was Japanese-held territory in the Korean peninsula. In those days, Japan was a country divided up among a number of clans, presided over by an emperor with an ill-defined supremacy and an ancestry traced back to the Sun Goddess. The Japanese did not occupy the whole of the territory of modern Japan, but lived in the main on the

This 19th-century Japanese triptych shows the Sun Goddess Amaterasu emerging from her cave to bathe the world in sunlight once more. The scene has been interpreted by some as representing the return of spring after winter. It may also have been inspired by a solar eclipse.

In Japanese mythology Izanagi ("the August Male") and his sister and wife Izanami ("the August Female"), shown in this 19th-century print, immersed a jewelled spear in the waters of the High Plains of Heaven. The drops that fell when they withdrew the spear became the island of Onogoro – the first solid land.

southern and central islands. Here were the mildest climate and the best agricultural prospects. In prehistoric times the introduction of rice growing and the fishing potential of Japanese waters had already made it possible for this mountainous country to feed a disproportionately large population, but pressure on land was to be a recurrent theme of Japanese history.

In 645 CE a political crisis in the dominant clan brought about its downfall and a new one arose, the Fujiwara. It was to preside over a great age of Japanese civilization and to dominate the emperors. There was more than political significance in the change. It also marked a conscious effort to redirect Japanese life along paths of renewal and reform. The direction could only be sought from the guidance offered by the highest example of civilization and power of which the Japanese were aware, and possibly the finest in the world at that time, that of imperial China, which was also an example of expanding, menacing power.

JAPAN'S RELATIONSHIP WITH CHINA

Its continuing and often changing relationship with China is another theme of Japanese history. Both peoples were of Mongoloid stock, though some Caucasoids whose presence it is difficult to account for also form a part of the Japanese ethnic heritage (these, the Ainus, were, at the beginning of the historical era, mainly to be found in the northeast). In prehistoric times Japan appears to have followed in the wake of the civilization of the mainland; bronze artifacts, for example, appear in the islands only in the first century or so BCE. Such innovations in the last millennium BCE may owe something

The arrival of Buddhism in Japan resulted in the introduction of the Chinese T'ang culture, which enriched Japanese art and science. The architecture of the Nara period (710–784), for example, imitated T'ang models, as seen in the Buddha Hall of the Todaiji shrine in Nara. The construction dates from the mid-8th century, but was largely rebuilt in 1709.

to immigrants displaced by the Chinese as they moved southwards on the mainland. But the first references to Japan in the Chinese records (in the third century CE) still depict a country not much affected by mainland events and Chinese influence was not very marked until the centuries following the Han collapse. Then, a vigorous Japanese intervention in Korea seems to have opened the way to closer contact. It was subsequently fostered by the movement of Buddhist students. Confucianism, Buddhism, and iron technology all came to Japan from China. There were attempts to bring about administrative changes on Chinese lines. Above all, Chinese writing had been brought to Japan and its characters were used to provide a written form of the native language. Yet cultural attraction and dependence had not meant political submission.

This 18th-century Japanese scroll depicts the death of the Buddha, a scene known in Japan as *nehanzu* or *parinirvana*. The dying Buddha is shown lying on his right side, facing north.

Shintoism

Shintoism has its origins in the animistic beliefs of early Japan. At the core of the Shinto religion are the cults of deities, which personify natural phenomena, including human beings, and who are called *kami*. Among these are the Sun Goddess (Amaterasu), the Moon God (Tsuki-yomi) and the Storm God (Susano).

Primitive Shinto ceremonies were simple and comprised ablutions and purification rituals. The arrival of Buddhism, however, produced a mutual influence that was to change both religions substantially, resulting in a syncretism known as Ryobu-Shinto (double Shinto). Some Shinto gods, such as Hachiman, the God of War, who is also called Bosatsu (Bodhisattva), have been adapted to Buddhist forms. Other important Shinto gods include Amida, Kannon and Jizo, the latter being closely linked with children, the souls of the dead and those who withstand pain.

The torii *(ceremonial gateway) at the Miyajima Shinto sanctuary, which is dedicated to Susano's three daughters.*

THE IMPORTANCE OF THE CLAN

The Japanese central administration was already well developed in scope and scale at the beginning of the period of centralization and major efforts of reform were made in the seventh and eighth centuries. Yet, in the end, Japan evolved not in the direction of a centralized monarchy but of what might be termed, in a Western analogy, feudal anarchy. For almost nine hundred years it is hard to find a political thread to Japanese history. Its social continuity is much more obvious. From the beginnings of the historical era, even down to the present day, the keys to the continuity and toughness of Japanese society have been the family and the traditional religion. The clan was an enlarged family, and the nation the most enlarged family of all. In patriarchal style, the emperor presided over the national family as did a clan leader over his clan or, even, the small farmer over his family. The focus of family and clan life was participation in the traditional rites, the religion known as Shinto, whose essence was the worship at the proper

Time chart (794–1867)

646
The Taika reforms aim to create a centralized state based on Chinese Sui and T'ang models

1185–1333
The Kamakura period of military feudalism. Shintoism is at its most splendid

1603–1867
The Tokugawa shogunate

500 — 1000 — 1500 — 2000

794–1185
The Heian period, characterized by the influence of Buddhism and Chinese culture

1274 and 1281
Mongol attempts to invade Japan

The *shogun* Yorimoto (1147–1199) made the city of Kamakura the Japanese capital, situated on a bay to the south of present-day Tokyo. Kamakura is famous for its 12th-century statue, the Great Buddha, which is 45 ft (14 m) high.

times of certain local or personal deities. When Buddhism came to Japan it was easily conjoined with this traditional way.

THE ECLIPSE OF THE EMPERORS

The institutional coherence of old Japan was less marked than its social unity. The emperor was its focus. From the beginning of the eighth century, though, the emperor's power was more and more eclipsed and so, in spite of the efforts of an occasional vigorous individual, it remained until the nineteenth century. This eclipse arose in part from the activities of the would-be reformers of the seventh century, for one of them was the founder of the great Fujiwara clan. In the next hundred years or so, his family tied itself closely to the imperial household by marriage. As children were frequently brought up in the household of their mother's family, the clan could exercise a crucial influence upon future emperors while they were children. In the ninth century the chief of the Fujiwara was made regent for the emperor – who was an adult – and for most of what is called the Heian period (794–1185: the name comes from that of the capital city, the modern Kyoto), that clan effectively controlled central government through marriage alliances and court office, its leaders acting in the emperor's name. The power of the Fujiwara did something to disguise the decline of the royal authority, but, in fact, the imperial clan was tending to become simply one among several which existed in the shade of the Fujiwara, each of them governing its own estates more or less independently.

THE KAMAKURA PERIOD

The displacement of the emperor became much more obvious after the passing of the power of the Fujiwara. The Kamakura period (1185–1333) was so called because power passed to a clan whose estates were in the area of that name, and the bypassing of the imperial court, which remained at Heian, became much more obvious. It was early in the Kamakura period that there appeared the first of a series of military dictators who bore the title of *shogun*. These ruled in the emperor's name but in fact with a large independence. The emperor lived on the revenues of his own estates, and as long as he acquiesced in the *shogun*'s intentions he would have military power behind him; when he did not, he would be overruled.

CENTRAL AUTHORITY FADES

The eclipse of the imperial power was so different from what had occurred in China, the model of the seventh-century reformers, that the explanation is not easy to see. It was complex. There was a steady progression through the centuries from the exercise of a usurped central authority in the emperor's name to the virtual disappearance of any central authority at all. No doubt there was a fundamental bias in the traditional clan loyalties of Japanese society and the topography of Japan which would have told against any central power; remote valleys provided lodgements for great magnates. But other countries have met these problems successfully: the Hanoverian governments of eighteenth-century Great Britain tamed the Scottish highlands with punitive expeditions and military roads. A more specific explanation can be seen in the way in which the land reforms of the seventh century, which were the key to political change, were in practice whittled away by the clans with influence at court. Some of these exacted privileges and exemptions, as did some landholding religious institutions. The most common example of the abuses which resulted from this was the granting of tax-free manors to noblemen who were imperial court officials by way of payment for carrying out their duties. The Fujiwara themselves were unwilling to check this practice. At a lower level, smaller proprietors would then seek to commend themselves and their land to a powerful clan in order to get assured tenure in return for rent and an obligation to provide service. The double result of such developments was to create a solid base for the power of local magnates while starving the central administrative structure of support from taxation. Taxes (in the form of a share of the crops) went not to the imperial administration but to the person to whom a manor had been granted.

GOVERNMENTAL STRUCTURES

Such a civil service as existed, unlike the Chinese, was firmly restricted to the aristocracy. Not being recruited by competition, it could not provide a foothold for a group whose interests might be opposed to the hereditary noble families. In the provinces, posts just below the highest level tended to go to the local notables, only the most senior appointments being reserved to civil servants proper.

No one planned that this should happen. Nor did anyone plan a gradual transition to military rule, whose origins lay in the need to make some of the families of the frontier districts responsible for defence against the still unsubdued Ainu peoples. Slowly the prestige of the

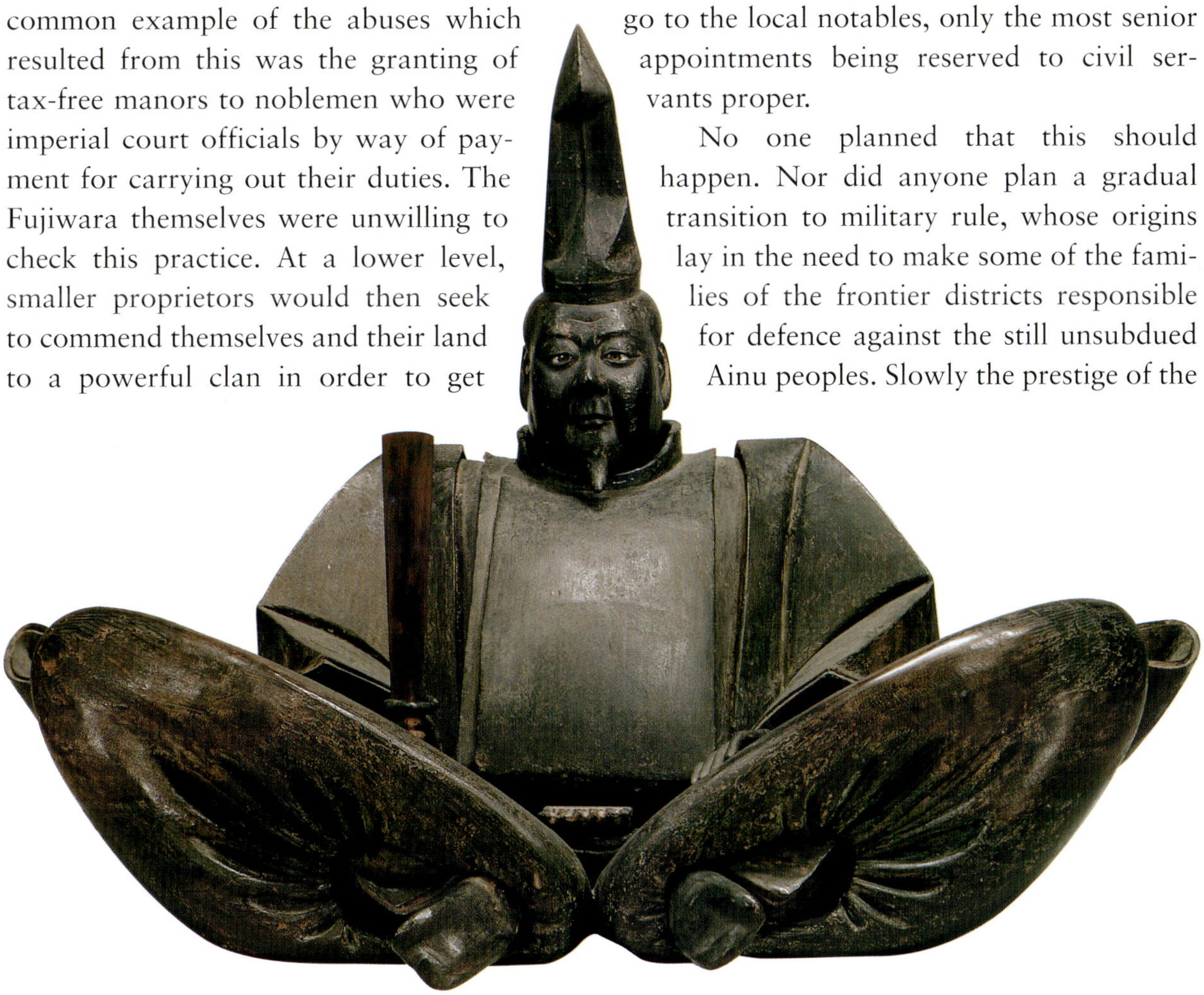

Yorimoto, who is represented by this 12th-century statue, was the head of the Minamoto clan. In 1192 he had himself designated the lifelong, hereditary chief of all the armies, which, in practice, meant that he became the absolute lord of Japan and signified the beginning of the shogunate era.

military clans drew to their leaders the loyalties of people seeking security in troubled times. And, indeed, there was a need for such security. Provincial dissidence began to express itself in outbreaks in the tenth century. In the eleventh there was clearly discernible an emerging class of manorial officers on the great estates. They enjoyed the real management and use of the lands of their formal masters and felt loyalties to the warrior clans in an elementary tie of service and loyalty. In this situation the Minamoto clan rose to a dominance which recreated central government in the early Kamakura period.

ISOLATION AND SECURITY

In one way internal power struggles were a luxury. The Japanese could indulge them because they lived in an island-state where no foreign intruder was ever more than occasionally threatening. Among other things, this meant that there was no need for a national army which might have mastered the clans. Although she came near to it in 1945, Japan has never been successfully invaded, a fact which has done much to shape the national psychology. The consolidation of the national territory was for the most part achieved in the ninth century when the peoples of the north were mastered and, after this, Japan rarely faced any serious external threat to her national integrity, though her relations with other states underwent many changes.

THE OUTSIDE WORLD

In the seventh century the Japanese had been ousted from Korea and this was the last time for many centuries that they were physically installed there. It was the beginning of a phase of cultural subservience to China which was matched by an inability to resist her on the mainland. Japanese embassies were sent to China in the interests of trade, good relations and cultural contact, the last one in the first half of the ninth century. Then, in 894, another envoy was appointed. His refusal to serve marks something of an epoch, for he

Kubilai Khan's ferocious armies met with defeat on the two occasions on which they tried to conquer Japan. This illustration, from *The Mongol Invasions Picture Scroll*, which dates from c.1293, shows a small Japanese vessel attacking a large Mongol ship during the second invasion.

gave it as his reason that China was too much disturbed and distracted by internal problems and that she had, in any case, nothing to teach the Japanese. Official relations were not resumed until the Kamakura period.

There were exploratory gestures in the thirteenth century. They did not prevent the expansion of irregular and private trade with the mainland in forms some of which looked much like freebooting and piracy. It may have been this which did much to provoke the two attempted Mongol invasions of 1274 and 1281. Both retired baffled, the second after grievous losses by storm – the *Kamikaze*, or "divine wind", which came to be seen in much the same light as the English saw the storms which shattered the Armada – and this was one of the greatest moments in strengthening the belief which the Japanese came to hold in their own invincibility and national greatness. Officially, the Mongols' motive had been the Japanese refusal to recognize their claim to inherit the Chinese pretensions to empire and to receive tribute from them. In fact, this conflict once more killed off the recently revived relations with China; they were not taken up again until the coming of Ming rule. By then the reputation of the Japanese as pirates was well established. They ranged far and wide through the Asian seas just as Drake and his companions ranged the Spanish Main. They had the support of many of the feudal lords of the south and it was almost impossible for the *shoguns* to control them even when they wished (as they often did) to do so for the sake of good relations with the Chinese.

One of the best-known symbols of the Japanese landscape and culture is Mount Fuji, which has inspired countless artists. This painting is by So-Ami, one of the finest artists of the *suibokuga* style, who lived in the middle of the 16th century.

JAPANESE CULTURE

THE COLLAPSE of the Kamakura shogunate in 1333 brought a brief and ineffective attempt to restore real power to the emperor, which ended when confronted with the realities of the military power of the clans. In the ensuing period neither *shogun* nor emperor often enjoyed assured power. Until the end of the sixteenth century civil warfare was almost continuous. Yet these troubles did not check the consolidation of a Japanese cultural achievement which remains across the centuries a brilliant and moving spectacle and still shapes Japanese life and attitudes even in an era of industrialism. It is an achievement notable for its power to borrow and adopt from other cultures without sacrificing its own integrity or nature.

Even at the beginning of the historical era, when the prestige of T'ang art makes the derivative nature of what is done in Japan very obvious, there was no merely passive acceptance of a foreign style. Already in the first of the great periods of high Japanese culture, in the eighth century, this is apparent in Japanese painting and a poetry already written in Japanese, though people for centuries still wrote works of art or learning in Chinese (it had something of the status long held by Latin in Europe). At this time, and still more during the climax of the Fujiwara ascendancy, Japanese art other than religious architecture was essentially a court art, shaped by the court setting and the work and enjoyment of a relatively narrow circle. It was hermetically sealed from the world of ordinary Japan by its materials, subject-matter and standards. The great majority of Japanese would never even see the products of what can now be discerned as the first great peak of Japanese culture. The peasant wove hemp and cotton; his womenfolk would be no more likely to touch the fine silks whose careful gradations of colour established the taste displayed by a great court lady's twelve concentric sleeves than he would be to explore the psychological complexities of the Lady Murasaki's subtle novel, the *Tale of Genji*, a study as compelling as Proust and almost as long. Such art had the characteristics to be expected of the art of an élite insulated from society by living in the compound of the imperial palace. It was beautiful, refined, subtle, and sometimes brittle, insubstantial and frivolous. But it already found a place for an emphasis which was to become traditional in Japan, that on simplicity, discipline, good taste and love of nature.

Much Kamakura art aimed to aggrandize the military classes, who had substituted the old nobility. This 14th-century illustration depicts the sea battle of Dannoura at which the Minamoto crushed the rival Taira clan in 1185.

The culture of the Heian court attracted criticism from provincial clan leaders who saw in it an effete and corrupting influence, sapping both the independence of the court nobles and their loyalty to their own clans. From the Kamakura period, a new subject-matter – the warrior – appears in both literature and painting. Yet, as the centuries passed, a hostile attitude to traditional arts changed into one of respect, and during the troubled centuries the warring magnates showed by their own support for them that the central canons of Japanese culture were holding fast. It was protected more and more by an insularity and even a cultural arrogance confirmed by the defeat of the Mongol invasions. A new, military, element, too, was added to this culture during the centuries of war, in part originating in criticism of the apparently effete court circles but then blending with their traditions. It was fed by the feudal ideal of loyalty and self-sacrificing service, by the warrior ideals of discipline and austerity, and by an aesthetic arising out of them. One of its characteristic expressions was an offshoot of Buddhism, Zen. Gradually there emerged a fusion of the style of the high nobility with the austere virtues of the *samurai* warrior which was to run through Japanese life down to the present day. Buddhism also left a visible mark on the Japanese landscape in its temples and the great statues of the Buddha himself. Overall, the anarchy was the most creative of all periods of Japanese culture, for in it there appeared the greatest landscape painting, the culmination of the skill of landscape gardening and the arts of flower arrangement, and the *No* drama.

THE ECONOMY

In particular areas, the lawlessness of these centuries often inflicted grave social and economic damage. As was long to be the case, most Japanese were peasants: they might suffer terribly from an oppressive lord, banditry, or the passage of an army of retainers from a rival fief. Yet such damage was nationally insignificant, it seems. In the sixteenth century a great burst of castle-building testifies to the availability of substantial resources, there was a prolonged expansion of the circulation of copper coinage, and Japanese exports – particularly the exquisite examples of the work of the swordsmiths – began to appear in the markets of China and Southeast Asia. By 1600 Japan's population stood at about eighteen million. Both its slow growth (it had somewhat more than trebled in five centuries) and its substantial urban component rested on a steady improvement in agriculture which had been able to carry the costs of civil strife and lawlessness as well. It was a healthy economic position.

EUROPEAN INTEREST

Sooner or later the Europeans were bound to come to find out more about the mysterious islands which produced such beautiful things. The first were the Portuguese who stepped ashore from Chinese ships, probably in 1543. Others followed in the next few years and in their own ships. It was a promising situation. Japan was virtually without a central government to undertake the regulation of intercourse with foreigners and many of the southern magnates were themselves highly interested in competing for foreign trade. Nagasaki, then a little village, was opened to the newcomers by one of them in 1570. This nobleman was a zealous Christian and had already built a church there; in 1549 the first Christian missionary had arrived, St Francis Xavier. Nearly forty years later Portuguese missionaries were forbidden, so much had the situation changed, though the ban was not at once enforced.

Among other things brought by the Portuguese to Japan were new food crops originally from the Americas – sweet potatoes, maize, sugar cane. They also brought muskets. The Japanese soon learnt to make them. This new weapon played an important part in assuring that the baronial wars of "feudal" Japan came to an end, as did those of medieval Europe, with the emergence of a preponderant power, a brilliant, humbly born soldier-dictator, Hideyoshi. His successor, Ieyasu, was one of his henchmen, a member of the Tokugawa family. In 1603 he revived

Several jars like this one, which dates from the 15th-century Muramachi shogunate, have been found in central Japan. Most served as vessels for saké, although some were used as funerary urns.

and assumed the old title of *shogun* and so inaugurated a period of Japanese history known as the "great peace", which lasted until a revolutionary change in 1868 but was itself an immensely creative period, in which Japan changed significantly.

THE TOKUGAWA SHOGUNATE

During the Tokugawa shogunate, for two and a half centuries, the emperor passed even further into the wings of Japanese politics and was firmly kept there. Court gave way to camp; the shogunate rested on a military overlordship. The *shoguns* themselves changed from being outstandingly important feudal lords to being in the first place hereditary princes and in the second the heads of a stratified social system over which they exercised viceregal powers in the name of the emperor and on his behalf. This régime was called the *bakufu* – the government of the camp. The *quid pro quo* provided by Ieyasu, the first Tokugawa *shogun*, was order and the assurance of financial support for the emperor.

The key to the structure was the power of the Tokugawa house itself. Ieyasu's origins had been pretty humble, but by the middle of the seventeenth century the clan appears to have controlled about one-quarter of Japan's rice-growing land. The feudal lords became in effect vassals of the Tokugawa, linked to the clan by a variety of ties. The term "centralized feudalism" has been coined to label this system. Not all the lords, or *daimyo*, were connected to the *shogun* in the same way. Some were directly dependent, being vassals with a hereditary family attachment to the Tokugawa family. Others were related to it by marriage, patronage or business. Others, less reliable, formed an outer category of those families which had only at length submitted. But all were carefully watched. The lords lived alternately at the *shogun's* court or on their estates; when they were on their estates, their families lived as potential hostages of the *shogun* at Edo, the modern Tokyo, his capital.

The Jesuit St Francis Xavier was sent as a missionary to Portugal's Eastern colonies by King John III. In 1549 St Francis arrived in Japan, where he travelled widely and founded a mission that was to flourish for 100 years. On the right in this illustration two Jesuit priests from one of the early Japanese missions are depicted.

SOCIAL RIGIDITY

Below the lords was a society strictly and legally separated into hereditary classes and the maintenance of this structure was the primary goal of the régime. The noble *samurai* were the lords and their retainers, the warrior rulers who dominated society and gave it its tone as did the gentry bureaucrats of China. They followed a spartan, military ideal symbolized by the two swords they carried, and were allowed to use on commoners guilty of disrespect. *Bushido*, their creed, stressed above all the loyalty owed by a person to his or her lord. The original links of the retainers with the land were virtually gone by the seventeenth century and they lived in the castle towns of their lords. The other classes were the peasants, the artisans and the merchants (the lowest in the social hierarchy because of their non-productive character); the self-assertive ethos of the merchant which emerged in Europe was unthinkable in Japan, in spite of the vigour of Japanese trade. As the aim of the whole system was stability, attention to the duties of one's station and confinement to them was determinedly enforced. Hideyoshi himself had supervised a great sword hunt whose aim was to take away these weapons from those who were not supposed to have them – the lower classes. Whatever the equity of this, it must have told in favour of order. Japan wanted stability and her society accordingly came to emphasize the things that could ensure it: knowing one's place, discipline, regularity, scrupulous workmanship, stoical endurance. At its best it remains one of humanity's most impressive social achievements.

THE EUROPEANS ARE EXPELLED

The Japanese system shared one particular weakness with the Chinese; it presumed effective insulation from external stimuli to change. It was for a long time threatened by the danger of a relapse into internal anarchy; there were plenty of discontented *daimyo* and restless swordsmen about in seventeenth-century Japan. By then, one obvious external danger came from Europeans. They had already brought to Japan imports which would have profound effects. Among them the most obvious were firearms, whose powerfully disruptive impact went beyond that which they achieved on their targets, and Christianity. This faith had at first been tolerated and even welcomed as something tempting traders from outside. In the early seventeenth century the percentage of Japanese Christians in the population was higher than it has ever been since. Soon, it has been estimated, there were over half a million of them. Nevertheless, this state of affairs did not last. Christianity has always had great subversive potential. Once this was grasped by Japan's rulers, a savage persecution began. It not only cost the lives of thousands of Japanese martyrs, who often suffered cruel deaths, but brought trade with Europe almost to an end. The English left and the Spanish were excluded in the 1620s. After the Portuguese had undergone a similar expulsion they rashly sent an embassy in 1640 to argue the toss; almost all of its members were killed. Japanese had already been forbidden to go abroad, or to return if they were already there, and the building of large ships was banned. Only the Dutch, who promised not to proselytize and were willing to trample on the cross, kept up Japan's

This detail of part of a folding screen depicts *samurai* warriors taking part in the siege of the castle of Osaka in 1615.

From a 17th-century folding screen, this detail shows Portuguese sailors unloading their merchandise in a Japanese port.

henceforth tiny contact with Europe. They were allowed a trading station on a tiny island in Nagasaki harbour.

After this, there was no real danger of foreigners exploiting internal discontent. But there were other difficulties. In the settled conditions of the "great peace", military skill declined. The *samurai* retainers sat about in the castle towns of their lords, their leisure broken by little except the ceremonial parade in outdated armour which accompanied a lord's progress to the city of Edo. When the Europeans came back in the nineteenth century equipped with up-to-date weapons, Japan's military forces would be technically unable to match them.

A CHANGING ECONOMY

The external military threat could, perhaps, hardly have been foreseen. Nor could another result of the general peace in which internal trade prospered. The Japanese economy became more dependent on money. Old relationships were weakened by this and new social stresses appeared. Payment in cash forced lords to sell most of the tax rice which was their subsistence to pay for their visits to the capital. At the same time, the market became a national one. Merchants did well: some of them soon had money to lend their rulers. Gradually the warriors became dependent on the bankers. Besides feeling a shortage of cash, those rulers found themselves sometimes embarrassed by their inability to deal with economic change and its social repercussions. If retainers were to be paid in coin, they might more easily transfer loyalty to another paymaster. Towns were growing, too, and by 1700 Osaka and Kyoto both had more than 300,000 inhabitants, while Edo may have had 800,000. Other changes were bound to follow such growth. Price fluctuations in the rice market of the towns sharpened hostility towards the wealthy dealers.

ECONOMIC GROWTH

In this changing economy we face one great paradox of Tokugawa Japan. While its rulers slowly came to show less and less ability to contain new challenges to traditional ways, those challenges stemmed from a fundamental fact – economic growth – which in historical perspective now appears the dominant theme of the era. Under the Tokugawa, Japan was developing fast. Between 1600 and 1850 agricultural production approximately doubled, while the population rose by less than half. Since the régime was not one which was able to skim off the new wealth for itself, it remained in society as savings for investment by those who saw opportunities, or went into a rising standard of living for many Japanese.

Dispute continues about the explanation of what seems to have been a successful stride to self-sustaining economic growth of a kind which was elsewhere to appear only in Europe. Some are obvious and have been touched upon: the passive advantages conferred by the seas around Japan which kept out invaders such as the steppe-borne nomads who time and again harried the wealth-producers of mainland Asia. The shogunate's own "great peace" ended feudal warfare and was another bonus. Then there were positive improvements to agriculture which resulted from more intensive cultivation, investment in irrigation, the exploitation of the new crops brought (originally from the Americas) by the Portuguese. But at this point the enquiry is already touching on reciprocal effects: the improvement of agriculture was possible because it became profitable to the producer, and it was profitable because social and governmental conditions were of a certain kind. Enforced residence of noblemen and their families at Edo not only put rice on the market (because the nobles had to find cash), but created a new huge urban market at the capital which sucked in both labour (because it supplied employment) and goods which it became more and more profitable to produce. Regional specialization (in textile manufacture, for example) was favoured by disparities in the capacity to grow food: most of Japanese industrial and handicraft production was, as in early industrial Europe, to be found in rural areas. Government helped, too; in the early years of the shogunate there was organized development of irrigation, standardizing of weights and currency. But for all its aspirations to regulate society, the government of the *bakufu* in the end probably favoured

Two Japanese ferry boats are shown lowering their sails in this 19th-century woodcut from Kuwana.

economic growth because it lacked power. Instead of an absolute monarchy, it came to resemble a balance-of-power system of the great lords, and was able to maintain itself only so long as there was no foreign invader to disturb it. As a result it could not obstruct the path to economic growth and divert resources from producers who could usefully employ them. Indeed, the economically quasi-parasitical *samurai* actually underwent a reduction in their share of the national income at a time when producers' shares were rising. It has been suggested that by 1800 the *per capita* income and life expectancy of the Japanese was much the same as that of their British contemporaries.

THE CONSEQUENCES OF ISOLATION

Much has been obscured by the more superficial but strikingly apparent features of the Tokugawa era. Some of these, of course, were important, but at a different level. The new prosperity of the towns created a clientèle for printed books and the coloured wood-block prints which were later to excite European artists' admiration. It also provided the audiences for the new *kabuki* theatre. Yet brilliant though it often was, and successful, at the deepest economic level (if undesignedly) as it was, it is not clear that the Tokugawa system could have survived much longer even without the coming of a new threat from the West in the nineteenth century. Towards the end of the period there were signs of uneasiness. Japanese intellectuals began to sense that somehow their isolation had preserved them from Europe but also had cut them off from Asia. They were right. Japan had already made for herself a unique historical destiny and it would mean that she faced the West in a way very different from the subjects of Manchu or Moghul.

In the Edo period a new artistic movement, which involved the production of xylographs or woodcuts with a purely popular character, emerged as a reaction against the traditional élitist painting. In these popular paintings women began to be represented as courtesans (*yujo* women) rather than geishas, who were the subject of traditional art. In this 18th-century piece three girls are depicted paddling in a river.

4 WORLDS APART

AFRICA AND THE AMERICAS moved towards civilization to rhythms very different from those operating elsewhere. Of course, this was not quite so true of Africa as of the Americas, which were long cut off by the oceans from all but fleeting contacts with the rest of the world. The Africans, by contrast, lived in a continent much of which was gradually Islamicized, and for a long time had at least peripheral encounters with first Arab and then European traders. These were of growing importance as time went by, though they did not suck Africa completely into the mainstream of world history until the late nineteenth century. This isolation, combined with an almost complete dependence for much of the story on archaeological evidence, makes much African and American history an obscure business.

This illustration, which depicts the arrival of Ethiopian legatees in ancient Rome to sue for peace, gives an idea of how Europeans living in the 15th century imagined Africans to look.

AFRICA

AFRICAN HISTORY BEFORE the coming of European trade and exploration is largely a matter of an internal dynamic we can barely discern, but we may presume folk-movements to have played a large part in it. There are many legends of migration and they always speak of movement from the north to the south and west. In each case, scholars have to evaluate the legend in its context, and with help from reference in Egyptian records, travellers' tales and archaeological discovery, but the general tendency is striking. It seems to register a general trend, the enrichment and elaboration of African culture in the north first and its appearance in the south only much later.

METALLURGICAL SKILLS

The kingdom of Kush, which had connexions with ancient Egypt, is a convenient place to begin the story of these cultural changes. By the fifth century BCE the Kushites had lost control of Egypt and retreated once more to Meroe, their capital in the south, but they had centuries of flourishing culture still ahead of them. From Egypt, probably, they had brought with them a hieroglyph (claims are now being made to have penetrated it). Certainly they diffused their knowledge to the south and west in the Sudan, where notable metallurgical skills were later to flourish among the Nubians and Sudanese. In the last few centuries BCE iron-working appears south of the Sahara, in central Nigeria. Its importance was recognized by its remaining the closely guarded secret of kings, but so valuable a skill slowly travelled southwards. By about the twelfth century CE it had penetrated the southeast, and the pygmies and the San people (previously known as Bushmen) of the south were the only Africans then still living in the Stone Age.

AGRICULTURE

Probably the greatest difference made by the spread of iron-working was to agriculture. It made possible a new penetration of the forests and better tilling of the soil (which may be connected with the arrival of new food-crops from Asia in the early Common Era), and so led to new folk-movements and population growth. Hunting and gathering areas were broken up by the coming of herdsmen and farmers who can be discerned already by about 500 CE in much of east and southeast Africa, in modern Zimbabwe and the Transvaal. Yet those Africans did not acquire the plough. Possibly the reason lies in the lack in most of the continent south of Egypt of an animal resistant enough to African diseases to draw one. One area where there were ploughs was Ethiopia, and there animals could be bred successfully, as the early use of the horse indicates. Horses were also bred for riding in the southern Sahara.

This suggests once again the important limiting factor of the African environment. Most of the continent's history is the story of response to influences from the outside – iron-working and new crops from the Near East, Asia, Indonesia and the Americas; steam engines and medicine from nineteenth-century Europe. These made it possible gradually to grapple with African nature. Without them, Africa south of the Sahara seems almost inert under the huge pressures exercised upon it by geography, climate and disease. It remained (with some exceptions) for the most part tied to a shifting agriculture, not achieving an intensive one; this was a positive response to difficult conditions but could not sustain more than a slow population growth. Nor did southern Africa arrive at the wheel, so it lagged behind in transport, milling and pottery.

CHRISTIAN AND ISLAMIC AFRICA

The story was different north of the Equator. Much Kushite history waits, in the most literal sense, to be uncovered, for few of the major cities have yet been excavated. It is known that in about 300 CE Kush was overthrown by Ethiopians. They were not then the unique people they were to become, with kings claiming descent from Solomon and for centuries the only Christian people in Africa outside Egypt. They were converted to

From the 11th century to the 14th century the Nigerian Ife culture was created by the Yoruba tribe, to which this bronze head of a king is attributed. The outstanding terracotta and bronze sculptures produced by the Yoruba have become a milestone in Africa's cultural history.

Time chart (500 BCE–900 CE)

	500 BCE		0		500 CE		1000 CE
Africa:	500 BCE The beginning of the Nox culture in northern Nigeria		c.300 CE The Kush kingdom is overthrown by Ethiopians		c.700 CE The Empire of Ghana enjoys great economic development and growth in trade	900 CE The Hausa settle in the Daura Kingdom of northern Nigeria	
The Americas:		c.400 BCE The decline of the Olmec civilization	c.300 CE The Teotihuacán civilization		600 CE The apogee of the Maya civilization in Mesoamerica		

Christianity by Copts only later in the fourth century; at that time they were still in touch with the classical Mediterranean world. But the Islamic invasions of Egypt placed between them and it a barrier which was not breached for centuries, during which the Ethiopians battled for survival against pagan and Muslim, virtually isolated from Rome or Byzantium. An Amharic-speaking people, they were the only literate non-Islamic African nation.

The only other place in Africa where Christianity established itself was in the Roman north. Here it had been a vigorous, if minority, cult. The violence of its dissensions and the pursuit of the Donatists as heretics probably explain its weakness when the Arab invasions brought it face to face with Islam. Except in Egypt, Christianity was extinguished in the Africa of the Arab states. Islam, on the other hand, was and has remained enormously successful in Africa. Borne by Arab invasion, it spread in the eleventh century right across to the Niger and western Africa. Arab sources therefore provide our main information about the non-literate African societies which stretched across the Sudan and Sahara after the passing of Kush. They were often trading communities and may reasonably be thought of as city-states; the most famous was Timbuctoo, impoverished by the time Europeans finally got there, but in the fifteenth century important enough to be the site of what has been described as an Islamic university. Politics and economics are still as closely intertwined in Africa as in any part of the world, and it is not surprising that the early kingdoms of black Africa should have appeared and prospered at the end of important trade routes where there was wealth to tap. Merchants liked stability.

Timbuctoo was founded by Tuareg nomads in c.1100 CE. It was absorbed into the Mali Empire in the late 13th century and became the main trading centre in Africa. Emperor Mansa Musa, the most famous of Mali's rulers, who reigned in the early 14th century, built palaces and mosques there, the best-known of which is the Great Mosque (Djingereyber). It is constructed of adobe and rubble and covered with clay.

GHANA

Another African state, the earliest recorded by the Arabs, had a name later taken by a modern nation: Ghana. Its origins are obscure, but may well have lain in the assertion of its supremacy by a people in the late pre-Common Era who had the advantage of iron weapons and horses. However this may be, the Ghana recorded by Arab chroniclers and geographers is already an important kingdom when it appears in the records in the eighth century CE. At its greatest extent, Ghana spanned an area about five hundred miles across the region framed to the south by the upper reaches of the Niger and Senegal and protected to the north by the Sahara. The Arabs spoke of it as "the land of gold"; the gold came from the upper Senegal and the

Christianity had already been prevalent in Egypt for more than 100 years when this 5th-century Coptic tapestry, clearly inspired by the art of the Eastern Roman Empire, was made. In the 7th century Egypt was conquered by the Arabs. At first the Christians were protected by their new overlords, but later they were enslaved until well into the 19th century.

Ashanti, and was passed by Arab traders up to the Mediterranean by trans-Saharan routes or through Egypt. The most important other commodities traded across the Sahara were salt and slaves. Ghana collapsed during the twelfth and thirteenth centuries.

MALI

Ghana's eclipse was followed by the preeminence of Mali, a kingdom whose ruler's wealth caused a sensation when in 1307 he made a pilgrimage to Mecca and another source of a name for a twentieth-century African state. Mali was even bigger than Ghana, taking in the whole Senegal basin and running about a thousand miles inland from the coast at the beginning of the fourteenth century. The Mali ruler is said to have had ten thousand horses in his stables. This empire broke up in the sixteenth century after defeat by the Moroccans. Other states were to follow. But, although in some cases the Arab records speak of African courts attended by men of letters, there is no native

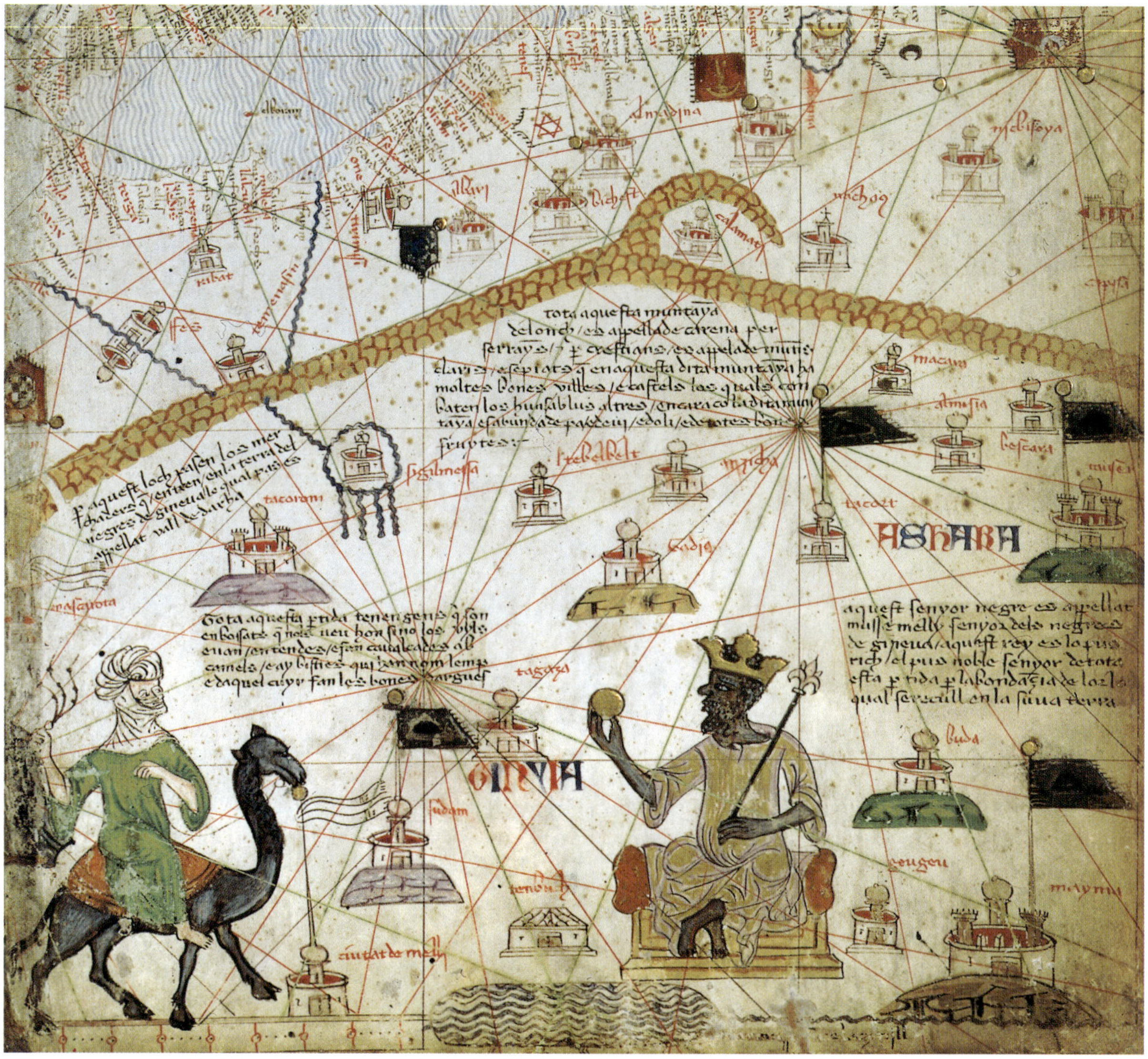

Mali's huge economic growth was a result of its trade with Arab merchants, who, at the end of the 12th century, had begun to exploit African gold. Legend has it that, as Emperor Mansa Musa travelled through Egypt during his pilgrimage to Mecca, he gave away so much gold that its value in Cairo dropped by 12 per cent. Musa's fame soon reached the Western world, as the Great Catalan Atlas (shown here), dated 1375, demonstrates.

documentation which enables us to reach these peoples. Clearly they remained pagan while their rulers belonged to the Islamic world. It may be that the dissolution of Ghana owed something to dissent caused by conversions to Islam. Arab reports make it obvious that the Islamic cult was associated with the ruler in the Sudanese and Saharan states but had also still to accommodate traditional practice from the pagan past – rather as early Christianity in Europe accepted a similar legacy. Nor did social custom always adapt itself to Islam: Arabic writers expressed shocked disapproval of the public nakedness of Mali girls.

SUB-SAHARAN AFRICA

Africa further south of the Sahara is even harder to get at. At the roots of the history which determined its structure on the eve of its absorption into world events was a folk-migration of the negroid peoples who speak languages of the group called Bantu. This is a term somewhat like "Indo-European", referring to identifiable linguistic characteristics, not genetic qualities. The detailed course of this movement is, of course, still highly obscure but its beginnings lie in eastern Nigeria, where there were early Bantu-speakers. From there they took their language and agriculture south, first into the Congo basin. There followed a rapid spread, round about the beginning of the Common Era, over most of southern Africa. This set the ethnic pattern of modern Africa.

Some peoples, speaking the language the Arabs called "Swahili" (from the Arabic word meaning "of the coast"), established towns on the east African coasts which were linked to mysterious kingdoms in the interior. This was before the eighth century CE, when the Arabs began to settle in these towns and turn them into ports. The Arabs called the region the land of the Zanz (from which was later to come the name of Zanzibar) and said that its peoples prized iron above gold. It is probable that these polities had some kind of trading relations with Asia even before Arab times; who the intermediaries were it is not possible to say, but they may have been Indonesians such as those who colonized Madagascar. The Africans had gold and iron to offer for luxuries and they also began the implantation of new crops from Asia, cloves and bananas among them.

RULING STRUCTURES

Even a vague picture of the working of the African states is hard to arrive at. Monarchy was by no means the rule in them and a sense of the importance of ties of kin seems to have been the only widespread characteristic of black African polities. Organization must have reflected the needs of particular environments and the possibilities presented by particular resources. Yet kingship was widely diffused. Again, the earliest signs are northern, in Nigeria and Benin. By the fifteenth century there are kingdoms in the region of the great eastern lakes and we hear of the kingdom of the Kongo, on the lower Congo river. There are not many signs of organization on this scale and African states were for a long time not to produce bureaucratized administration or standing armies. The powers of kings must have been limited, not only by custom and respect for tradition, but by the lack of resources to bind people's allegiance beyond the ties imposed by kinship and respect. No doubt this accounts for the transitory and fleeting nature of many of these "states". Ethiopia was an untypical African country.

ZIMBABWE

Some remarkable traces remain of these dim and shadowy kingdoms. A high level of culture in the east African interior in about the twelfth century is demonstrated by the remains of mine-workings, roads, rock paintings,

In the late 15th century the Portuguese established trade relations with Benin in western Africa: their collaboration was to prove highly profitable for both kingdoms. African craftsmen began to work for the Portuguese, combining motifs from the two cultures in their work. This ivory salt-cellar is an example of this syncretic influence.

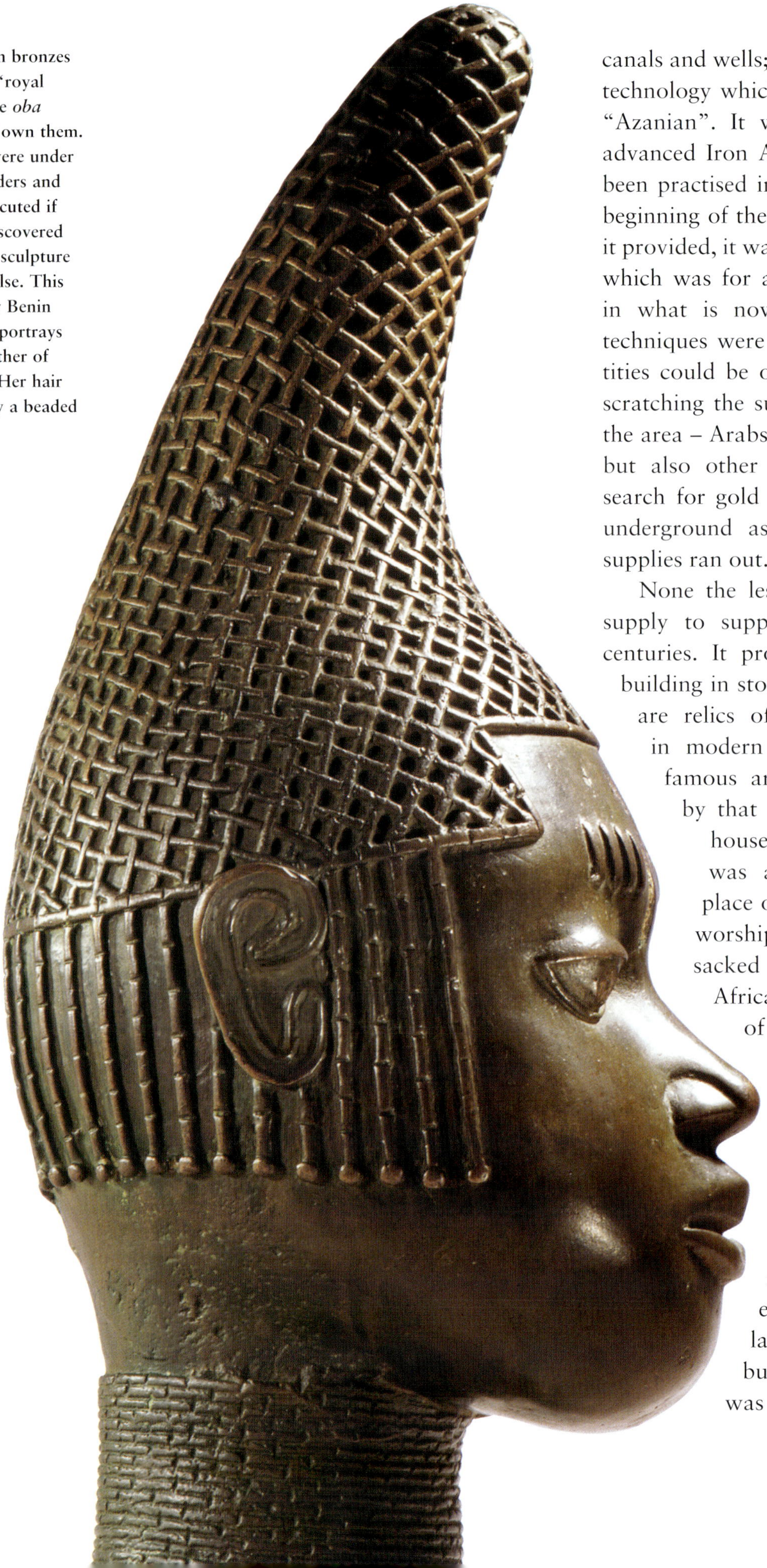

The Benin bronzes were a "royal art": only the *oba* (king) could own them. Craftsmen were under his direct orders and could be executed if they were discovered producing a sculpture for anyone else. This 16th-century Benin bronze bust portrays Idia, the mother of Oba Esigie. Her hair is covered by a beaded coral cap.

canals and wells; these were the products of a technology which archaeologists have called "Azanian". It was the achievement of an advanced Iron Age culture. Agriculture had been practised in the region since about the beginning of the Common Era. On the basis it provided, it was possible to exploit the gold which was for a long time easily accessible in what is now Zimbabwe. Only simple techniques were needed at first; large quantities could be obtained by little more than scratching the surface. This drew traders to the area – Arabs first, and later Portuguese – but also other Africans as migrants. The search for gold had in the end to be taken underground as the most easily available supplies ran out.

None the less there was a rich enough supply to support a "state" lasting four centuries. It produced the only significant building in stone in southern Africa. There are relics of it in hundreds of places in modern Zimbabwe, but the most famous are at the place itself called by that name (which means "stone houses"). From about 1400 this was a royal capital, the burial place of kings and a sacred site for worship. So it remained until it was sacked in about 1830 by another African people. The Portuguese of the sixteenth century had already reported a great fortress built of dry-stone masonry but only in the nineteenth century have we records by Europeans of what we know to be this site. They were amazed to find massive walls and towers in carefully shaped stone, laid in courses without mortar but with great accuracy. There was disinclination to believe that

Africans could have produced anything so impressive; some suggested the Phoenicians should have the credit and a few romantics toyed with the idea that Zimbabwe had been put there by the masons of the Queen of Sheba. Today, remembering the world of other Iron Age peoples in Europe and the civilizations of America, such hypotheses do not seem necessary. The Zimbabwe ruins may reasonably be attributed to the Africans of the fifteenth century.

AFRICAN CULTURE

Advanced as East Africa was, its peoples failed to arrive at literacy for themselves; like the early Europeans, they were to acquire it from other civilizations. Perhaps the absence of a need for careful records of land, or of crops which could be stored, is a part of the explanation. Whatever the reason, the absence of literacy was a handicap in acquiring and diffusing information and in consolidating government. It was also a cultural impoverishment: Africa would not have a native tradition of learned sages from whom would come scientific and philosophical skill. On the other hand, the artistic capacity of black Africa was far from negligible, as the achievement of Zimbabwe, or the bronzes of Benin, which captivated later Europeans, show.

THE AMERICAS

ISLAM HAD BEEN AT WORK in Africa for nearly eight hundred years (and before that there had been the influence of Egypt on its neighbours) by the time the Europeans arrived in America, to discover civilizations which had achieved much more than those of Africa and appeared to have done so without stimuli from the outside. This has seemed so improbable to some people that much time has been spent investigating and discussing the possibility that the elements of civilization were implanted in the Americas by trans-Pacific voyagers a very long time ago. Most scholars find the evidence inconclusive. If there was such a contact in remote times, it had long since ceased. There is no unequivocal trace of connexion between the Americas and any other continent between the time when the first Americans crossed the Bering Straits and the landings of Vikings. There is then none thereafter until the Spanish arrived at the end of the fifteenth century. To an even greater degree than Africa, and for a longer time, we must assume the Americas to have been cut off from the rest of the world.

Representing a king, this piece is one of the remarkable Benin bronze plaques, most of which were taken to England in 1897 by members of a British expedition. The kingdom of Benin, which was founded in the 12th century, reached its heyday in the 15th century, when Lagos (now the capital of Nigeria) was founded.

The pre-imperialist Americas

This map shows the empires that ruled in the Americas before Spanish explorers and imperialists landed there.

NORTH AMERICAN PEOPLES

Their isolation accounts for the fact that, even in the nineteenth century, pre-agricultural peoples still survived in North America. On the eastern plains of the modern United States there were "Indians" (as Europeans later came to call them) practising agriculture before the arrival of Europeans, but further west other communities were then still hunting and gathering. They would go on doing so, though with important changes of techniques as first the horse and metal, brought by Europeans, and then firearms were added to their technical equipment. Further west still, there were peoples on the west coast who fished or collected their subsistence on the seashore, again in ways fixed since time immemorial. Far to the north, a *tour de force* of specialization has enabled the Eskimos to live with great efficiency in an all but intolerable environment; this pattern survives in its essentials even today. Yet although the Indian cultures of North America are respectable achievements in their overcoming of environmental challenge, they are not civilization. For the American achievement in indigenous civilization it is necessary to go south of the Rio Grande. Here were to be found a series of major civilizations linked by common dependence on the cultivation of maize and by possessing pantheons of nature gods, but strikingly different in other ways.

MESOAMERICAN CIVILIZATIONS

In Mesoamerica the Olmec foundation proved very important. The calendars, hieroglyphics and the practice of building large ceremonial sites which mark so much of the region in later times may all be ultimately derived from it; the gods of Mesoamerica were already known in Olmec times, too. Between the beginning and the fourth century of the Common Era the successors of the Olmecs built the first great American city, Teotihuacán, in what is now Mexico. It was for two or three centuries a major trading centre and probably of outstanding religious importance, for it contained a huge complex of pyramids and great public buildings. Mysteriously, it was destroyed in about the seventh century, possibly by one of a series of waves of invaders moving southwards into the valley of central Mexico. These movements began an age of migration and warfare which was to last until the coming of the Spaniards, and produced several brilliant regional societies.

Teotihuacán

One of the most impressive ancient ceremonial centres in Latin America is, without a doubt, Teotihuacán (City of the Gods), located in a valley near the present-day city of Mexico. Mythology stated that the gods had convened at the site to create the world for the fifth time. The city's most famous buildings, the Pyramids of the Sun and the Moon, were founded around the year 100 CE. Many temples, squares and houses were constructed around them – the houses are believed to have provided lodgings for the priests who made up the most important social class.

Between the middle of the 4th century and the end of the 5th century CE, the city reached the height of its glory: the Avenue of the Dead, a thoroughfare lined with the ruins of more than 75 temples, dates from this time. Next to it stands the Temple of Quetzalcoatl, the exterior of which is decorated with the famous heads of winged serpents.

All this splendour was probably made possible by improvements in agricultural techniques. The resulting increased harvests then led to population growth, and to the expansion of commerce. This in turn gave rise to the appearance of extensive trade networks, established to discover new sources of raw materials.

The Avenue of the Dead, seen here from the Pyramid of the Sun, leads to the smaller Pyramid of the Moon.

THE MAYA

THE MOST REMARKABLE Mesoamerican societies were those formed by the Maya cultures of Yucatán, Guatemala and northern Honduras. Their setting was extraordinary, given its appearance today. Virtually all the great Maya sites lie in tropical rain-forest, whose animals and insects, climate and diseases demand great efforts if its resources are to be tapped by agriculture. Yet the Maya not only maintained huge populations for many centuries with rudimentary agricultural techniques (they had no ploughs or metal tools and long depended on burning and clearing land to use it for a couple of seasons before moving on), but also raised stone buildings comparable to those of ancient Egypt.

Many Maya sites may remain undiscovered in the jungle, but enough have now been found to reconstruct an outline of Maya history and society, both of which have in the past few decades been shown to have been much more complex than was once thought. The earliest traces of Maya culture have been discerned in the third and fourth centuries BCE; it blossomed into its greatest period between the sixth and ninth centuries CE, when its finest buildings, sculpture and pottery were produced. Maya cities of that era contained great ceremonial complexes, combinations of temples, pyramids, tombs and ritual courts, often covered with hieroglyphic writing. Religion played an important part in the government of this culture, endorsing the dynastic rulers of the cities in ceremonies in which bloodshed and sacrifice played a signal part.

THE MAYA CALENDAR

Maya religious practice consisted of the performance of regular acts of intercession and worship in a cycle calculated from a calendar derived from astronomical observation. Many scholars have found this the only Maya achievement worthy of comparison with the buildings, and it was indeed a great feat of mathematics. Through the calendar, enough of Maya thinking can be grasped to make it evident that this people's religious leaders had an idea of time much vaster than that of any other civilization of which we have knowledge; they calculated an antiquity of hundreds of thousands of years. They may even have arrived at the idea that time has no beginning.

The stone hieroglyphs and three surviving books tell us something of this calendar and have provided a chronology for Maya dynasties. The Maya of the classical era used to put up dated monuments every twenty years to record the passage of time, the last of them dated to 928. By then, Maya civilization was past its peak. For all the skill of its builders and craftsmen in jade and obsidian, it had considerable limitations. The makers of the great temples never achieved the arch, nor could they employ carts in their operations, for the Maya never discovered the wheel, while the religious world in whose shadows they lived was peopled by two-headed dragons, jaguars and grinning skulls. As for its political achievement, Maya society had long been based on patterns of alliances tying together the cities in two dynastic agglomerations whose history is set out in the hieroglyph of the monuments. At its greatest extent, the largest Maya city may have had as many as 40,000 inhabitants, with a dependent rural population far greater than that of Maya America today.

THE DECLINE OF THE MAYA

Maya civilization was highly specialized. Like the Egyptian, it required a huge investment of

The Maya codices

The Maya codices constitute one of the most splendid expressions of Maya art. These documents consist of folded leaves of paper (made from tree bark covered with whitewash), on which representations of the gods, leaders and hieroglyphs were drawn. Most of the codices vanished when the Spanish arrived; some Spaniards, such as the first Bishop of Yucatán, Diego de Landa, gave orders that the Maya documents should be systematically destroyed.

Only four pre-conquest codices survive today, three of which are named after the cities in which they are now held. The 13th-century Dresden Codex contains articles about astronomy and astrology. The Paris Codex, only a fragment of which has been found, contains information about divination and ceremonial rituals. The Madrid Codex, also known as the Tro-cortesian Codex, was found in two fragments. It is made up of 56 sheets of text describing the various rituals that the Maya priests used to predict the future.

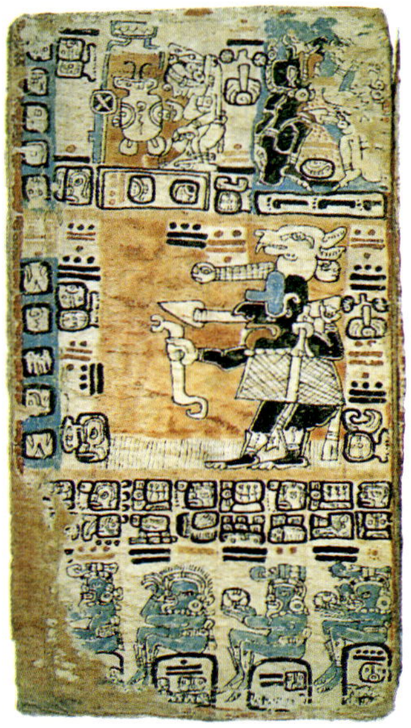

The Madrid Codex, from which this detail is taken, shows a large number of gods, priests and Maya nobles.

labour in unproductive building, but the Egyptians had done much more. Perhaps Maya civilization was overloaded at an early date. Soon after its beginning a people from the valley of Mexico, probably Toltec, seized Chichen Itza, the greatest Maya site, and from this time the jungle centres of the south began to be abandoned. The invaders brought metal with them and also the Mexican practice of sacrificing prisoners of war. Their gods begin to appear in sculpture at the Maya sites. Seemingly, there was also a shift of power from priests to secular rulers among the Maya, and there was a contemporaneous cultural recession marked by cruder pottery and sculpture and a decline in the quality of the hieroglyph, too. By the end of the eleventh century the Maya political order had collapsed, though a few cities were to flicker back to life at a lower level of cultural and material existence during the next couple of centuries. Chichen Itza was finally abandoned in the thirteenth century and the centre of Maya culture shifted to another site, sacked in its turn, possibly after a peasant rising in about 1460. With that, the Maya story goes into eclipse until the twentieth century. In the sixteenth century Yucatán passed into the hands of the Spanish, though only in 1699 did the last Maya stronghold fall to them.

The Spaniards were only in the most formal sense the destroyers of Maya civilization. It had already collapsed from within by the time they arrived. Explanation is not easy, given our information, and it is tempting to fall back on metaphor: Maya civilization was the answer to a huge challenge and could meet it for a time, but only with a precarious political structure vulnerable to outside influence, and at the cost of narrow specialization and burdens which were huge in relation to the resources available to support them. Even before foreign invasion, as political fragmentation occurred, the irrigation arrangements of which the archaeologists have discovered the remains were falling into desuetude and decay. As decisively as elsewhere in the Americas, the native culture left behind no living style, no technology of note, no literature, no political or religious institution of significance. Only in the language of the Maya peasantry did the past retain some foothold. What the Maya left behind were wondrous ruins, which would long bemuse and fascinate those who had later to try to explain them.

The Maya used two calendars. One was ritual and consisted of a combination of 13 numerals and 20 named days, resulting in 260-day cycles. The solar calendar, however, was made up of 365 days, divided into 18 months of 20 days each, with five days added to the end. Every 52 solar calendar years, the two types of calendar coincided on one day. This bas-relief, from the city of Palenque, bears a hieroglyph referring to a unit of time that is equivalent to 7,200 days.

THE AZTECS

WHILE MAYA SOCIETY was in its final decay, one of the last peoples to arrive in the valley of Mexico won an hegemony there which amazed the Spanish more than anything they later found in Yucatán. These were the Aztecs, who had entered the valley in about 1350 CE, overthrowing the Toltecs who then exercised supremacy there. They

This illustration from the Axcatitlán Codex represents the Aztecs' long journey from their nomadic origins in northern Mexico to their definitive settlement at Tenochtitlán, the city from which they ruled a huge empire.

settled in two villages on marshy land at the edge of Lake Texcoco; one of these was called Tenochtitlán and it was to be the capital of an Aztec empire which expanded in less than two centuries to cover the whole of central Mexico. Aztec expeditions went far south into what was later the republic of Panama, but showed no diligence in settlement. The Aztecs were warriors and preferred an empire of tribute: their army gave them the obedience of some thirty or so minor tribes or states which they left more or less alone, provided the agreed tribute was forthcoming. The gods of these peoples were given the compliment of inclusion in the Aztec pantheon.

The centre of Aztec civilization was Tenochtitlán, the capital they had built up from the village. It stood in Lake Texcoco on a group of islands connected to the lake shores by causeways, one of which was five miles long and took eight horsemen abreast. The Spanish left excited descriptions of this city: its magnificence, said one, exceeded that of Rome or Constantinople. It probably contained about 100,000 inhabitants at the beginning of the sixteenth century and to its maintenance went what was received from the subject peoples. By comparison with European cities it was an astonishing place, filled with temples and dominated by huge artificial pyramids, yet its magnificence seems to have been derivative, for the Aztecs exploited the skills of their subjects. Not a single important invention or innovation of Mexican culture can confidently be assigned to the post-Toltec period. The Aztecs controlled, developed and exploited the civilization that they found.

AZTEC CULTURE

When the Spanish arrived in the early sixteenth century, the Aztec Empire was still expanding. Not all of its subject peoples were completely subdued, but Aztec rule ran from coast to coast. At its head was a semi-divine but elected ruler, chosen from a royal family. He directed a highly ordered and centralized society, making heavy demands on its members for compulsory labour and military service, but also providing them with an annual subsistence. It was a civilization pictographically literate, highly skilled in agriculture and the handling of gold, but knowing nothing of the plough, iron-working or the wheel. Its central rituals – which greatly shocked the Spaniards – included human sacrifice; no less than 20,000 victims were killed at the dedication of the great pyramid of Tenochtitlán. Such holocausts re-enacted a cosmic drama which was at the heart of Aztec mythology; it taught that the gods had been obliged to sacrifice themselves to give the sun the blood it needed as food.

RELIGION AND WEAKNESS

Aztec religion struck Europeans by its revolting details – the tearing out of victims' hearts, the flayings and ceremonial decapitations – but its bizarre and horrific accompaniments were less significant than its profound political and social implications. The importance of sacrifice meant that a continual flow of victims was needed. As these were usually supplied by prisoners of war – and because death in battle was also a route to the paradise of the sun for the warrior – a state of peace in the Aztec Empire would have been disastrous from a religious point of view. Hence the Aztecs did not really mind that their dependencies were only loosely controlled and that revolts were frequent. Subject tribes were allowed to keep their own rulers and governments so that punitive raids could be made upon them at the slightest excuse. This ensured that the empire could not win the loyalty of the subject peoples; they were bound to welcome the Aztec collapse when it came. Religion was also to affect in other ways the capacity to respond to the threat from Europeans, notably in the Aztecs' desire to take prisoners for sacrifice rather than to kill their enemies in battle, and in their belief that one day their great god, Quetzalcoatl, white-skinned and bearded, would return from the east, where he had gone after instructing his people in the arts.

Altogether, for all its aesthetic impressiveness and formidable social efficiency, the feel of Aztec civilization is harsh, brutal and unattractive. Few civilizations of which we know much have pressed so far their demands on their members. It seems to have lived always in a state of tension, a pessimistic civilization, its members uneasily aware that collapse was more than a possibility.

PERU

To the south of Mexico and Yucatán lay several other cultures, distinct enough in their degree of civilization but none of them were so remarkable as the most distant, the Andean civilization of Peru. The Mexican peoples still lived for the most part in the Stone Age; the Andeans had got much further than this. They had also created a true state. If the Maya excelled among the American cultures in the elaborate calculations of their calendar, the Andeans were far ahead of their neighbours in the complexity of their government. The imagination of the Spaniards was captured by Peru even more than by Mexico, and the reason was not simply its

This 15th-century bas-relief, known as the "Sun Stone", represents the Aztec solar calendar. In the central circle is the face of the Sun God. The second circle shows the fifth sun and the talons of the solar god. The third circle comprises 20 hieroglyphs representing the days. Eight solar rays alternate with eight hieroglyphs of stylized feathers and "precious water" (representing blood) in 40 blocks to make up the next circle. Finally, the outer ring shows the sun disc surrounded by two enormous serpents.

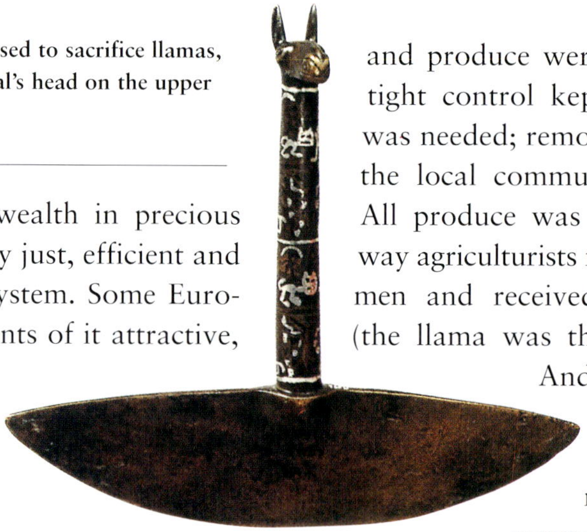

This ceremonial knife was used to sacrifice llamas, as the carving of the animal's head on the upper part of the handle indicates.

immense and obvious wealth in precious metals, but its apparently just, efficient and highly complex social system. Some Europeans soon found accounts of it attractive, for it required an almost total subordination of the individual to the collective.

INCA GOVERNMENT

Andean society was ruled by the Incas. In the twelfth century a people from Cuzco began to extend its control over earlier centres of civilization in Peru. Like the Aztecs, they began as neighbours of those longer civilized than themselves; they were barbarians who soon took over the skills and fruits of higher cultures. At the end of the fifteenth century the Incas ruled a realm extending from Ecuador to central Chile, their conquest of the coastal areas being the most recent. This was an astonishing feat of government, for it had to contend with the natural obstacles provided by the Andes. The Inca state was held together by about ten thousand miles of roads passable in all weathers by chains of runners who bore messages either orally or recorded in *quipu*, a code of knots in coloured cords. With this device elaborate records were kept. Though pre-literate, the Andean Empire was formidably totalitarian in the organization of its subjects' lives. The Incas became the ruling caste of the empire, its head becoming *Sapa Inca* – the "only Inca". His rule was a despotism based on the control of labour. The population was organized in units, of which the smallest was that of ten heads of families. From these units, labour service and produce were exacted. Careful and tight control kept population where it was needed; removal or marriage outside the local community was not allowed. All produce was state property; in this way agriculturists fed herdsmen and craftsmen and received textiles in exchange (the llama was the all-purpose beast of Andean culture, providing wool as well as transport, milk and meat). There was no commerce. Mining for precious metals and copper resulted in an exquisite adornment of Cuzco which amazed the Spaniards when they came to it. Tensions inside this system were not dealt with merely by force, but by the resettlement of loyal populations in a disaffected area and a strict control of the educational system in order to inculcate the notables of conquered peoples with the proper attitudes.

INCA CULTURE

Like the Aztecs, the Incas organized and exploited the achievements of culture which they found already to hand, though less brutally. Their aim was integration rather than obliteration and they tolerated the cults of conquered peoples. Their own god was the sun. The absence of literacy makes it hard to penetrate the mind of this civilization, but it is noticeable that, though in a different way, the Peruvians seem to have shared the Aztecs' preoccupation with death. Accidents of climate, as in Egypt, favoured its expression in rites of mummification; the dry air of the high Andes was as good a preservative as the sand of the desert. Beyond this it is not easy to say what divisions among the conquered peoples persisted and were expressed in the survival of tribal cults. When a challenge appeared from

On a high mountain ridge, around 45 miles (70 km) northwest of Cuzco, stand the ruins of the Inca city of Machu Picchu. A large rectangular plaza, surrounded by small stone houses, lies at the heart of the settlement. Terraces that were used for farming line the mountainside down to the Urubamba river, which flows along the valley floor 2,000 ft (600 m) below the city.

Europe it became apparent that Inca rule had not eliminated discontent among its subjects, for all its remarkable success.

THE LOST CIVILIZATIONS

All the American civilizations were in important and obvious ways very different from those of Asia or Europe. A complete literacy escaped them, though the Incas had good enough record-keeping processes to run complex governmental structures. Their technologies, though they had certain skills at a high level, were not so developed as those already long known elsewhere. Though these civilizations provided satisfactory settings and institutions for cultures of intense (but limited) power, the contribution of the indigenous Americans to the world's future was not to be made through them, therefore. It had in fact already been made before they appeared, through the obscure, unrecorded discoveries of primitive cultivators who had first discovered how to exploit the ancestors of tomatoes, maize, potatoes and squash. In so doing they had unwittingly made a huge addition to the resources of humanity. The glittering civilizations built on that in the Americas, though, were fated in the end to be no more than beautiful curiosities in the margin of world history, ultimately without progeny.

5 EUROPE: THE FIRST REVOLUTION

FEW TERMS HAVE SUCH misleading connotations as the "Middle Ages". A wholly Eurocentric usage meaning nothing in the history of other traditions, the phrase embodies the negative idea that no interest attaches to certain centuries except their position in time. They were first singled out and labelled by people in the fifteenth and sixteenth centuries who wanted to recapture a classical antiquity long cut off from them. In that remote past, they thought, people had done and made great things; a sense of rebirth and quickening of civilization upon them, they could believe that in their own day great things were being done once more. But in between two periods of creativity they saw only a void – *Medio Evo*, *Media Aetas*, the Middle Ages – defined just by falling in between other ages, and in itself dull, uninteresting, barbaric.

The Church tried to fill the economic, social and ideological vacuum created in the West by the collapse of the Roman Empire in Europe. Pope Urban VI (1378–1389), portrayed in this engraving, was a key figure in one of the major religious conflicts of the Middle Ages: the Great Schism.

THE "MIDDLE AGES"

It was not long before people could see that there was a little more to this period of a thousand or so years of European history than a mere void. One way in which they gained perspective was by looking for the origins of what they knew; in the seventeenth century the English talked about a "Norman Yoke" supposedly laid on their ancestors and in the eighteenth century the French idealized their aristocracy by attributing its origins to Frankish Conquest. Such reflexions, nonetheless, were very selective; in so far as the Middle Ages were thought of as a whole it was still, even

Time chart (711–1558)

711–1492 The Spanish Reconquest

1000–1300 Europe's first universities are founded

1066 The Norman conquest of England

1122 The Concordat of Worms (the Investiture Contest)

c.1200 The beginning of Venetian commercial and military power

1337–1558 The Hundred Years' War

500 — 1000 — 1500

two hundred years ago, usually with contempt. Then, quite suddenly, came a great change. Men and women started to idealize those lost centuries as vigorously as their forebears had ignored them. Europeans began to fill out their picture of the past with historical novels about chivalry and their countryside with mock baronial castles inhabited by cotton-spinners and stockbrokers. More important, a huge effort of scholarship was then brought to bear on the records of these times. This was an improvement, but still left impediments to understanding, some of which are still with us. People came to idealize the unity of medieval Christian civilization and the seeming stability of its life, but in so doing blurred the huge variety within it.

AN AGE OF CHANGE

It is still very hard to be sure we understand the European Middle Ages, although one crude distinction in this great tract of time nevertheless seems obvious enough. The centuries between the end of antiquity and the year 1000 or so now look very much like an age of foundation. Certain great markers then laid out the patterns of the future, though change was slow and its staying power still uncertain. Then, in the eleventh century, a change of pace can be sensed. New developments quicken and become discernible. It becomes clear, as time passes, that they are opening the way to something quite different. An age of adventure and revolution is beginning in Europe, and it will go on until

The continent of Europe was personified in Greek myth as the youthful beauty Europa. She is seized and carried over the sea by Zeus in the form of a bull in this version depicted by François Boucher's *Rape of Europa*, which was painted in 1747.

European history merges with the first age of global history.

This makes it hard to say when the Middle Ages "end". In many parts of Europe, they were still going strong at the end of the eighteenth century, the moment at which Europe's first independent offshoot had just come into existence across the Atlantic. Even in the new United States, there were many people who, like millions of Europeans, were still gripped by a supernatural view of life, and traditional religious views about it, much as medieval men and women had been five hundred years earlier. Many Europeans then still lived lives which in their material dimensions were still those of their medieval forerunners, too. Yet at that moment, the Middle Ages were in some countries long over in any important sense. Old institutions had gone or were crumbling, taking unquestioned traditions of authority with them. In many places, something we can recognize as the life of the modern world was already going on. This first became possible, then likely, and finally unavoidable in what can now be seen as Europe's second formative phase, and the first of her revolutionary eras.

Leo IX was appointed pontiff at the Council of Worms in 1048. His papacy was marked by a determined attempt to reform the Church. Leo's efforts to win over Byzantium, however, failed and led to the excommunication of Cerularius, the patriarch of Constantinople; both are portrayed in this 15th-century manuscript illustration.

THE CHURCH

THE CHURCH is a good place to begin the story of Europe's first revolutionary era. By "the Church" as an earthly institution, Christians mean the whole body of the faithful, lay and cleric alike. In this sense the Church came to be the same thing as European society during the Middle Ages. By 1500 only a few Jews, visitors and slaves stood apart from the huge body of people who (at least formally) shared Christian beliefs. Europe was Christian. Explicit paganism had disappeared from the map between the Atlantic coasts of Spain and the eastern boundaries of Poland. This was a great qualitative as well as a quantitative change. The religious beliefs of Christians were the deepest spring of a whole civilization which had matured for hundreds of years and was not yet threatened seriously by division or at all by alternative mythologies. Christianity had come to define Europe's purpose and to give its life a transcendent goal. It was also the reason why Europeans first became conscious of themselves as members of a particular society.

Nowadays, non-Christians are likely to think of something else as "the Church". People use the word to describe ecclesiastical institutions, the formal structures and organizations which maintain the life of worship and discipline of the believer. In this sense, too, the Church had come a long way by 1500. Whatever qualifications and ambiguities hung about them, its successes were huge; its failures might be great, too, but within the Church there were plenty of men who confidently insisted on the Church's power (and duty) to put them right. The Roman Church which had been a backwater of ecclesiastical life in late antiquity was, long before the fall of Constantinople, the possessor and focus of unprecedented power and influence. It had not only acquired new independence and importance but also had given a new temper to the Christian life since the eleventh century. Christianity then had become both more disciplined and more aggressive. It had also become more rigid: many doctrinal and liturgical practices dominant until our day are less than a thousand years old.

ECCLESIASTICAL REFORMS

The most important changes took roughly from 1000 to 1250, and they constituted a revolution. Their beginnings lay in the Cluniac movement. Four of the first eight abbots of Cluny were later canonized: seven of them were outstanding men. They advised popes, acted as their legates, served emperors as ambassadors. They were men of culture, often of noble birth, sprung from the greatest families of Burgundy and the West Franks (a fact which helped to widen Cluny's influence) and they threw their weight behind the moral and spiritual reform of the Church. Leo IX, the pope with whom papal reform really begins, eagerly promoted Cluniac ideas. He spent barely six months of his five years' pontificate at Rome; instead, he visited synods in France and Germany, correcting local practice, checking interference with the Church by lay magnates, punishing clerical impropriety, imposing a new pattern of ecclesiastical discipline. Greater standardization of practice within the Church was one of the first results. It begins to look more homogeneous.

Another outcome was the founding of a second great monastic order, the Cistercians (so named after the place of their first house, at Cîteaux), by monks dissatisfied with Cluny and anxious to return to the original strictness of the Benedictine rule, in particular by resuming the practical and manual labour Cluny had abandoned. A Cistercian monk, St Bernard, was to be the greatest leader and preacher of both Christian reform and crusade in the twelfth century, and his order had widespread influence both on monastic discipline and upon ecclesiastical architecture. It, too, pushed the Church towards greater uniformity and regularity.

INVESTITURE

The success of reform was also shown in the fervour and moral exaltation of the crusading movement, often a genuinely popular manifestation of religion. But new ways also aroused opposition, some of it among churchmen themselves. Bishops did not

Pope Urban II is depicted consecrating one of the churches at Cluny in this 12th-century miniature.

Henry IV, accompanied by Hugo, abbot of Cluny, is depicted here imploring Countess Matilda of Tuscany to intercede on his behalf with Pope Gregory VII.

always like papal interference in their affairs and parochial clergy did not always see a need to change inherited practices which their flock accepted (clerical marriage, for example). The most spectacular opposition to ecclesiastical reform came in the great quarrel which has gone down in history as the Investiture Contest. The attention given to it has been perhaps slightly disproportionate and, some would say, misleading. The central episodes lasted only a half-century or so and the issue was by no means clear-cut. The very distinction of Church and State implicit in some aspects of the quarrel was in anything like the modern sense still unthinkable to medieval people. The specific administrative and legal practices at issue were by and large quite soon the subject of agreement and many clergy felt more loyalty to their lay rulers than to the Roman Pope. Much of what was at stake, too, was very material. What was in dispute was the sharing of power and wealth within the ruling classes who supplied the personnel of both royal and ecclesiastical government in Germany and Italy, the lands of the Holy Roman Empire. Yet other countries were touched by similar quarrels – the French in the late eleventh century, the English in the early twelfth – because there was a transcendent theoretical principle at stake which did not go away: what was the proper relationship of lay and clerical authority?

HILDEBRAND

The most public battle of the Investiture Contest was fought just after the election of Pope Gregory VII in 1073. Hildebrand (Gregory's name before his election: hence the adjective "Hildebrandine" sometimes used of his policies and times) was a far from attractive person, but a pope of great personal and moral courage. He had been one of Leo IX's advisers and fought all his life for the independence and dominance of the papacy within western Christendom. He was an Italian, but not a Roman, and this, perhaps, explains why before he was himself pope he played a prominent part in the transfer of papal election to the college of cardinals, and the exclusion from it of the Roman lay nobility. When reform became a matter of politics and law rather than morals and manners (as it did during his twelve years' pontificate) Hildebrand was likely to provoke rather than avoid conflict. He was a lover of decisive action without too nice a regard for possible consequences.

Perhaps strife was already inevitable. At the core of reform lay the ideal of an independent Church. It could only perform its task, thought Leo and his followers, if free from lay interference. The Church should stand apart from the state and the clergy should live lives different from laymen's lives: they should be a distinct society within Christendom. From this ideal came the attacks on simony (the buying of preferment), the campaign against the marriage of priests, and a fierce struggle over the exercise of hitherto uncontested lay interference in appointment and promotion. This last gave its name to the long quarrel over lay "investiture": who rightfully appointed to a vacant bishopric, the temporal ruler or the Church? The right was symbolized in the act of giving his ring and staff to the new bishop.

Further potential for trouble lay in more mundane issues. Perhaps the emperors were bound to find themselves in conflict with the papacy sooner or later, once it ceased to be in need of them against other enemies, for they inherited big, if shadowy claims of authority from the past which they could hardly abandon without a struggle. In Germany the Carolingian tradition had subordinated the Church to a royal protection which easily blurred into domination. Furthermore, within Italy the empire had allies, clients and interests to defend. Since the tenth century, both the emperors' practical control of the papacy and their formal authority had declined. The new way of electing popes left the emperor with a theoretical veto and no more. The working relationship, too, had deteriorated in that some popes had already begun to dabble in troubled waters by seeking support among the emperor's vassals.

THE CLASH WITH HENRY IV

The temperament of Gregory VII was no emollient in this delicate situation. Once elected, he took his throne without imperial

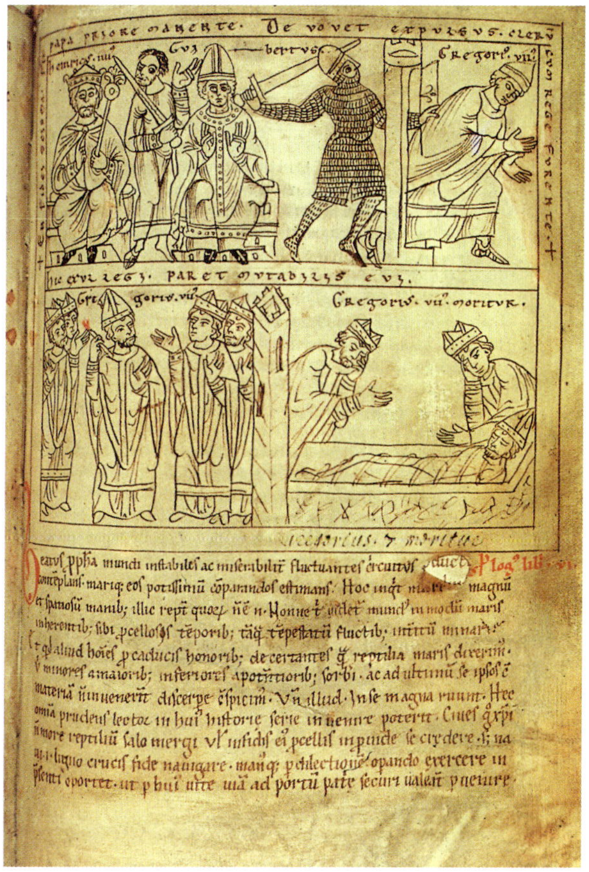

Scenes from the life of Pope Gregory VII, who was born c.1020 in the Italian region of Tuscany. Having worked in the service of the papal *curia* for more than 20 years, notably as an emissary to France and Germany, he was elected pope on 22 April 1073.

assent, simply informing the emperor of the fact. Two years later he issued a decree on lay investiture. Curiously, what it actually said has not survived, but its general content is known: Gregory forbade any layman to invest a cleric with a bishopric or other ecclesiastical office, and excommunicated some of the emperor's clerical councillors on the grounds that they had been guilty of simony in purchasing their preferment. To cap matters, Gregory summoned Henry IV, the Holy Roman Emperor, to Rome to appear before him and defend himself against charges of misconduct.

Henry responded at first through the Church itself; he got a German synod to declare Gregory deposed. This earned him excommunication, which would have mattered less had he not faced powerful enemies in Germany who now had the pope's support. The result was that Henry had to give way.

This illustration graphically encapsulates the resolution of the confrontation between pope and emperor. God is shown handing St Peter's keys, the symbol of spiritual power, to the pope and a sword, the symbol of secular power, to the emperor.

To avoid trial before the German bishops presided over by Gregory (who was already on his way to Germany), Henry came in humiliation to Canossa, where he waited in the snow barefoot until Gregory would receive his penance in one of the most dramatic of all confrontations of lay and spiritual authority. But Gregory had not really won. Not much of a stir was caused by Canossa at the time. The pope's position was too extreme: he went beyond canon law to assert a revolutionary doctrine, that kings were but officers who could be removed when the pope judged them unfit or unworthy. This was almost unthinkably subversive to people whose moral horizons were dominated by the idea of the sacredness of oaths of fealty; it foreshadowed later claims to papal monarchy but was bound to be unacceptable to any king.

Investiture ran on as an issue for the next fifty years. Gregory lost the sympathy he had won through Henry's bullying and it was not until 1122 that another emperor agreed to a concordat which was seen as a papal victory, though one diplomatically disguised. Yet Gregory had been a true pioneer; he had differentiated clerics and laymen as never before and had made unprecedented claims for the distinction and superiority of papal power. More would be heard of them in the next two centuries. Though his immediate successors acted less dramatically than he, they steadily pressed papal claims to papal advantage. Urban II used the first crusade to become the diplomatic leader of Europe's lay monarchs; they looked to Rome, not the empire. Urban also built up the Church's administrative machine; under him emerged the *curia*, a Roman bureaucracy which corresponded to the household administrations of the English and French kings. Through it the papal grip on the Church itself was strengthened. In 1123, a historic date, the first ecumenical council was held in the West and its decrees were promulgated in the pope's own name. And all the time, papal jurisprudence and jurisdiction ground away; more and more legal disputes found their way from the local church courts to papal judges, whether resident at Rome, or sitting locally.

THE PAPAL MONARCHY

Prestige, dogma, political skill, administrative pressure, judicial practice and the control of more and more benefices all buttressed the new ascendancy of the papacy in the Church. By 1100 the groundwork was done for the emergence of a true papal monarchy. As the investiture contest receded, secular princes were on the whole well disposed to Rome and it appeared that no essential ground had

St Thomas à Becket (1118–1170) was appointed chancellor of England by Henry II in 1154. In 1162 he was chosen as archbishop of Canterbury, being ordained as a priest only the day before his consecration. As a consequence of his actions in defence of the independence of the Church, Becket was exiled to France in 1164, from where he threatened to excommunicate the English king. In 1170 Becket returned to England, where he was murdered in Canterbury Cathedral by the king's knights – an event depicted in this 14th-century manuscript illustration.

been lost by the papacy. There was indeed a spectacular quarrel in England over the question of clerical privilege and immunity from the law of the land which would be an issue of the future; immediately, it led to the murder (and then the canonization) of Becket, the archbishop of Canterbury. But on the whole, the large legal immunities of clergy were not much challenged. Under Innocent III papal pretensions to monarchical authority reached a new theoretical height. True, Innocent did not go quite so far as Gregory. He did not claim an absolute plenitude of temporal power everywhere in western Christendom, but he said that the papacy had by its authority transferred the empire from the Greeks to the Franks. Within the Church his power was limited by little but the inadequacies of the bureaucratic machine through which he had to operate. Yet papal power was still often deployed in support of the reforming ideas – which shows that much remained to be done.

Clerical celibacy became more common and more widespread. Among new practices which were pressed on the Church in the thirteenth century was that of frequent individual confession, a powerful instrument of control in a religiously minded and anxiety-ridden society. Among doctrinal innovations, the theory of transubstantiation, that by a mystical process the body and blood of Christ were actually present in the bread and wine used in the communion service, was imposed from the thirteenth century onwards.

THE GREAT GOTHIC CATHEDRALS

The final christening of Europe in the central Middle Ages was a great spectacle. Monastic reform and papal autocracy were wedded to

Gothic architecture

The term Gothic, first used by the Florentine writer Giorgio Vasari, defines an architectural style which developed in Europe at the beginning of the 12th century and lasted until the end of the 15th century. It originated in France where, during the 12th and 13th centuries, the most notable Gothic cathedrals were constructed, including Chartres (built on the site of the old Romanesque cathedral), Amiens, Paris (the true centre of Gothic culture) and Reims.

Chartres Cathedral was built between 1195 and 1240 and has been referred to as an incarnation of medieval thought. With its 10,000 painted and sculpted figures, it represents one of the greatest endeavours ever carried out in the name of Christian education.

The emergence of the Gothic style heralded an architectural and artistic revolution. Some of the most representative elements of this impressive architectural style include pointed arches, the disappearance of partition walls, windows divided up by columns and curved-stone decorations, pinnacles on buttresses, and finials on towers and spires.

Gothic art spread throughout Europe and had clearly differentiated phases: the "classic Gothic" style, the best examples of which can be found in France; the "late Gothic" style, which developed in the 14th century (the most important characteristic of which was the recognition of artistic individuality); and a final "flamboyant" period, characterized partly by its asymmetry.

The ambulatory around the sanctuary of Chartres Cathedral.

In this 14th-century Gothic mural from the Cerco church in Artajona (northeastern Spain), various scenes from the life of St Saturnin are depicted. The saint was the first bishop of the French city of Toulouse during the 3rd century.

intellectual effort and the deployment of new wealth in architecture to make this the next peak of Christian history after the age of the Fathers. It was an achievement whose most fundamental work lay, perhaps, in intellectual and spiritual developments, but it became most visible in stone. What we think of as "Gothic" architecture was the creation of this period. It produced the European landscape which, until the coming of the railway, was dominated or punctuated by a church tower or spire rising above a little town. Until the twelfth century the major buildings of the Church were usually monastic; then began the building of the astonishing series of cathedrals, especially in northern France and England, which remains one of the great glories of European art and, together with castles, constitutes the major architecture of the Middle Ages. There was great popular enthusiasm, it seems, for these huge investments, though it is difficult to penetrate to the mental attitudes behind them. Analogies might be sought in the feeling of twentieth-century enthusiasts for space exploration, but this omits the supernatural dimension of these great buildings. They were both offerings to God and an essential part of the instrumentation of evangelism and education on earth. About their huge naves and aisles moved the processions of relics and the crowds of pilgrims who had come to see them. Their windows were filled with the images of the biblical story which was the core of European culture; their façades were covered with the didactic representations of the fate awaiting just and unjust. Christianity achieved in them a new publicity and collectiveness. Nor is it possible to assess the full impact of these great churches on the imagination of medieval Europeans without reminding ourselves how much greater was the contrast their splendour presented to the reality of everyday life than any imaginable today.

THE FRANCISCANS

The power and penetration of organized Christianity were further reinforced by new religious orders. Two were outstanding: the mendicant Franciscans and Dominicans, who in England came to be called respectively the Grey and Black Friars, from the colours of their habits. The Franciscans were true revolutionaries: their founder, St Francis of Assisi, left his family to lead a life of poverty among the sick, the needy and the leprous. The followers

St Francis of Assisi

St Francis of Assisi was born into a noble family in 1181. In 1206 he enlisted in the pontifical army, which was fighting against the emperor. Before going into combat, however, St Francis had a vision that prompted him to leave the army and dedicate himself to prayer and charity. After two years of living as a hermit, he began to attract disciples and in 1210 Pope Innocent III approved the Franciscan Rule.

The new rule's key element was its ideal of poverty, in imitation of Christ's own rejection of material wealth, described in the New Testament. In 1212, with his sister Clare, St Francis founded the female branch of his rule, later known as the Poor Clares. Between 1213 and 1214, after a thwarted trip to the Holy Land, St Francis settled in Spain where he tried to evangelize the Muslims. In 1219 he undertook a journey to Palestine and Egypt, where he attempted to convert the sultan. In 1221, in collaboration with Cardinal Ugolino of Conti, the first written rule of the Franciscan Order was compiled.

An illness contracted on his journey to the East was the cause of St Francis' death on 3 October 1226. He was canonized by Pope Gregory IX in 1228. In 1980 St Francis was designated patron saint of ecology.

Giotto (1266–1336) painted three huge cycles of frescos representing the life of St Francis of Assisi. This mural from Santa Croce in Florence shows St Francis trying to convert the Egyptian sultan.

who soon gathered about him eagerly took up a life directed towards the imitation of Christ's poverty and humility. There was at first no formal organization and Francis was never a priest, but Innocent III, shrewdly seizing the opportunity of patronizing this potentially divisive movement instead of letting it escape from control, bade them elect a Superior. Through him the new fraternity owed and maintained rigorous obedience to the Holy See. They could provide a counterweight to local episcopal authority because they could preach without the licence of the bishop of the diocese. The older monastic orders recognized a danger and opposed the Franciscans, but the friars prospered, despite internal quarrels. In the end they acquired a considerable administrative structure, but they always remained peculiarly the evangelists of the poor and the mission field.

THE DOMINICANS AND THE PERSECUTION OF HERETICS

The Dominicans were founded to further a narrower end. Their founder was a Castilian priest who went to preach in the Languedoc to heretics, the Albigensians. From his companions grew a new preaching order; when Dominic died in 1221 his seventeen followers had become over five hundred friars. Like the Franciscans, they were mendicants vowed to poverty, and like them, too, they threw themselves into missionary work. But their impact was primarily intellectual and they became a great force in a new institution of great importance, just taking shape: the first Western universities. Dominicans came also to provide many of the personnel of the Inquisition, an organization to combat heresy which appeared in the early thirteenth century. From the fourth century onwards, churchmen had urged the persecution of heretics. Yet the first papal condemnation of them did not come until 1184. Only under Innocent III did persecution come to be the duty of Catholic kings. The Albigensians were certainly not Catholic, but there is some doubt whether they should really be regarded even as Christian heretics. Their beliefs reflect Manichaean doctrines. They were dualists, some of whom rejected all material creation as evil. Like those of many later heretics, heterodox religious views were taken to imply aberration or at least nonconformity in social and moral practices. Innocent III seems to have decided to persecute the Albigensians after the murder of a papal legate in the Languedoc, and in 1209 a crusade was launched against them. It attracted many laymen (especially from northern France) because of the chance it offered for a quick grab at the lands and homes of the Albigensians, but it also marked a great innovation: the joining of State and Church in Western Christendom to crush by force dissent which might place either in danger. It was for a long time an effective device, though never completely so.

In judging the theory and practice of medieval intolerance it must be remembered that the danger in which society was felt to stand from heresy was appalling: its members might face everlasting torment. Yet persecution

In this painting by the Spanish artist Pedro Berruguete (c.1450–1504), St Dominic is depicted overseeing the burning of the Albigensians' books, a fate only the Holy Bible was spared.

did not prevent the appearance of new heresies again and again in the next three centuries, because they expressed real needs. Heresy was, in one sense, an exposure of a hollow core in the success which the Church had so spectacularly achieved. Heretics were living evidence of dissatisfaction with the outcome of a long and often heroic battle. Other critics would also make themselves heard in due course and different ways. Papal monarchical theory provoked counter-doctrine; thinkers would argue that the Church had a defined sphere of activity which did not extend to meddling in secular affairs. As individuals became more conscious of national communities and respectful of their claims, this would seem more and more appealing. The rise of mystical religion, too, was another phenomenon always tending to slip outside the ecclesiastical structure. In movements like the Brethren of the Common Life, following the teachings of the mystic Thomas à Kempis, laymen created religious practices and devotional forms which often escaped from clerical control.

THE WORLDLINESS OF THE MEDIEVAL CHURCH

Mystical religious movements expressed the great paradox of the medieval Church. It had risen to a pinnacle of power and wealth. It deployed lands, tithes, and papal taxation in the service of a magnificent hierarchy whose worldly greatness reflected the glory of God and whose lavish cathedrals, great monastic churches, splendid liturgies, learned foundations

Lincoln Cathedral in England was constructed between 1123 and 1233. This view down the central aisle gives an impression of the grandeur of this building and of the many other similar cathedrals that were erected in Europe in the Gothic period.

and libraries embodied the devotion and sacrifices of the faithful. Yet the point of this huge concentration of power and grandeur was to preach a faith at whose heart lay the glorification of poverty and humility and the superiority of things not of this world.

The worldliness of the Church drew increasing criticism. It was not just that a few ecclesiastical magnates lolled back upon the cushion of privilege and endowment to gratify their appetites and neglect their flocks. There was also a more subtle corruption inherent in power. The identification of the defence of the faith with the triumph of an institution had given the Church an increasingly bureaucratic and legalistic face. The point had arisen as early as the days of St Bernard; even then, there were too many ecclesiastical lawyers, it was said. By the mid-thirteenth century legalism was blatant. The papacy itself was soon criticized. At the death of Innocent III the Church of comfort and of the sacraments was already obscured behind the granite face of centralization. The claims of religion were confused with the assertiveness of an ecclesiastical monarchy demanding freedom from constraint of any sort. It was already difficult to keep the government of the Church in the hands of men of spiritual stature; Martha was pushing Mary aside, because administrative and legal gifts were needed to run a machine which more and more generated its own purposes. A higher authority than that of the pope, some argued, lay in an ecumenical council.

BONIFACE VIII

In 1294 a hermit of renowned piety was elected pope. The hopes this roused were quickly dashed. Celestine V was forced to resign within a few weeks, seemingly unable to impose his reforming wishes on the *curia*.

The claim to papal supremacy

"The faith commands us to recognize only one and holy Church, which has only one body and one head: it has two swords, a spiritual one and a material one; both swords, the spiritual and the material, are under the power of the Church and must be used for the Church; one for the priests, the other for the kings and warriors, but according to the priest's instructions and when he permits it … . He represents spiritual power sent to instruct man on earth, and correct him when he is not good. Consequently, when the earthly power is led astray it should be put back on the right path by the spiritual, as should be the inferior spiritual power by the superior, but the supreme power can only be corrected by God and not by any man. Therefore whoever opposes this power established by God opposes the order of God."

An extract from Boniface VIII's papal bull, *Unam Sanctam* (November, 1302).

His successor was Boniface VIII. He has been called the last medieval pope because he embodied all the pretensions of the papacy at its most political and its most arrogant. He was by training a lawyer and by temperament far from a man of spirituality. He quarrelled violently with the kings of both England and France and in the Jubilee of 1300 had two swords carried before him to symbolize his possession of temporal as well as spiritual power. Two years later he asserted that a belief in the sovereignty of the pope over every human being was necessary to salvation.

Under him the long battle with kings came to a head. Nearly a hundred years before, England had been laid under interdict by the pope; this terrifying sentence forbade the administration of any of the sacraments while the king remained unrepentant and

A 16th-century portrait of the humanist Italian writer Francesco Petrarch (1304–1374), who spent much of his life in papal Avignon.

unreconciled. Men and women could not have their children baptized or obtain absolution for their own sins, and those were fearful deprivations in a believing age. King John had been forced to yield. A century later, things had changed. Bishops and their clergy were often estranged from Rome, which had undermined their authority, too. They could sympathize with a stirring national sense of opposition to the papacy whose pretensions reached their peak under Boniface. When the kings of France and England rejected his authority they found churchmen to support them. They also had resentful Italian noblemen to fight for them. In 1303 some of them (in French pay) pursued the old pope to his native city and there seized him with, it was said, appalling physical indignity. His fellow-townsmen released Boniface and he was not (like Celestine, whom he had put in prison) to die in confinement, but die he did, no doubt of shock, a few weeks later.

This was only the beginning of a bad time for the papacy and, some would claim, for the Church. For more than four centuries it was to face recurrent and mounting waves of hostility which, though often heroically met, ended by calling Christianity itself in question. Even by the end of Boniface's reign, the legal claims he had made were almost beside the point; no one stirred to avenge him. Now spiritual failure increasingly drew fire; henceforth the papacy was to be condemned more for standing in the way of reform than for claiming too much of kings. For a long time, though, criticism had important limits. The notion of autonomous, self-justified criticism was unthinkable in the Middle Ages: it was for failures in their traditional religious task that churchmen were criticized.

THE AVIGNON PAPACY

In 1309 a French pope brought the papal *curia* to Avignon, a town belonging to the king of Naples but overshadowed by the power of the French kings whose lands overlooked it. There was to be a preponderance of French cardinals, too, during the papal residence at Avignon (which lasted until 1377). The English and Germans soon believed the popes had become the tool of the French kings and took steps against the independence of the Church in their own territories. The imperial electors declared that their vote required no approval or confirmation by the pope and that the imperial power came from God alone.

At Avignon the popes lived in a huge palace, whose erection was a symbol of their decision to stay away from Rome, and whose luxury was a symbol of growing worldliness. The papal court was of unexampled magnificence, attended by a splendid train of servitors and administrators paid for by ecclesiastical taxation and misappropriation.

The Great Schism at Avignon

In 1309 Pope Clement V fixed his residence in Avignon at the request of the French king Philip the Fair. The reasons for this papal exodus from Rome were complex. The role of the pope as the visible head of Christianity and as arbiter in conflicts between the various monarchies was in decline. The burgeoning power of the national monarchies and the appearance of new social sectors were making it impossible for the pope to control European politics.

In 1377 Gregory XI moved the pontifical headquarters back to Rome; he died one year later in the Eternal City. In the campaign to choose his successor, two factions emerged, one pro-Italian and the other formed mainly by French cardinals. Urban VI was elected but then rejected by the French cardinals, who, on 20 September 1378, appointed Robert of Geneva as pope, under the name of Clement VII. This brought about the Great Schism of Avignon.

This imposing palace-fortress was the headquarters of the popes during the years they spent in Avignon. Its construction, begun by Benedict XII (1333–1342), was continued by Clement VI and completed in the time of Innocent VI (1352–1366).

Unfortunately the fourteenth century was a time of economic disaster; a much-reduced population was being asked to pay more for a more costly (and, some said, extravagant) papacy. Centralization continued to breed corruption – the abuse of the papal rights to appoint to vacant benefices was an obvious instance – and accusations of simony and pluralism had more and more plausibility. The personal conduct of the higher clergy was more and more obviously at variance with apostolic ideals. A crisis arose among the Franciscans themselves, some of the brothers, the "spirituals", insisting that they take seriously their founder's rule of poverty, while their more relaxed colleagues refused to give up the wealth which had come to their order. Theological issues became entangled with this dispute. Soon there were Franciscans preaching that Avignon was Babylon, the scarlet whore of the Apocalypse, and that the papacy's overthrow was at hand, while a pope, asserting that Christ Himself had respected property, condemned the ideal of apostolic poverty and unleashed the Inquisition against the "spirituals". They were burned for their preachings, but not before they had won audiences.

THE GREAT SCHISM

The exile in Avignon fed a popular anti-clericalism and anti-papalism different from that of kings exasperated against priests who would not accept their jurisdiction. Many of the clergy themselves felt that rich abbeys and worldly bishops were a sign of a Church that had become secularized. This was the irony that tainted the legacy of Gregory VII. Criticism eventually rose to the point at which the papacy returned to Rome in 1377, only to face the greatest scandal in the history of the Church, a "Great Schism". Secular monarchs set on having quasi-national churches in their own realms, and the college of twenty or so cardinals, manipulating the papacy so as to maintain their own revenues and position, together brought about the election of two popes, the second by the French cardinals alone. For thirty years popes at Rome and Avignon simultaneously claimed the headship of the Church. Eight years afterwards there was a third contender as well. As the schism wore on, the criticism directed against the papacy became more and more virulent. "Antichrist" was a favourite term of abuse for the claimant to the patrimony of St Peter. It was complicated by the involvement of secular rivalries, too. For the Avignon pope, broadly, there stood as allies France, Scotland, Aragon and Milan; the Roman was supported by England, the German emperors, Naples and Flanders.

THE CONCILIAR MOVEMENT

The schism at one moment seemed to promise renovation and reformation. The instrument to which reformers turned was an ecumenical or general council of the Church; to return to the days of the apostles and the Fathers for a means to put the papal house in order sounded good sense to many Catholics. Unfortunately, it did not turn out well. Four councils were held. The first, held at Pisa in 1409, struck out boldly, proclaiming the deposition of both popes and choosing another. This meant there were now three pretenders to the chair of St Peter; moreover, when the new one died after a few months, another was elected whose choice was said to be tainted by simony (this was the first John XXIII, now no longer recognized as a pope and the victim of one of Gibbon's most searing judgments). The next council (Constance, 1414–18) removed John (though he had summoned it), got one of his competitors to abdicate and then deposed the third pretender. At last there could be a fresh start; the schism was healed. In 1417 a new pope was elected, Martin V. This was a success, but some people had hoped for more; they had sought reform and the council had been diverted from that. Instead it had devoted its time to heresy, and support for reform dwindled once the unity of the papacy was restored. After another council (Siena, 1423–4) had been dissolved by Martin V for urging reform ("that the Supreme Pontiff should be called to account was perilous," he declared), the last met at Basle (1431–49), but was ineffective long before its dissolution. The conciliar movement had not achieved the desired reform and papal power was restored. The principle that there existed an alternative conciliar source of authority inside the Church was always henceforth regarded with suspicion at Rome. Within a few years it was declared heresy to appeal from the pope to a general council.

PAPAL AUTHORITY WEAKENED

The Church had not risen to the level of the crisis now upon it. The papacy had maintained its superiority, but its victory was only partial; secular rulers had reaped the benefits of anti-papal feeling in new freedoms for national Churches. As for the moral authority of Rome, that had clearly not been restored and one result would be a more damaging movement for reform three-quarters of a century later. The papacy now began to look more and more Italian, and so it was to remain. There were some dismal popes to come in the next two centuries, but that did less damage to the Church than the evolution of their See towards becoming just one more Italian state.

WYCLIF AND HUS

Heresy, always smouldering, had burst out in a blaze of reforming zeal during the conciliar period. Two outstanding men, Wyclif and Hus, focused the discontents to which schism had given rise. They were first and foremost reformers, though the English Wyclif was a teacher and thinker rather than a man of action. Hus, a Bohemian, became the leader of a movement which involved national as well as ecclesiastical issues; he exercised huge influence as a preacher in Prague. He was condemned by the council of Constance for heretical views on predestination and property and was burned in 1415. The great impulse given by Wyclif and Hus flagged as their criticisms were muffled, but they had tapped the nerve of national anti-papalism which was to prove so destructive of the unity of the Western Church. Catholics and Hussites were still disputing Bohemia in bitter civil wars twenty years after Hus' death. Meanwhile, the papacy itself made concessions in its diplomacy with the lay monarchies of the fifteenth century.

CHANGES IN POPULAR RELIGION

Religious zeal in the fifteenth century more and more appeared to bypass the central apparatus of the Church. Fervour manifested itself in a continuing flow of mystical writing and in new fashions in popular religion. A new obsession with the agony of the Passion was reflected in art; new devotions to saints, a craze for flagellation, outbreaks of dancing frenzy all show a heightened excitability. An outstanding example of the appeal and power of a popular preacher can be seen in Savonarola, a Dominican whose immense success made him for a time moral dictator of Florence in the 1490s. But religious fervour often escaped the formal and ecclesiastical structures.

In the fourteenth and fifteenth centuries much of the emphasis of popular religion was individual and devotional. Another impression of the inadequacy of both vision and machinery within the hierarchies is to be found, too, in a neglect of missionary work outside Europe.

The execution of the convicted heretic John Hus is depicted in this 15th-century drawing. The accused had been paraded through the streets of Constance wearing a hat decorated with two devils arguing over which one would get his soul. The last words Hus spoke were: "I will die today in the light of the truth of the Gospel which I have preached and taught."

A RELIGIOUS CIVILIZATION

All in all, the fifteenth century leaves a sense of withdrawal, an ebbing after a big effort which had lasted nearly two centuries. Yet to leave the medieval Church with that impression uppermost in our minds would be to risk a

The central panel of *The Last Judgment*, a triptych by the German artist Stephan Lochner. Painted between 1435 and 1440, this was originally an altarpiece for the church of St Lawrence in Cologne.

grave misunderstanding of a society made more different from our own by religion than by any other factor. Europe was still Christendom and was so even more consciously after 1453. Within its boundaries, almost the whole of life was defined by religion. The Church was for most men and women the only recorder and authenticator of the great moments of their existence – their marriages, their children's births and baptisms, their deaths. Many of them wholly gave themselves up to it: a much greater proportion of the population became monks and nuns than is the case today, but though they might think of withdrawal to the cloister from a hostile everyday, what they left behind was no secular world such as ours, wholly distinct from and indifferent to the Church. Learning, charity, administration, justice and huge stretches of economic life all fell within the ambit and regulation of religion. Even when laymen attacked churchmen, they did so in the name of the standards the Church had itself taught them and with appeals to the knowledge of God's purpose it gave them. Religious myth was not only the deepest spring of a civilization, it was still the life of everyone. It defined human purpose and did so in terms of a transcendent good. Outside the Church, the community of all believers, lay only paganism. The devil – conceived in a most material form – lay in wait for those who strayed from the path of grace. If there were some bishops and even popes among the errant, so much the worse for them. Human frailty could not compromise the religious view of life. God's justice would be shown and He would divide sheep from goats on the Day of Wrath when all things would end.

PRINCIPALITIES AND POWERS

MOST PEOPLE TODAY are used to the idea of the State. It is generally agreed that the world's surface is divided up between impersonal organizations working through officials marked out in special ways, and that such organizations provide the final public

Europe in the Middle Ages

This map shows European political divisions between the 13th and 15th centuries.

This 16th-century miniature depicts an attack on a castle. Medieval castles were not merely military establishments: they also served as centres of political power and social organization, and were often crucial to the local economy.

authority for any given area. Often, states are thought in some way to represent people or nations. But whether they do or not, states are the building blocks from which most of us would construct a political account of the modern world.

None of this would have been intelligible to a European in 1000; five hundred years later much of it might well have been, depending on who the European was. The process by which the modern state emerged, though far from complete by 1500, is one of the markers which delimit the modern era of history. The realities had come first, before principles and ideas. From the thirteenth century onwards many rulers, usually kings, were able for a variety of reasons to increase their power over those they ruled. This was often because they could keep up large armies and arm them with the most effective weapons. Iron cannons were invented in the early fourteenth century; bronze followed, and in the next century big cast-iron guns became available. With their appearance, great men could no longer brave the challenges of their rulers from behind the walls of their castles. Steel crossbows, too, gave a big advantage to those who could afford them. Many rulers were by 1500 well on the way to exercising a monopoly of the use of armed force within their realms. They were arguing more, too, about the frontiers they shared, and this expressed more than just better techniques of surveying. It marked a change in emphasis within government, from a claim to control persons who had a particular relationship to the ruler to one to control people who lived in a certain area. Territorial was replacing personal dependence.

ROYAL BUREAUCRACIES

Over territorial agglomerations, royal power was increasingly exercised directly through officials who, like weaponry, had to be paid for. A kingship which worked through vassals known to the king, who did much of his work for him in return for his favours and who supported him in the field when his needs went beyond what his own estates could supply, gave way to one in which royal government was carried out by employees, paid for by taxes (more and more in cash, not kind), the raising of which was one of their most important tasks. The parchment of charters and rolls began by the sixteenth century to give way to the first trickles and rivulets of what was to become the flood of modern bureaucratic paper.

Such a sketch hopelessly blurs this immensely important and complicated change. It was linked to every side of life: to religion and the sanctions and authority it embodied; to the economy, the resources it offered and the social possibilities it opened or closed; to ideas and the pressure they exerted on still plastic institutions. But the upshot is not in doubt. Somehow, Europe was beginning by

1500 to organize itself differently from the Europe of Carolingians and Ottonians. Though personal and local ties were to remain for centuries overwhelmingly the most important ones for most Europeans, society was institutionalized in a different way from that of the days when even tribal loyalties still counted. The relationship of lord and vassal which, with the vague claims of pope and emperor in the background, so long seemed to exhaust political thought, gave way to an idea of princely power over all the inhabitants of a domain which, in extreme assertions (such as that of Henry VIII of England that a prince knew no external superior save God) was really quite new.

THE APPEAL OF MONARCHY

Necessarily, changes in political thinking neither took place everywhere in the same way nor at the same pace. By 1800 France and England would have been for centuries unified in a way that Germany and Italy were still not. But wherever it happened, the centre of the process was usually the steady aggrandizement of royal families. Kings enjoyed great advantages. If they ran their affairs carefully they had a more solid power base in their usually large (and sometimes very large) domains than had noblemen in their smaller estates. The kingly office had a mysterious aura about it, reflected in the solemn circumstances of coronations and anointings. Royal courts and laws seemed to promise a more independent, less expensive justice than could be got from the local feudal lords. Kings could therefore appeal not only to the resources of the feudal structure at whose head – or somewhere near it – they stood, but also to other forces outside. One of these, which was slowly revealed as of growing importance, was the sense of nationhood.

Under the newly empowered monarchs, medieval society's institutions were very different from those that had existed when tribal loyalties still held sway. This manuscript illustration, dated c.1460, shows the judges of "The King's Bench", who made up England's highest court, and one which had originally sat only in the presence of the king himself.

NATIONHOOD

The idea of nationhood is another concept taken for granted nowadays, but we must be careful not to antedate it. No medieval state was national in our sense. Nevertheless, by 1500 the subjects of the kings of England and France could often think of themselves as different from aliens who were not their fellow-subjects, even if they might also regard people who lived in the next village as virtually foreigners. Even two hundred years earlier this sort of distinction was being made between those born within and those born outside the realm and the sense of community of the native-born was steadily enhanced. One symptom was the appearance of belief in national patron saints; though churches had been dedicated to him under the Anglo-Saxon kings, only in the fourteenth century did

His tripartite *Divine Comedy* is the best-known work by the poet Dante Alighieri (1265–1321). This illustration depicts a scene described in verse 33 of the poem's first section, the *Inferno*.

St George's red cross on a white background became a kind of uniform for English soldiers when he was recognized as official protector of England (his exploit in killing the dragon had only been attributed to him in the twelfth century and may be the result of mixing him up with a legendary Greek hero, Perseus). Others were the writing of national histories (already foreshadowed by the Dark Age histories of the Germanic peoples) and the discovery of national heroes. In the twelfth century a Welshman more or less invented the mythological figure of Arthur, while an Irish chronicler of the same period built up an unhistorical myth of the High King Brian Boru and his defence of Christian Ireland against the Vikings. Above all, there was more vernacular literature. First Spanish and Italian, then French and English began to break through the barrier set about literary creativity by Latin. The ancestors of these tongues are recognizable in twelfth-century romances such as the Song of Roland which transformed a defeat of Charlemagne by Pyrenean mountaineers into the glorious stand of his rearguard against the Arabs, or the Poem of the Cid, the epic of a Spanish national hero. With the fourteenth century came Dante, Langland and Chaucer, each of them writing in a language which we can read with little difficulty.

THE IMPORTANCE OF LOCAL COMMUNITIES

We must not exaggerate the immediate impact of the growing sense of nationhood. For centuries yet, family, local community, religion or trade were still to be the focus of most people's loyalties. Such national institutions as they could have seen growing among them would have done little to break into this conservatism; in few places was it more than a matter of the king's justices and the king's tax gatherers – and even in England, in some ways the most national of late medieval states, many people might never have seen either. The rural parishes and little towns of the Middle Ages, on the other hand, were real communities, and in ordinary times provided enough to think about in the way of social responsibilities. We really need another word than "nationalism" to suggest the occasional and fleeting glimpses of a community of the realm which might once in a while touch a medieval man, or even the irritation which might suddenly burst out in a riot against the presence of foreigners, whether workmen or merchants. (Medieval anti-semitism, of course, had different roots.) Yet such hints of national feeling occasionally reveal the slow consolidation of support for new states in western Europe.

THE ANGLO-NORMANS

The first western European states to cover anything like the areas of their modern successors were England and France. A few thousand Normans had come over from France after the invasion of 1066 to Anglo-Saxon England to form a new ruling class. Their leader, William the Conqueror, gave them lands, but retained more for himself (the royal estates were larger than those of his Anglo-Saxon predecessors) and asserted an ultimate lordship over the rest: he was to be lord of the land and all men held what they held either directly or indirectly of him. He inherited the prestige and machinery of the old English monarchy, too, and this was important, for it raised him decisively above his fellow-Norman warriors. The greatest of them became William's earls and barons, the lesser ones among them knights, ruling England at first from the wooden and earth castles which they spread over the length of the land.

They had conquered one of the most civilized societies in Europe, which went on under the Anglo-Norman kings to show unusual vigour. A few years after the Conquest, the English government carried out one of the most remarkable administrative

The legend of King Arthur, which clearly follows in the Celtic tradition, made its first literary appearance in the 12th-century tale *The History of the Kings of England* by Geoffrey of Monmouth. A scene from the legend is evoked in this illustration from a 14th-century manuscript of *The Quest for the Holy Grail*: while King Arthur is dying, Sir Bedivere flings the king's sword (Excalibur) into the water, where it is seized by the Lady of the Lake.

Chaucer's *Canterbury Tales*

"A KNIGHT ther was, and that a worthy man,
That fro the tyme that he first bigan
To riden out, he loved chivalrie,
Trouthe and honour, fredom and curteisie.
Ful worthy was he in his lordes werre,
And therto hadde he riden, no man ferre,
As wel in cristendom as in hethenesse,
And evere honoured for his worthynesse.
At Alisaundre he was whan it was wonne.
Ful ofte tyme he hadde the bord bigonne
Aboven alle nacions in Pruce;
In Lettow hadde he reysed and in Ruce,
No Cristen man so ofte of his degree.
In Gernade at the seege eek hadde he be
Of Algezir, and riden in Belmarye.
At Lyeys was he and at Satalye,
Whan they were wonne; and in the Grete See
At many a noble armee hadde he be."

An extract from the "General Prologue" to *The Canterbury Tales* (c.1387–c.1400) by Geoffrey Chaucer, edited by A. C. Spearing.

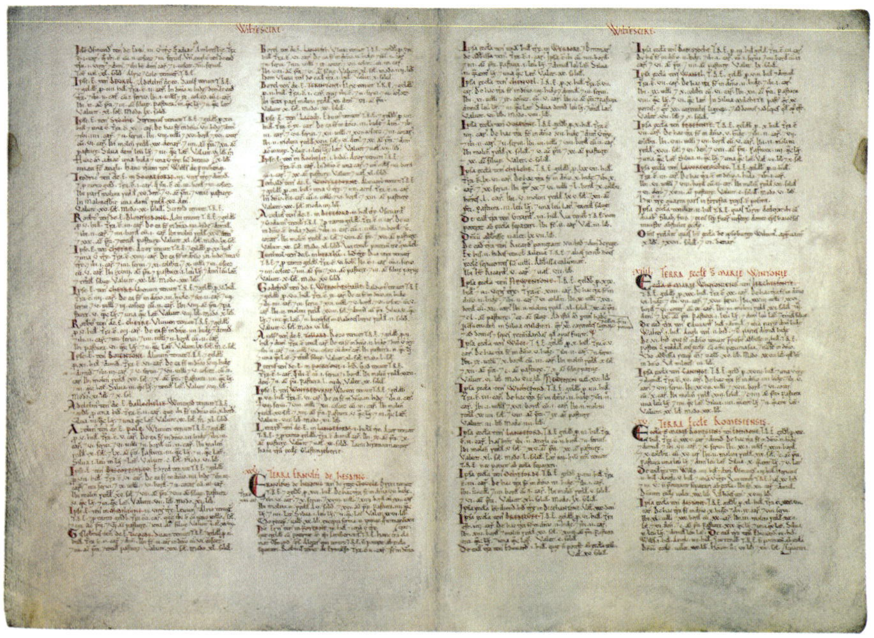

William the Conqueror commissioned the Domesday Book in 1085 and it was completed three years later. The book, of which two of the Wiltshire folios are shown here, listed the kingdom's taxable wealth and resources in great detail.

acts of the Middle Ages, the compilation of the Domesday Book, a huge survey of England for royal purposes. The evidence was taken from juries in every shire and hundred, and its minuteness deeply impressed the Anglo-Saxon chronicler who bitterly noted ("it is shameful to record, but did not seem shameful for him to do") that not an ox, cow or pig escaped the notice of William's men. In the next century there was rapid, even spectacular, development in the judicial strength of the Crown. Though minorities and weak kings from time to time led to royal concessions to the magnates, the essential integrity of the monarchy was not compromised. The constitutional history of England is for five hundred years the story of the authority of the Crown. This owed much to the fact that England was separated from possible enemies, except to the north, by water; it was hard for foreigners to interfere in her domestic politics and the Normans were to remain her last successful invaders.

For a long time, though, the Anglo-Norman kings were more than kings of an island state. They were heirs of a complex inheritance of possessions and feudal dependencies which at its furthest stretched far into southwestern France. Like their followers, they still spoke Norman French. The loss of most of their "Angevin" inheritance (the name came from Anjou) at the beginning of the twelfth century was decisive for France as well as for England. A sense of nationhood was nurtured in each of them by their quarrels with one another.

THE CAPETIANS

The Capetians had hung on grimly to the French crown. From the tenth century to the fourteenth their kings succeeded one another in unbroken hereditary succession. They added to the domain lands which were the basis of royal power. The Capetians' lands were rich, too. They fell in the heartland of modern France, the cereal-growing area round Paris called the Ile de France, which was for a long time the only part of the country bearing the old name of Francia, thus commemorating the fact that it was a fragment of the old kingdom of the Franks. The domains of the first Capetians were thus distinguished from the other west Carolingian territories, such as Burgundy; by 1300 their vigorous successors had expanded "Francia" to include Bourges, Tours, Gisors and Amiens. By then the French kings had also acquired Normandy and other feudal dependencies from the kings of England.

THE HUNDRED YEARS' WAR

In the fourteenth century (and later) the great fiefs and feudal principalities existing in what is now France make it improper to think of the Capetian kingdom as a monolithic unity. Yet it was a unity of sorts, though much rested on the personal tie. During the fourteenth century that unity was greatly enhanced by a long struggle with England, remembered by the misleading name of the Hundred Years' War. In fact, English and French were only sporadically at war between 1337 and 1453. Sustained warfare was difficult to keep up – it was too expensive. Formally, though, what was at stake was the maintenance by the kings of England of territorial and feudal claims on the French side of the Channel; in 1350 Edward III had quartered his arms with those of France. There were therefore always likely to be specious grounds to start fighting again, and the opportunities it offered to English noblemen for booty and ransom money made war seem a plausible investment to many of them.

For England, these struggles supplied new elements to the infant mythology of nationhood (largely because of the great victories won at Crécy and Agincourt) and generated a long-lived distrust of the French. The Hundred Years' War was important to the French monarchy because it did something to check feudal fragmentation and broke down somewhat the barriers between Picard and Gascon, Norman and French. In the long run, too, French national mythology benefited; its greatest acquisition was the story and example of Joan of Arc whose astonishing career accompanied the turning of the balance of the long struggle against the English, though few of the French at the time knew she existed. The two long-term results of the war which mattered most were that Crécy soon led to the English conquest of Calais, and that England was the loser in the

In 1429 Joan of Arc (1412–1431) led the French armies to victory against the English in Orleans. The following year Joan fell into the hands of the English, who had her declared guilty of heresy and burned her at the stake, as depicted in this 15th-century illustration. "La Pucelle", as she was affectionately known, was canonized in 1920.

The main events of the Hundred Years' War

The name is conventionally applied to a period of intermittent Anglo-French struggle in pursuit of English claims to the French crown. After performing homage for his lands in Aquitaine to the King of France, the English king Edward III quarrelled with his overlord, which led to open hostilities:

1337 Edward III proclaims himself King of France, in right of his mother.

1340–47 The English are victors at Sluys (naval, 1340) and Crécy (1346), and Calais is captured (1347).

1355–6 Raids by the Black Prince across France from the southwest; the French are defeated at Poitiers.

1360 The Treaty of Brétigny ends the first phase of the war. Edward is given an enlarged, sovereign duchy of Aquitaine.

1369–72 The French re-open the conflict, the English fleet is defeated at La Rochelle (1372) and the loss of Aquitaine begins a steady decline of the English position.

1399 The deposition of Richard II (who was married in 1396 to a daughter of Charles VI of France) renews French hostility.

1405–6 The French arrive in Wales and attack English lands in Guienne.

1407 The outbreak of civil war in France is exploited by the English.

1415–19 Henry V reasserts the claim to the French throne. Alliance with Burgundy and the defeat of the French at Agincourt are followed by the English re-conquest of Normandy (1417–19).

1420 The Treaty of Troyes confirms the conquest of Normandy. Henry V marries the daughter of the King of France and is recognized as the regent of France.

1422 The death of both Henry V and Charles VI of France. The infant Henry VI succeeds to the English throne; the war is successfully continued by the English with Burgundian help.

1429 The intervention of Joan of Arc saves Orleans; Charles VII is crowned at Reims.

1430 Henry VI has himself crowned King of France.

1436 The English lose Paris after the collapse of the Anglo-Burgundian alliance.

1444 The Treaty of Tours: England concedes the Duchy of Maine.

1449 The Treaty of Tours is broken by the English, resulting in the collapse of English resistance under concerted French pressure.

1453 The English defeat at Castillon ends their effort to reconquer Gascony; the English are left with only Calais and the Channel Islands and the struggle peters out in their abortive expeditions of 1474 and 1492.

1558 Calais is lost to France (but the title of King of France is retained by English kings down to George III – and the French coat of arms is displayed in *The Times* newspaper's device until 1932).

long run. Calais was to be held by the English for two hundred years and opened Flanders (where a cluster of manufacturing towns was ready to absorb English wool and later cloth exports), to English trade. England's ultimate defeat meant that her territorial connexion with France was virtually at an end by 1500 (though in the eighteenth century George III was still entitled "King of France"). Once more, England became almost an island. After 1453 French kings could push forward with the consolidation of their state undisturbed by the obscure claims of England's kings, from which the wars had sprung. They could settle down to establish their sovereignty over their rebellious magnates at their leisure. In each country, war in the long run strengthened the monarchy.

A depiction of the Battle of Crécy, the most important of the early English victories in the Hundred Years' War.

SPAIN

Progress towards a future national consolidation was also to be seen in Spain. She achieved a measure of unity by the end of the fifteenth century which was mythologically underpinned by the Reconquest. The long struggle against Islam gave Spanish nationhood a quite special flavour from the start because of its intimate connexion with Christian faith and fervour; the Reconquest was a crusade uniting men of different origins. Toledo had been a Christian capital again in the mid-twelfth century. A hundred years later,

Ferdinand II of Aragon and Isabella I of Castile, whose marriage had united their two kingdoms, were supporters of the great Genoese explorer, Christopher Columbus. Three scenes from the journey during which Columbus discovered America are depicted in this tapestry. In the left-hand section Queen Isabella is shown giving the navigator her jewels to help finance the voyage. In the right-hand section he is portrayed about to set sail on the *Santa Maria*. The central section of the tapestry depicts Columbus at the Spanish court, having just returned from his first journey.

Seville belonged to the kingdom of Castile and the crown of Aragon ruled the great Arab city of Valencia. In 1340, when the last great Arab offensive was defeated, success brought the threat of anarchy as the turbulent nobles of Castile strove to assert themselves. The monarchy took the burghers of the towns into alliance. The establishment of stronger personal rule followed the union of the crowns of Aragon and Castile by the marriage in 1479 of *Los Reyes Católicos*, "the Catholic Monarchs", Ferdinand of Aragon and Isabella of Castile. This made easier both the final expulsion of the Moors and the eventual creation of one nation, though the two kingdoms long remained formally and legally separate. Only Portugal in the peninsula remained outside the framework of a new Spain; she clung to an independence often threatened by her powerful neighbour.

GERMANY

Little sign of the groundplans of future nations was to be found in Italy and Germany. Potentially, the claims of the Holy Roman Emperors were an important and broad base for political power. Yet after 1300 they had lost virtually all the special respect due to their title. The last German to march to Rome and force his coronation as emperor did so in 1328, and it proved an abortive effort. A long thirteenth-century dispute between rival emperors was one reason for this. Another was the inability of the emperors to consolidate monarchical authority in their diverse dominions.

In Germany the domains of successive imperial families were usually scattered and disunited. The imperial election was in the hands of great magnates. Once elected, emperors had no special capital city to provide a centre for a nascent German nation. Political circumstances led them more and more to devolve such power as they possessed. Important cities began to exercise imperial powers within their territories. In 1356 a document traditionally accepted as a landmark in German constitutional history (though only a registration of established fact), the Golden Bull, named seven electoral princes who acquired the exercise of almost all the imperial rights in their own lands. Their jurisdiction, for example, was henceforth absolute; no appeals lay from their courts to the emperor. What persisted in this situation of attenuated imperial power was a reminiscence of the mythology which would still prove a temptation to many vigorous princes.

An Austrian family, the house of Habsburg, eventually succeeded to the imperial throne. Theirs was to be a great name: Habsburgs were to provide emperors almost without break from the accession of Maximilian I, who became emperor in 1493 and opened his house's greatest era, to the end of the empire in 1806. And even then they were to survive another century as the rulers of a great state. They began with an important advantage: as German princes went, they were rich. But their most important resources only became available after a marriage which in the end brought them the inheritance of the duchy of Burgundy, the most affluent of all fifteenth-century European states and one including much of the Netherlands. Other inheritances and marriages would add Hungary and Bohemia to their possessions. For the first time since the thirteenth century, it seemed possible that an effective political unity might be imposed on Germany and central Europe; Habsburg family interest in uniting the scattered dynastic territories now had a possible instrument in the imperial dignity.

German eastward expansion

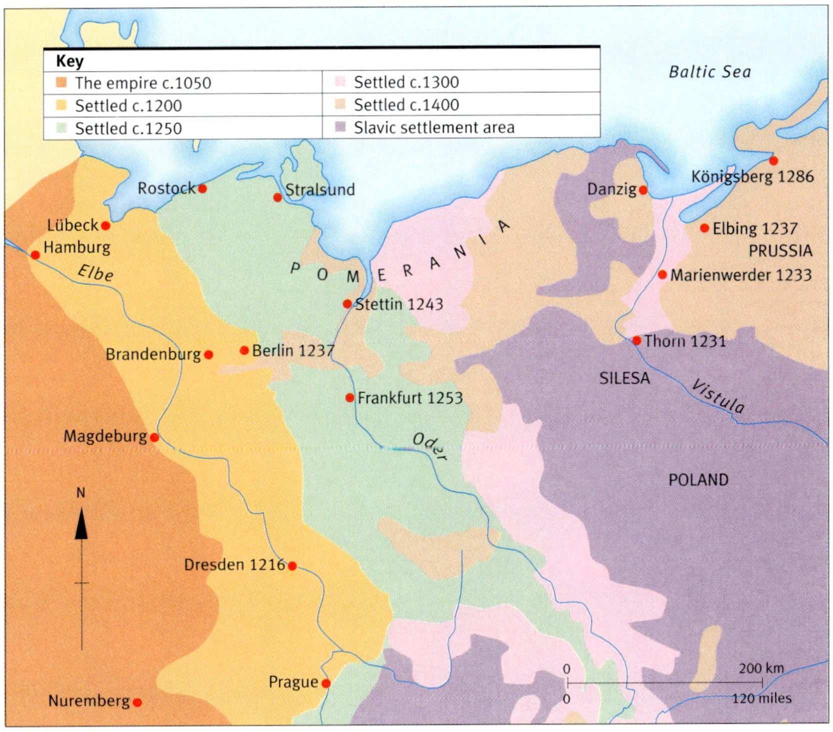

From the 12th to the 15th centuries the territories of Germany expanded eastwards. Its borders eventually shaped the kingdom of France to the west and the kingdoms of Burgundy, Italy and the Papal States to the south, as well as the territories of the Polish Slavic peoples and the kingdom of Hungary to the east.

ITALY

By the fifteenth century the empire had virtually ceased to matter in Italy. The struggle to preserve it there had long been tangled with Italian politics: the contestants in feuds which tormented Italian cities called themselves Guelph and Ghibelline long after those names ceased to mean, as they once did, allegiance respectively to pope or emperor. After the fourteenth century there was no imperial domain in Italy and emperors hardly went there except to be crowned with the Lombard crown. Imperial authority was delegated to "vicars" who made of their vicariates units almost as independent as the electorates of

Italian cities became thriving centres of trade and industry during the Middle Ages. Many banks, such as the one depicted in this 14th-century illustration, enjoyed great prosperity.

Germany. Titles were given to these rulers and their vicariates, some of which lasted until the nineteenth century; the duchy of Milan was one of the first. But other Italian states had different origins. Besides the Norman south, there were the republics, of which Venice, Genoa and Florence were the greatest.

The city republics represented the outcome of two great trends sometimes interwoven in early Italian history, the "communal" movement and the rise of commercial wealth. In the tenth and eleventh centuries, in much of north Italy, general assemblies of the citizens had emerged as effective governments in many towns. They described themselves sometimes as *parliamenta* or, as we might say, town meetings, and represented municipal oligarchies who profited from a revival of trade beginning to be felt from 1100 onwards. In the twelfth century the Lombard cities took the field against the emperor and beat him. Thereafter they ran their own internal affairs.

VENICE

The greatest beneficiary of the revival of trade after 1100 was Venice, and she contributed much to it. Formally a dependency of Byzantium, she was long favoured by the detachment from the troubles of the European mainland given to her by her position on a handful of islands in a shallow lagoon. Refugees had already fled to her from the Lombards. Besides offering security, geography also imposed a destiny; Venice, as its citizens loved later to remember, was wedded to the sea, and a great festival of the republic long commemorated it by the symbolic act of throwing a ring into the waters of the Adriatic. Venetian citizens were forbidden to acquire estates on the mainland and instead turned their energies to commercial empire overseas. Venice became the first west European city to live by trade. She was also the most successful of the pillagers of the Eastern Empire and fought and won a long struggle with Genoa for commercial supremacy in the East. Yet there was enough to go round: Genoa, Pisa and the Catalan ports all prospered with the revival of Mediterranean trade with the East.

LIMITED MONARCHICAL POWER

Much of the political groundplan of modern Europe was in being by 1500. Portugal, Spain, France and England were recognizable in their modern form, though in Italy and Germany, where vernacular language defined nationhood, there was no correspondence between the nation and the State. That institution, too, was still far from enjoying the firmness it later acquired. The kings of France were not kings of Normandy but dukes. Different titles symbolized different legal and practical powers in different provinces. There were many such complicated survivals; constitutional relics everywhere cluttered up the idea of monarchical sovereignty, and they could provide excuses for rebellion. One explanation of the success of Henry VII, the first of the Tudors, was that by judicious marriages he drew much of the remaining poison from the bitter struggle of great families which had bedevilled the English crown in the fifteenth-century Wars of the Roses, but there were still to be feudal rebellions to come.

REPRESENTATION

One limitation on monarchical power had appeared which has a distinctly modern look. In the fourteenth and fifteenth centuries can be found the first examples of the representative, parliamentary bodies which are so characteristic of the modern state. The most famous of them all, the English parliament, was the most mature by 1500. Their origins are complex and have been much debated. One root is Germanic tradition, which imposed on a ruler the obligation of taking

This engraving of the English parliament depicts representatives at the House of Commons in Westminster on 13 April 1640. The assembly is presided over by King Charles I.

counsel from his great men and acting on it. The Church, too, was an early exponent of the representative idea, using it, among other things, to obtain taxation for the papacy. It was a device which united towns with monarchs, too: in the twelfth century representatives from Italian cities were summoned to the diet of the empire. By the end of the thirteenth century most countries had seen examples of representatives with full powers being summoned to attend assemblies which princes had called to find new ways of raising taxation.

This was the nub of the matter. New resources had to be tapped by the new (and more expensive) state. Once summoned, princes found representative bodies had other advantages. They enabled voices other than those of the magnates to be heard. They provided local information. They had a propaganda value. On their side, the early parliaments (as we may loosely call them) of Europe were discovering that the device had advantages for them, too. In some of them the thought arose that taxation needed consent and that someone other than the nobility had an interest and therefore ought to have a voice in the running of the realm.

WORKING AND LIVING

FROM AROUND THE YEAR 1000 another fundamental change was under way in Europe: it began to get richer. As a result, more Europeans slowly acquired a freedom of choice almost unknown in earlier times; society became more varied and complicated. Slow though it was, this was a revolution; wealth at last began to grow faster than population. This was by no means obvious everywhere to the same degree and was punctuated by a bad setback in the fourteenth century. Yet the change was decisive and launched Europe on a career of economic growth lasting to our own day.

POPULATION GROWTH

One crude but by no means misleading index is the growth of population. Only approximate estimates can be made but they are based on better evidence than is available for any earlier period. The errors they contain are unlikely much to distort the overall trend. They suggest that a Europe of about forty million people in 1000 grew to sixty million

This detail is from a mural painted by Ambrogio Lorenzetti in Siena's Palazzo Pubblico in around 1338. It is part of an allegory representing the effects of good government on a city and depicts Siena as a peaceful, prosperous town, whose people are shown trading and dancing in the streets.

or so in the next two centuries. Growth then seems to have further accelerated to reach a peak of about seventy-three million around 1300, after which there is indisputable evidence of decline. The total population is said to have gone down to about fifty million by 1360 and only to have begun to rise in the fifteenth century. Then it began to go up again, and overall growth has been uninterrupted ever since.

Of course, the rate of increase varied even from village to village. The Mediterranean and Balkan lands did not succeed in doubling their population in five centuries and by 1450 had relapsed to levels only a little above those of 1000. The same appears to be true of Russia, Poland and Hungary. Yet France, England, Germany and Scandinavia probably trebled their populations before 1300 and after bad setbacks in the next hundred years still had twice the population of the year 1000. Contrasts within countries could be made, too, sometimes between areas very close to one another, but the general effect is indisputable: population grew overall as never before, but unevenly, the north and west gaining more than the Mediterranean, the Balkans and eastern Europe.

AGRICULTURAL DEVELOPMENT

The explanation for population growth lies in food supply, and therefore in agriculture. It was for a long time the only possible major source of new wealth. More food was obtained by bringing more land under cultivation and by increasing its productivity. Thus began the rise in food production which has gone on ever since. Europe had great natural advantages (which she has retained) in her moderate temperatures and good rainfall, and these, combined with a physical relief whose predominant characteristic is a broad northern plain, have always given her a large area of potentially productive agricultural land. Huge areas of it still wild and forested in 1000 were brought into cultivation in the next few centuries.

Land was not short in medieval Europe and a growing population provided the labour to clear and till it. Though slowly, the landscape changed. The huge forests were gradually cut into as villages pushed out their fields. In some places, new colonies were deliberately established by landlords and rulers. The building of a monastery in a remote spot – as many were built – was often the beginning of a new nucleus of cultivation or stock-raising in an almost empty desert of scrub and trees. Some new land was reclaimed from sea or marsh. In the east, much was won in the colonization of the first German *Drang nach Osten*. Settlement there was promoted as consciously as it was later to be promoted in Elizabethan England in the first age of North American colonization.

The breaking in of fresh land slowed down by about 1300. There were even signs of over-population. The first big increase in the cultivated and grazed area was over, and an indispensable increase in productivity had occurred. Some say that in places it roughly doubled output. In part it was the slow result of more cultivation, the effect of regular fallows and cropping, of the slow enrichment of the soil, but new crops had been introduced, too. Although grain-growing was still the main business of the cultivator in northern Europe, the appearance of beans and peas of various sorts in larger quantities from the tenth century onwards meant that more nitrogen was being returned to the soil. Cause and effect are difficult to disentangle in economic history; other suggestive signs of change go along with these. In the thirteenth century the first manuals of agricultural practice appear and the first agricultural book-keeping,

This illustration, from a French 15th-century Book of Hours, shows work to be done on the land in March. A farmer is using the new symmetrical plough, which increased yields by digging more deeply than had previously been possible.

a monastic innovation. More specialized cultivation brought a tendency to employ wage labourers instead of serfs carrying out obligatory work. By 1300 it is likely that most household servants in England were recruited and paid as free labour, and probably a third of the peasants as well. The bonds of servitude were relaxing and a money economy was spreading slowly into the countryside.

THE HARDSHIP OF PEASANT LIFE

Some peasants benefited from the emerging fiscal economy, but increased wealth usually went to the landlord who took most of the profits. Most still lived poor and cramped lives, eating coarse bread and various grain-based porridges, seasoned with vegetables and only occasionally fish or meat. Calculations suggest each peasant consumed about two thousand calories daily (almost exactly the figure calculated for the average daily intake of a Sudanese in 1988), and this had to sustain him or her for very laborious work. If peasants grew wheat they did not eat its flour, but sold it to the better-off, keeping barley or rye for their own food. They had little elbow-room to better themselves. Even when their lord's legal grip through bond labour became less firm, the lord still had practical monopolies of mills and carts, which the peasants needed to work the land. "Customs", or taxes for protection, were levied without regard to distinctions between freeholders and tenants and could hardly be resisted.

URBAN GROWTH

More cash crops for growing markets gradually changed the self-sufficient manor into a unit producing for sale. Its markets were to be found in towns which grew steadily between 1100 and 1300; urban population increased faster than rural. This is a complicated phenomenon. The new town life was in part a revival going hand in hand with the revival of trade, in part a reflexion of growing population. It is a chicken-and-egg business to decide which comes first. A few new towns grew up around a castle or a monastery. Sometimes this led to the establishment of a market. Many new towns, especially in

Germany, were deliberately settled as colonies. On the whole, long-established towns grew bigger – Paris may have had about eighty thousand inhabitants in 1340 and Venice, Florence and Genoa were probably comparable – but few were so big. Fourteenth-century Germany had only fifteen towns of more than ten thousand inhabitants, and London, with about thirty-five thousand, was then by far the biggest English city. Of the great medieval towns, only those in the south had been important Roman centres (though many in the north, of course, had, like London, Roman nuclei). New cities tended to be linked distinctively to economic possibilities. They were markets, or lay on great trade-routes such as the Meuse and Rhine, or were grouped in an area of specialized production such as Flanders, where already in the late twelfth century Ypres, Arras and Ghent were famous as textile towns, or Tuscany, also a cloth-producing region. Wine was one of the first agricultural commodities to loom large in international trade and this underpinned the early growth of Bordeaux. Ports often became the metropolitan centres of maritime regions, as did Genoa and Bruges.

TRADE

The commercial revival was most conspicuous in Italy, where trade with the outside world was resumed, above all by Venice. In that great commercial centre banking for the first time separated itself from the changing of money. By the middle of the twelfth century, whatever the current state of politics, Europeans enjoyed continuing trade not only with Byzantium but with the Arab Mediterranean. Beyond those limits, an even wider world was involved. In the early fourteenth century trans-Saharan gold from Mali relieved a bullion shortage in Europe. By then, Italian merchants had long been at work in Central Asia and China. They sold slaves from Germany and central Europe to the Arabs of Africa and the Levant. They bought Flemish and English cloth and took it to Constantinople and the Black Sea. In the thirteenth century the first voyage was made from Italy to Bruges; before this the Rhine, Rhône and overland routes had been used.

Grain merchants are portrayed trading their wares in Florence, Italy, in this 14th-century painting.

European trade in the 13th century

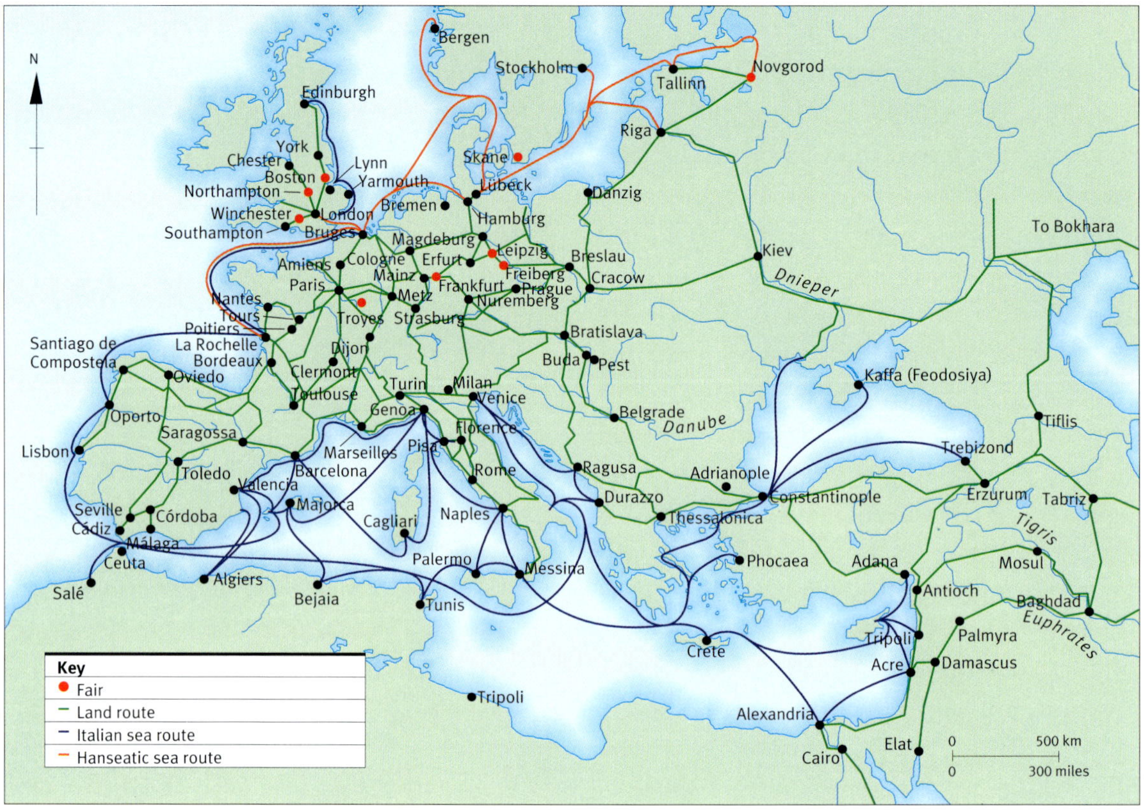

This map represents the most important trade routes and commercial fairs in 13th-century Europe.

Roads were built across Alpine passes. Trade fed on trade and the northern European fairs drew other merchants from the northeast. The German towns of the Hanse, the league which controlled the Baltic, provided a new outlet for the textiles of the West and the spices of the East.

TECHNOLOGY

Through the expansion of trade, European economic geography was revolutionized. In Flanders and the Low Countries economic revival soon began to generate a population big enough to stimulate agricultural innovation. Everywhere, towns which could escape from the cramping monopolies of the earliest manufacturing centres enjoyed the most rapid new prosperity. One visible result was a great wave of building. It was not only a matter of the houses and guildhalls of newly prosperous cities; it left a glorious legacy in Europe's churches, not only the great cathedrals, but the scores of magnificent parish churches of little English towns.

Building was a major expression of medieval technology. The architecture of a cathedral posed engineering problems as complex as those of a Roman aqueduct; in solving them, the engineer was slowly to emerge from the medieval craftsmen. Medieval technology was not in a modern sense science-based, but it achieved much by the accumulation of experience and reflexion on it. Possibly its most important achievement was the harnessing of other forms of energy to do the work of muscles and, therefore, to deploy muscle-power more effectively and productively. Winches, pulleys and inclined planes thus eased the shifting of heavy loads, but change was most obvious in agriculture, where metal tools had been becoming more common since the tenth century. The iron plough had made available the heavier soils of valley lands; since it required oxen to pull it, the evolution of a more efficient yoke followed and with it more efficient traction. The whipple-tree and the shoulder collar for the horse also made possible bigger loads. There were not many such innovations, but they were sufficient to effect a considerable increase in the cultivators' control of the land. They also imposed new demands. Using horses meant that more grain had to be grown to feed them, and this led to new crop rotations.

Another innovation was the spread of milling; both windmills and watermills, first known in Asia, were widely spread in Europe even by 1000. In the centuries to come they were put to more and more uses. Wind often replaced muscle-power in milling foodstuffs, as it had already done in the evolution of better ships; water was used when possible to provide power for other industrial operations. It drove hammers both for cloth-fulling and for forging (here the invention of the crank was of the greatest importance), an essential element in a great expansion of Europe's metallurgical

Long-distance trade was increasingly common from the 12th century. This 15th-century miniature shows a trade ship's merchandise being unloaded in a European port.

Leonardo da Vinci

As well as being one of the greatest artists of all time, Leonardo da Vinci was one of the founders of modern scientific thought – he solved many of the important technical problems of his time. Leonardo's designs (from flying machines to an early concept for the automobile) have come down to us through thousands of drawings, notes and sketches found on loose sheets of paper and in notebooks. Leonardo reflected a new empiricism: he was educated in an artisan's workshop and never learnt Latin (the language of official culture).

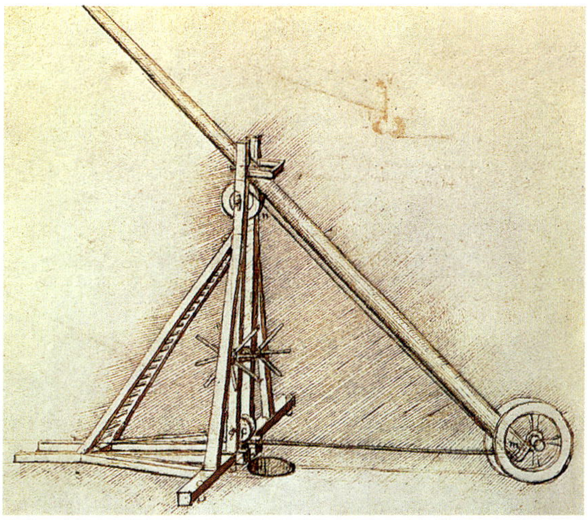

A drawing by Leonardo da Vinci of a machine to manufacture files for working metal or wood.

This 15th-century illustration is a detail from the altar-piece of the church of St Michael in Avila, in the Spanish region of Old Castile. It shows the church under construction.

industry in the fifteenth century, and one closely connected with rising demand for an earlier technological innovation of the previous century, artillery. Water-driven hammers were also used in paper-making. The invention of printing soon gave this industry an importance which may even have surpassed that of the new metal-working of Germany and Flanders. Print and paper had their own revolutionary potential, too, because books made the diffusion of techniques faster and easier in the growing pool of craftsmen and artificers able to use such knowledge. Some innovations were simply taken over from other cultures; the spinning-wheel came to medieval Europe from India (though the application of a treadle to it to provide drive with the foot seems to have been a European invention of the sixteenth century).

EARLY BANKING

Whatever qualifications are needed, it is clear (if only from what was to follow) that by 1500 a technology was available which was already embodied in a large capital investment. It was making the accumulation of further capital for manufacturing enterprises easier than ever before. The availability of this capital must have been greater, moreover, as new devices eased business. Medieval Italians invented much of modern accountancy as well as new credit instruments for the financing of international trade. The bill of exchange appears in the thirteenth century, and with it and the first true bankers we are at the edge of modern capitalism. Limited liability appears in Florence in 1408. Yet though such a change from the past was by implication colossal, it is easy to get it out of proportion if we do not recall its scale. For all the magnificence of its palaces, the goods shipped by medieval Venice in a year could all have fitted comfortably into one large modern ship.

A FRAGILE ECONOMY

The economic changes were also precarious. For centuries, economic life was fragile, never far from the edge of collapse. Medieval agriculture, in spite of such progress as had been made, was appallingly inefficient. It abused the land and exhausted it. Little was consciously put back into it except manure. As new land

Large-scale commercial trade generated a great deal of wealth for the major medieval cities such as Bristol, London, Bruges and, above all, Venice and Genoa. Genoese bankers and money-changers are shown at work in this 14th-century miniature.

The burial of some of the victims of the Black Death at Tournai in 1349 is depicted in this manuscript illustration.

became harder to find, family holdings got smaller; probably most European households farmed less than eight acres in 1300. Only in a few places (the Po valley was one) was there a big investment in collective irrigation or improvement. Above all, agriculture was vulnerable to weather; two successive bad harvests in the early fourteenth century reduced the population of Ypres by a tenth. Local famine could rarely be offset by imports. Roads had broken down since Roman times, carts were crude and for the most part goods had to be carried by packhorse or mule. Water transport was cheaper and swifter, but could rarely meet the need. Commerce could have its political difficulties, too; the Ottoman onslaught brought a gradual recession in Eastern trade in the fifteenth century. Demand was small enough for a very little change to determine the fate of cities: cloth production in Florence and Ypres fell by two-thirds in the fourteenth century.

DEPOPULATION AND DISORDER

It is very difficult to generalize but about one thing there is no doubt: a great and cumulative setback occurred during the fourteenth century. There was a sudden rise in mortality, not occurring everywhere at the same time, but notable in many places after a series of bad harvests round about 1320. This started a slow decline of population which suddenly became a disaster with the onset of attacks of epidemic disease. These are often called by the name of one of them, the "Black Death" of 1348–50 and the worst single attack. It was of bubonic plague, but no doubt it masked many other killing diseases which swept Europe with it and in its wake. Europeans died of typhus, influenza and smallpox, too; all contributed to a great demographic disaster. In some areas a half or a third of the population may have died; over Europe as a whole the total loss has been calculated as a quarter. A papal enquiry put the figure at more than forty million. Toulouse was a city of thirty thousand in 1335 and a century later only eight thousand lived there; fourteen hundred died in three days at Avignon.

There was no universal pattern, but all Europe shuddered under these blows. In extreme cases a kind of collective madness broke out. Pogroms of Jews were a common expression of a search for scapegoats or those guilty of spreading the plague; the burning of witches and heretics was another. The European psyche bore a scar for the rest of the Middle Ages, which were haunted by the imagery of death and damnation in painting, carving and literature. The fragility of settled order illustrated the precariousness of the balance of food and population. When disease killed enough people, agricultural production would collapse; then the inhabitants of the towns would die of famine if they were not already dying of plague. Probably a plateau of productivity had already been reached by about 1300. Both available techniques and easily accessible new land for cultivation had reached a limit and some have seen signs of population pressure treading close upon

This miniature shows a penitential procession of the Dutch Flagellants of Doonik in 1349. The Flagellants were one of the many fanatical groups that emerged as a result of the horrors of the plague epidemic.

resources even by that date. From this flowed the huge setback of the fourteenth century and then the slow recovery in the fifteenth.

PEASANT RISINGS AND GAINS

It is scarcely surprising that an age of such colossal dislocations and disasters should have been marked by violent social conflicts. Everywhere in Europe the fourteenth and fifteenth centuries brought peasant risings. The French *jacquerie* of 1358 which led to over thirty thousand deaths, and the English Peasants' Revolt of 1381 which for a time captured London, were especially notable. The roots of rebellion lay in the ways in which landlords had increased their demands under the spur of necessity and in the new demands of royal tax collectors. Combined with famine, plague and war they made an always miserable existence intolerable. "We are made men in the likeness of Christ, but you treat us like savage beasts," was the complaint of English peasants who rebelled in 1381. Significantly, they appealed to the Christian standards of their civilization; the demands of medieval peasants were often well formulated and effective but it is anachronistic to see in them a nascent socialism.

Demographic disaster on such a scale paradoxically made things better for some of the poor. One obvious and immediate result was a severe shortage of labour; the pool of permanently under-employed had been brutally dried up. A rise in real wages followed. Once the immediate impact of the fourteenth-century disasters had been absorbed the standard of living of the poor may have slightly risen, for the price of cereals tended to fall. The tendency for the economy, even in the countryside, to move on to a money basis was speeded up by the labour shortage. By the sixteenth century, serf labour and servile status had both receded a long way in western Europe, particularly in England. This weakened the manorial structure and the feudal relationships clustered about it. Landlords were also suddenly confronted with a drop in their rent incomes. In the previous two centuries the habits of consumption of the better-off had become more expensive. Now property-owners suddenly ceased to grow more prosperous. Some landlords could adapt. They could, for example, switch from cultivation which required much labour to sheep-running which required little. In Spain there were still even possibilities of taking in more land and living directly off it. Moorish estates were the reward of the soldier of the Reconquest. Elsewhere, many landlords simply let their poorer land go out of cultivation.

RANK AND STATUS

The results are very hard to pin down, but they were bound to stimulate further and faster social change. Medieval society changed dramatically, and sometimes in oddly assorted ways, between the tenth century and the sixteenth. Even at the end of that age, though, it seems still almost unimaginably remote. Its obsession with status and hierarchy is one index of this. Medieval European men and women were defined by their legal status. Instead of being an individual social atom, so to speak, each person was the point at which a number of coordinates met. Some of them were set by birth, and the most obvious expression of this was the idea of nobility. The noble society which was to remain a reality in some places until the twentieth century was already present in its essentials in the thirteenth. Gradually, warriors had turned into landowners. Descent then became important because there were inheritances to argue about. One indicator was the rise of the sciences of heraldry and genealogy, which have since had a profitable life right down to our own day. New titles appeared as distinctions within the nobility ripened. The first English duke was created in 1337, an expression of the tendency to find ways of singling out the greater magnates from among their peers. Symbolic questions

Hunting was a favourite occupation of European noblemen and landowners. This oil painting, which dates from 1529, is entitled *Elector Frederick the Wise's Deerhunt.* Among the figures in the foreground are Elector Frederick III of Saxony, the Holy Roman Emperor (Maximilian I of Habsburg), and Elector John the Constant of Ernestine Saxony.

of precedence became of intense interest; rank was at stake. From this rose the dread of disparagement, the loss of status which might follow for a woman from an unequal marriage or for a man from contamination by a lowly occupation. For centuries it was to be assumed that only arms, the Church or the management of his own estates were fit occupations for a nobleman in northern Europe. Trade, above all, was closed to him except through agents. Even when, centuries later, this barrier gave way, hostility to retail trade was the last thing to be abandoned by those who cared about these things. When a sixteenth-century French king called his Portuguese cousin "the grocer king" he was being rude as well as witty and no doubt his courtiers appreciated the sneer.

The investiture of a medieval knight is portrayed in this 14th-century illustration.

CHIVALROUS VALUES

The values of the nobility were, at bottom, military. Through their gradual refinement there emerged slowly the notions of honour, loyalty and disinterested self-sacrifice which were to be held up as models for centuries to well-born boys and girls. The ideal of chivalry articulated these values and softened the harshness of a military code. It was blessed by the Church, which provided religious ceremonies to accompany the bestowal of knighthood and the knights' acceptance of Christian duties. The heroic figure who came supremely to embody the notion was the mythological English King Arthur, whose cult spread to many lands. It was to live on in the ideal of the gentleman and gentlemanly conduct, however qualified in practice.

Of course, it never worked as it should have done. But few great creative myths do; neither did the feudal theory of dependence, nor does democracy. The pressures of war and, more fundamentally, economics, were always at work to fragment and confuse social obligations. The increasing unreality of the feudal concept of lord and vassal was one factor favouring the growth of kingly power. The coming of a money economy made further inroads, service had increasingly to be paid for in cash, and rents became more important than the services that had gone with them. Some sources of feudal income remained fixed in terms made worthless by changes in real prices. Lawyers evolved devices which enabled new aims to be realized within a "feudal" structure more and more unreal and worm-eaten.

MERCHANTS

Medieval nobility was for a long time very open to new entrants, but usually this became less and less true as time passed. In some

Urban growth led to an increase in the number of private businesses in medieval Europe. A butcher's shop is represented in this Italian manuscript dating from the 14th century.

places attempts were actually made to close for ever a ruling caste. Yet European society was all the time generating new kinds of wealth and even of power which could not find a place in the old hierarchies and challenged them. The most obvious example was the emergence of rich merchants. They often bought land; it was not only the supreme economic investment in a world where there were few, but it might open the way to a change of status for which landownership was either a legal or a social necessity. In Italy merchants sometimes themselves became the nobility of trading and manufacturing cities. Everywhere, though, they posed a symbolic challenge to a world which had, to begin with, no theoretical place for them. Soon they evolved their own social forms, guilds, mysteries and corporations, which gave new definitions to their social role.

The rise of the merchant class was almost a function of the growth of towns; that is to say that merchants were inseparably linked with the most dynamic element in medieval European civilization. Unwittingly, at least at first, towns and cities held within their walls much of the future history of Europe. Though their independence varied greatly in law and practice, there were parallels in other countries to the Italian communal movement. Towns in the German east were especially independent, which helps to explain the appearance there of the powerful Hanseatic League of more than a hundred and fifty free towns. The Flemish towns also tended to enjoy a fair degree of freedom: French and English towns usually had less. Yet lords everywhere sought the support of towns against kings, while kings sought the support of townsmen and their wealth against overmighty subjects. They gave towns charters and privileges. The walls which surrounded the medieval city were the symbol as well as a guarantee of its immunity. The landlords' writ did not run in them and sometimes their anti-feudal implication was even more explicit: villeins, for example, could acquire their freedom in some towns if they lived in them for a year and a day. "The air of the town makes men free," said a German proverb. The communes, and within them the guilds were associations of free men for a long time isolated in a world unfree. The burgher – the *bourgeois*, the dweller in *bourg* or borough – was a man who stood up for himself in a universe of dependence.

THE DIFFERENTIATION OF EUROPEAN HISTORY

Much of the history behind the emergence of the *bourgeoisie* remains obscure because it is for the most part the history of obscure individuals. The wealthy merchants who became the typically dominant figures of the new town life and fought for their corporate privileges are visible enough, but their humbler predecessors are usually not. In earlier times

The Hanseatic League

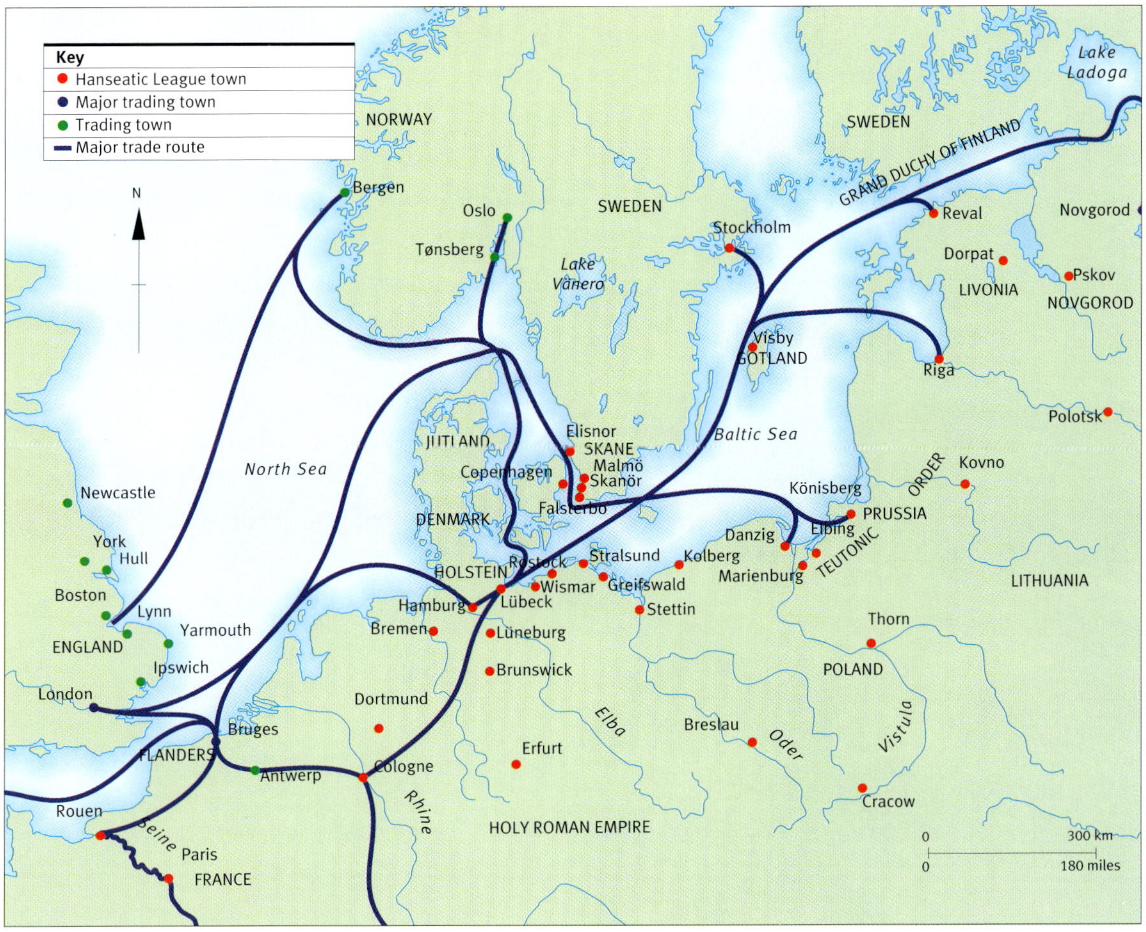

The economic community of the Teutonic Hanse appeared in the middle of the 14th century, although its origins date back to the 11th century. The attempt by the Danish king Valdemar IV (1340–1375) to monopolize trade in the Baltic resulted in the union of several cities and, consequently, the foundation of the Hanseatic League. In 1375 Emperor Charles IV recognized the Hanse's economic monopoly in the coastal territories of the Baltic. The League's "capital" was in the city of Lübeck and the great master of the Teutonic Order was its only prince. The Hanse of the Seventeen Cities (an organization set up by various merchants in the Netherlands and northern France) had similar characteristics, as did the Hanse of London.

a merchant can have been little but the pedlar of exotica and luxuries which the medieval European estate could not provide for itself. Ordinary commercial exchange for a long time hardly needed a middleman: craftsmen sold their own goods and cultivators their own crops. Yet somehow in the towns there emerged traders who dealt between them and the countryside, and their successors were to be those who used capital to order in advance the whole business of production for the market.

In the blossoming of urban life lies buried also much which made European history different from that of other continents. Neither in the ancient world (except, perhaps,

Nuns usually came from privileged backgrounds – the working classes could not afford to pay the large dowry required to enter into a convent. On this panel from a 15th-century polyptych, Blessed Humility (a beatified nun) is portrayed reading aloud from the Bible in a convent refectory.

classical Greece) nor in Asia or America, did city life develop the political and social power it came to show in Europe. One reason was the absence of destructively parasitic empires of conquest to eat away at the will to betterment; Europe's enduring political fragmentation made rulers careful of the geese which laid the golden egg they needed to compete with their rivals. A great sack of a city was a noteworthy event in the European Middle Ages; it was the inescapable and recurrent accompaniment of warfare in much

of Asia. This, of course, could not be the whole story. It also must have mattered that, for all its obsession with status, Europe had no caste system such as that of India, no stultifying ideological homogeneity so intense as China's. Even when rich, the city-dwellers of other cultures seem to have acquiesced in their own inferiority. The merchant, the craftsman, the lawyer and the doctor had roles in Europe, though, which at an early date made them more than simple appendages of landed society. Their society was not closed to change and self-advancement; it offered routes to self-improvement other than the warrior's or the court favourite's. Townsmen were equal and free, even if some were more equal than others.

WOMEN

It need not surprise us that practical, legal and personal freedom was much greater for men than for women (though there were still those of both sexes who were legally unfree at the bottom of society). Whether they were of noble or common blood, women suffered, by comparison with their menfolk, from important legal and social disabilities, as they did in every civilization which had ever existed. Their rights of inheritance were often restricted; they could inherit a fief, for example, but could not enjoy personal lordship, and had to appoint men to carry out the obligations that went with it. In all classes below the highest there was much drudgery to be done by women; until the twentieth century European peasant women worked on the land as women do in Africa and Asia today.

There were theoretical elements in the subjection of women and a large contribution was made to them by the Church. In part this was a matter of its traditionally hostile stance towards sexuality. Its teaching had never been able to find any justification for sex except the link with the reproduction of the species. Woman being seen as the origin of Man's Fall and a standing temptation to concupiscence, the Church threw its weight behind the domination of society by men. Yet this is not all there is to be said. Other societies have done more to seclude and oppress women than Christendom, and the Church at least offered women the only respectable alternative to domesticity available until modern times; the history of the female religious is studded with outstanding women of learning, spirituality and administrative gifts. The position of at least a minority of well-born women, too, was marginally bettered by the idealization of women in the chivalric codes of behaviour of the thirteenth and fourteenth centuries. There lay in this a notion of romantic love, and an entitlement to service, a stage towards a higher civilization.

Yet such ideas can have affected very few. Among themselves, medieval European women were more equal before death than would be rich and poor in Asia today, but, then, so were men. Women lived less long than men, it seems, and frequent confinements and a high mortality rate no doubt explain this. Medieval obstetrics remained, as did other branches of medicine, rooted in Aristotle and Galen; there was nothing better available. But men died young, too. Aquinas lived only to forty-seven and philosophy is not nowadays thought to be physically exacting. This was about the age to which a man of twenty in a medieval town might normally expect to survive: he was lucky to have got as far already and to have escaped the ferocious toll of infant mortality which imposed an average life of about thirty-three years and a death rate about twice that of modern industrial countries. Judged by the standards of antiquity, so far as they can be grasped, this was of course by no means bad.

Women often helped their husbands in their work, although there are many examples of women who had jobs or businesses of their own. Unmarried women generally did the same work as men. This 7th-century illustration shows men and women toiling together in the fields.

THE COLLECTION OF INFORMATION

This reminds us of one last novelty in the huge variety of the Middle Ages; they left behind the means for us to measure just a little more of the dimensions of human life. From these centuries come the first collections of facts upon which reasoned estimates can be made. When in 1085 William the Conqueror's officers rode out into England to interrogate its inhabitants and to record its structure and wealth in the Domesday Book, they were unwittingly pointing the

The *Triumph of Death* is portrayed by an anonymous 15th-century Sicilian artist. Death could never be far from the thoughts of medieval Europeans, ill-equipped as they were to combat disease.

way to a new age. Other collections of data, usually for tax purposes, followed in the next few centuries. Some have survived, together with the first accounts which reduce farming and business to quantities. Thanks to them, historians can talk with a little more confidence about late medieval society than about that of any earlier time.

In this painting, which is dated 1434, Jan Van Eyck portrayed the rich Italian merchant Arnolfini and his betrothed, members of the growing urban bourgeoisie.

6 NEW LIMITS, NEW HORIZONS

In the Near East Europeans were until very recently called "Franks", a word first used in Byzantium to mean Western Christians. It caught on elsewhere and was still being used in various distortions and mispronunciations from the Persian Gulf to China a thousand years later. This is more than just a historical curiosity; it is a helpful reminder that non-Europeans were struck from the start by the unity, not the diversity, of the Western peoples and long thought of them as one.

EUROPE LOOKS OUTWARDS

The roots of the idea of European unity can be seen even in the remote beginnings of Europe's long and victorious assault on the world, when a relaxation of pressure on her eastern land frontier and northern coasts at last began to be felt. By 1000 CE or so, the barbarians were checked; then they began to be Christianized. Within a short space of time Poland, Hungary, Denmark and Norway came to be ruled by Christian kings. One last great threat, the Mongol onslaught, still lay ahead, it is true, but that was at that time unimaginable. By the eleventh century, too, the rolling back of Islam had already begun. The Islamic threat to southern Europeans diminished because of the decline into which the Abbasid caliphate had fallen in the eighth and ninth centuries.

THE CRUSADES

The struggle with Islam was to continue vigorously until the fifteenth century. It was given unity and fervour by religion, the deepest source of European self-consciousness.

The participants of the People's Crusade set off for Jerusalem ahead of the armies of the First Crusade in 1096. They were massacred by the Seljuk Turks in Anatolia, as this contemporary illustration shows.

Christianity bound people together in a great moral and spiritual enterprise. But that was only one side of the coin. It also provided a licence for the predatory appetites of the military class which dominated lay society. They could despoil the pagans with clear consciences. The Normans were in the vanguard, taking south Italy and Sicily from the Arabs, a task effectively complete by 1100. (Almost incidentally they swallowed the last Byzantine possessions in the West as well.) The other great struggle in Europe against Islam was the epic of Spanish history, the Reconquest, whose climax came in 1492, when Granada, the last Muslim capital of Spain, fell to the armies of the Catholic Monarchs.

The Spaniards had always seen the Reconquest as a religious cause, and as such it had drawn warriors from all over Europe since its opening in the eleventh century. It had benefited from the same religious revival and quickening of vigour in the West which expressed itself in a succession of great enterprises in Palestine and Syria. The Crusades, as they came to be called, went on for more than two centuries, and though they were to be unsuccessful in their aim of delivering the Holy Land from Islamic rule they would leave profound marks not only on the Levant, but also on European society and psychology. The first four were the most important. The earliest and most successful was launched in 1096. Within three years the crusaders recaptured Jerusalem, where they celebrated the triumph of the Gospel of Peace by an appalling massacre of their prisoners, women and children included. The Second Crusade (1147–9), in contrast, *began* with a successful massacre (of Jews in the Rhineland), but thereafter, though the presence of an emperor and a king of France gave it greater importance than its predecessor, it was a disaster. It failed to recover Edessa, the city whose loss had largely provoked it, and did much to discredit St Bernard, its most fervent advocate (though it had a by-product of some importance when an English fleet took Lisbon from the Arabs and it passed into the hands of the King of Portugal). Then in 1187 Saladin recaptured Jerusalem for Islam. The

Richard the Lionheart was one of the main protagonists in the Third Crusade, together with Philip II of France and Emperor Frederick I Barbarossa. One of its most significant achievements was the taking of Acre in 1191 (the illustration shows a scene from the siege), although Jerusalem, the crusaders' prime objective, remained in the hands of Saladin.

Time chart (1095–1498)

1095	Urban II proclaims the First Crusade at the Council of Clermont
1120	Order of the Knights Templar is founded
1309	The papacy is transferred to Avignon
1453	Constantinople falls to the Turks
1492	Columbus crosses the Atlantic and discovers the New World
1498	Vasco da Gama circumnavigates the Cape of Good Hope and reaches India

Scale: 1000 – 1200 – 1400 – 1600

The Crusades

Conventionally, the Crusades were the series of expeditions directed from Western Christendom to the Holy Land whose aim was to recover the Holy Places from their Islamic rulers. Those who took part were assured by papal authority of certain spiritual rewards including indulgences (remission of time spent in purgatory after death) and the status of martyr in the event of death on the expedition. The first four expeditions were the most important and made up what is usually thought of as the crusading era.

1095 Urban II proclaims the First Crusade at the Council of Clermont.

1099 The capture of Jerusalem and foundation of the Latin Kingdom.

1144 The Seljuk Turks capture the (Christian) city of Edessa, whose fall inspires St Bernard's preaching of a new crusade (1146).

1147–9 The Second Crusade is a failure (its only significant outcome is the capture of Lisbon by an English fleet – and its transfer to the King of Portugal).

1187 Saladin reconquers Jerusalem for Islam.

1189 The launch of the Third Crusade, which fails to recover Jerusalem.

1192 Saladin allows pilgrims access to the Holy Sepulchre.

1202 The Fourth Crusade, the last of the major crusades, which culminates in the capture and sack of Constantinople by the crusaders (1204) and the establishment of a "Latin Empire" there.

1212 The so-called "Children's Crusade".

1216 The Fifth Crusade captures Damietta in Egypt, soon lost again.

1228–9 The emperor Frederick II (excommunicate) undertakes a crusade and recaptures Jerusalem, crowning himself king.

1239–40 Crusades by Theobold of Champagne and Richard of Cornwall.

1244 Jerusalem is retaken for Islam.

1248–54 Louis IX of France leads a crusade to Egypt where he is taken prisoner, ransomed and sets out on a pilgrimage to Jerusalem.

1270 Louis IX's second crusade, against Tunis, where he dies.

1281 Acre, the last Christian foothold in the Levant, falls to Islam.

There were many other expeditions to which the title of "crusade" was given, sometimes formally. Some were directed against non-Christians (Moorish Spain and the Slav peoples), some against heretics (such as the Albigensians), some against monarchs who had offended the papacy. There were also further futile expeditions to the Near East. In 1464 Pius II failed to obtain support for what proved to be a last attempt to mount a further crusade to that region.

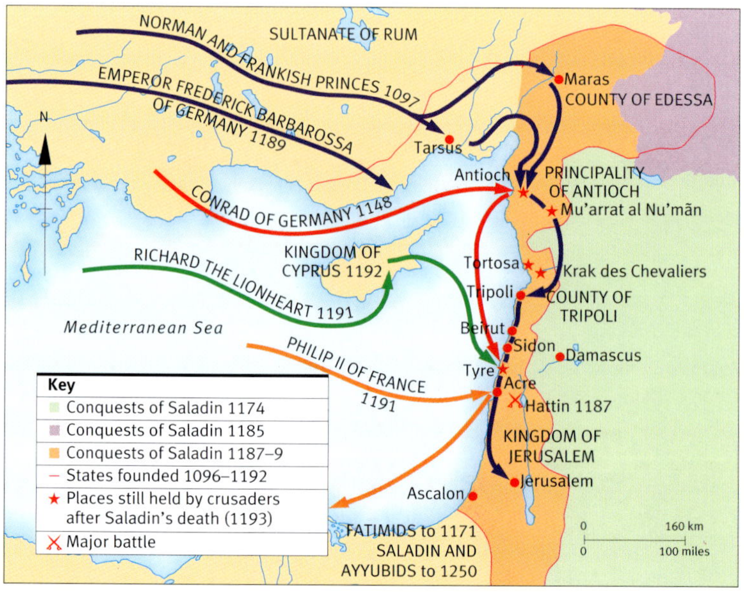

This map shows the routes of the first four crusades.

Third Crusade which followed (1189–1192) was socially the most spectacular. A German emperor (drowned in the course of it) and the kings of England and France all took part. They quarrelled and the crusaders failed to recover Jerusalem. No great monarch answered Innocent III's appeal to go on the next crusade, though many land-hungry magnates did. The Venetians financed the expedition, which left in 1202. It was at once diverted by interference in the dynastic troubles of Byzantium, which suited the Venetians, who helped to recapture Constantinople for a deposed emperor. There followed the terrible sack of the city in 1204 and that was the end of the Fourth Crusade, whose monument was the establishment of a "Latin Empire" at Constantinople which survived there for only a half-century.

One of the crusaders' most famous possessions was Krak des Chevaliers, a castle located in Syria near Tripoli, which was used as a surveillance centre. From 1142 the castle was held by the Knights Hospitallers, who managed to resist Muslim assaults until 1271, when the castle was taken by Sultan Baybars I.

THE CRUSADERS AND THE EUROPEAN OUTLOOK

Several more crusades set out in the thirteenth century, but though they helped to put off a little longer the dangers which faced Byzantium, crusading to the holy land was dead as an independent force. Its religious impulse could still move people, but the first four crusades had too often shown the

The crusaders take Jerusalem

"Our pilgrims, once in the city, chased and killed the Saracens as far as the Temple of Solomon, where they had regrouped and from where they confronted our people in the fiercest fighting of the day, to the point where the whole temple glistened with their blood. In the end, after having defeated the pagans, our people took possession in the temple of a large number of women and children, whom they killed or spared as they pleased. In the upper level of the temple of Solomon, a large group of pagans of both sexes had taken refuge, to whom Tancred and Gaston de Bearn had given their standards as safe-keeping. The crusaders immediately spread all over the city, making off with gold, silver, horses, mules and pillaging the houses that overflowed with riches. Afterwards, absolutely ecstatic and crying with joy, they went to worship at the Sepulchre of our Saviour Jesus and paid their debt with Him. The next morning, our people scaled the roof of the temple and attacked the Saracens, both men and women, and drawing their swords, they beheaded them. Some of them threw themselves off the Temple roof. On seeing this spectacle, Tancred became very indignant."

An anonymous chronicler recounts the taking of Jerusalem by the crusaders on 15 July 1099, during the First Crusade.

This illustration shows the French king Louis IX (1215–1270) setting out on his ill-fated final crusade, which culminated in the surrender of his troops. The captured crusaders were taken to Cairo. In the peace treaty negotiated there the Christians had to give up Damietta.

unpleasant face of greed. They were the first examples of European overseas imperialism, both in their characteristic mixture of noble and ignoble aims, and in their abortive settler colonialism. Whereas in Spain, and on the pagan marches of Germany, Europeans were pushing forward a frontier of settlement, they tried in Syria and Palestine to transplant Western institutions to a remote and exotic setting as well as to seize lands and goods no longer easily available in the West. They did this with clear consciences because their opponents were infidels who had by conquest installed themselves in Christianity's most sacred shrines. "Christians are right, pagans are wrong," said the Song of Roland and that probably sums up well enough the average crusader's response to any qualms about what he was doing.

THE CRUSADERS

The brief successes of the First Crusade had owed much to a passing phase of weakness and anarchy in the Islamic world, and the feeble transplants of the Frankish states and the Latin Empire of Constantinople soon collapsed. But there were important and permanent results. As we noted, the crusades had embittered still further the division of Western from Eastern Christendom: the first warriors to sack Constantinople had been crusaders. Secondly, the crusaders had cherished and intensified the sense of unbridgeable ideological separation between Islam and Christianity. The Crusades both expressed and helped to forge the special temper of Western Christianity, giving it a militant tone and an aggressiveness which would make its missionary work more potent in the future when it would have technological superiority on its side as well, but also more ruthless. In it lay the roots of a mentality which, when secularized, would power the world-conquering culture of the modern era. The Reconquest was scarcely to be complete before the Spanish would look to the Americas for the battlefield of a new crusade.

Yet Europe was not impervious to Islamic influence. In these struggles she imported and invented new habits and institutions. Wherever they encountered Islam, whether in the crusading lands, Sicily or Spain, western Europeans found things to admire. Sometimes they took up luxuries not to be

The early military orders and the Knights Templar

From the time of St Augustine, the Catholic Church supported the idea of using arms in its defence. Hundreds of knights from all over Europe took part in the Spanish Reconquest, many of whom later went on to spearhead the Christian armies which travelled to the Near East with the intention of liberating the Holy Places. It is in this context that the military orders were born, combining the religious spirit of the monastic order with the warrior ideal of the knightly order.

Many medievalists believe that the origins of the military orders lie in the Muslim world, in the famous *ribats* – frontier castles where the faithful offered temporary military service. Some experts hold that there are parallels between the Christian idea of Holy War and the Islamic *jihad*. Other scholars reject these theories, in the belief that the military orders had Latin origins and emerged from the internal transformations which were taking place within the Catholic Church during that period.

The first military orders – the Hospitallers and the Templars – were founded at the beginning of the 12th century. The Order of the Knights of the Temple, or Templars, was established in 1120 by Hugh of Payns, a French knight, who had long dreamed of creating a new religious order of knights whose role would be to protect pilgrims. From the foundation of their order, the Templars received substantial donations, making it one of the best-funded orders in Christendom. The Templar Rule was approved at the Council of Troyes in 1129, having been enthusiastically defended by St Bernard of Clairvaux.

This picture by the Spanish painter Casado de Alisal depicts Pope Alexander III confirming the foundation of the Order of Santiago in 1170.

found at home: silk clothes, the use of perfumes and new dishes. One habit acquired by some crusaders was that of taking more frequent baths. This may have been unfortunate, for it added the taint of religious infidelity to a habit already discouraged in Europe by the association of bath-houses with sexual licence. Cleanliness had not yet achieved its later quasi-automatic association with godliness.

MILITARY ORDERS

One institution crystallizing the militant Christianity of the high Middle Ages was the military order of knighthood. It brought together soldiers who professed vows as members of a religious order and of an accepted discipline to fight for the faith. Some of these orders became very rich, owning endowments in many countries. The Knights of St John of Jerusalem (who are still in existence) were to be for centuries in the forefront of the battle against Islam. The Knights Templar rose to such great power and prosperity that they were destroyed by a French king who feared them, and the Spanish military orders of Calatrava and Santiago were in the forefront of the Reconquest.

Another military order operated in the

north, the Teutonic Knights, the warrior monks who were the spearhead of Germanic penetration of the Baltic and Slav lands. There, too, missionary zeal combined with greed and the stimulus of poverty to change both the map and the culture of a whole region. The colonizing impulse which failed in the Near East had lasting success further north. German expansion eastwards was a huge folk-movement, a centuries-long tide of men and women clearing forest, planting homesteads and villages, founding towns, building fortresses to protect them and monasteries and churches to serve them. When the crusades were over, and the narrow escape from the Mongols had reminded Europe that it could still be in danger, this movement went steadily on. Out on the Prussian and Polish marches, the soldiers, among whom the Teutonic Knights were outstanding,

This painting, which dates from c.1600, represents a 13th-century battle between Turkish troops and the Knights of the Teutonic Order. One of the German knights in the foreground is carrying a flag bearing the emblem of the Teutonic cross.

provided its shield and cutting-edge at the expense of the native peoples. This was the beginning of a cultural conflict between Slav and Teuton which persisted down to the twentieth century. The last time that the West threw itself into the struggle for Slav lands was in 1941: many Germans saw "Barbarossa" (as Hitler's attack on Russia was named in memory of a medieval emperor) as another stage in a centuries-old civilizing mission in the East. In the thirteenth century a Russian prince, Alexander Nevsky, Grand Duke of Novgorod, had to beat off the Teutonic Knights (as Russians were carefully reminded by a great film in 1937) at a moment when he also faced the Tatars on another front.

THE SHAPING OF THE RUSSIAN STATE

While the great expansion of the German East between 1100 and 1400 made a new economic, cultural and racial map, it also raised yet another barrier to the union of the two Christian traditions. Papal supremacy in the West made the Catholicism of the late medieval period more uncompromising and more unacceptable than ever to Orthodoxy. From the twelfth century onwards Russia was more and more separated from western Europe by her own traditions and special historical experience. The Mongol capture of Kiev in 1240 had been a blow to Eastern Christianity as grave as the sack of Constantinople in 1204. It also broke the princes of Muscovy. With Byzantium in decline and the Germans and Swedes on their backs, they were to pay tribute to the Mongols and their Tatar successors of the Golden Horde for centuries. This long domination by a nomadic people was another historical experience sundering Russia from the West.

Tatar domination had its greatest impact on the southern Russian principalities, the area where the Mongol armies had operated. A new balance within Russia appeared; Novgorod and Moscow acquired new importance after the eclipse of Kiev, though both paid tribute to the Tatars in the form of silver, recruits and labour. Their emissaries, like other Russian princes, had to go to the Tatar capital at Sarai on the Volga, and make their separate arrangements with their conquerors. It was a period of the greatest dislocation and confusion in the succession patterns of the Russian states. Both Tatar policy and the struggle to survive favoured those which were most despotic. The future political tradition of Russia was thus now shaped by the Tatar experience as it had been by the inheritance of imperial ideas from Byzantium. Gradually Moscow emerged as the focus of a new centralizing trend. The process can be discerned as early as the reign of Alexander Nevsky's son, who was prince of Muscovy. His successors had the support of the Tatars, who found them efficient tax gatherers. The Church offered no resistance and the metropolitan archbishopric was transferred from Vladimir to Moscow in the fourteenth century.

Meanwhile, a new challenge to Orthodox Christianity had arisen in the West. A Roman Catholic but half-Slav state had emerged which was to hold Kiev for three centuries. This was the medieval duchy of Lithuania, formed in 1386 in a union by marriage which incorporated the Polish kingdom and covered much of modern Poland, Prussia, the Ukraine and Moldavia. Fortunately for the Russians, the Lithuanians fought the Germans, too; it was they who shattered the Teutonic Knights at Tannenberg in 1410. Harassed by the Germans and the Lithuanians to the west, Muscovy somehow survived by exploiting divisions within the Golden Horde.

Ivan IV, known as Ivan the Terrible, ruled over Russia from 1533 to 1584. He ruthlessly eliminated his enemies, making full use of the despotic powers with which his grandfather, Ivan the Great, had invested the Russian monarchy.

The fall of Constantinople brought a great change to Russia; Eastern Orthodoxy had now to find its centre there, and not in Byzantium. Russian churchmen soon came to feel that a complex purpose lay in such awful events. Byzantium, they believed, had betrayed its heritage by seeking religious compromise at the Council of Florence. "Constantinople has fallen", wrote the metropolitan of Moscow, "because it has deserted the true Orthodox faith ... There exists only one true Church on earth, the Church of Russia." A few decades later, at the beginning of the sixteenth century, a monk could write to the ruler of Muscovy in a quite new tone: "Two Romes have fallen, but the third stands and a fourth will not be. Thou art the only Christian sovereign in the world, the lord of all faithful Christians."

IVAN THE GREAT

The end of Byzantium came when other historical changes made Russia's emergence from confusion and Tatar domination possible and likely. The Golden Horde was rent by dissension in the fifteenth century. At the same time, the Lithuanian state began to crumble. These were opportunities, and a ruler who was capable of exploiting them came to the throne of Muscovy in 1462. Ivan the Great (Ivan III) gave Russia something like the definition and reality won by England and France from the twelfth century onwards. Some have seen him as the first national ruler of Russia. Territorial consolidation was the foundation of his work. When Muscovy swallowed the republics of Pskov and Novgorod, his authority stretched at least in theory as far as the Urals. The oligarchies which had ruled them were deported, to be replaced by men who held lands from Ivan in return for service. The German merchants of the Hanse who had dominated the trade of these republics were expelled, too. The Tatars made another onslaught on Moscow in 1481 but were beaten off, and two invasions of Lithuania gave Ivan much of White Russia and Little Russia in 1503. His successor took Smolensk in 1514.

Ivan the Great was the first Russian ruler to take the title of "Tsar". It was a conscious evocation of an imperial past, a claim to the heritage of the Caesars, the word in which it originated. In 1472 Ivan married a niece of the last Greek emperor. He was called "autocrat by the grace of God" and during his reign the double-headed eagle was adopted, which was to remain part of the insignia of Russian rulers until 1917. This gave a further Byzantine colouring to Russian monarchy and Russian history, which became still more unlike that of western Europe. By 1500 western Europeans already recognized a distinctive kind of monarchy in Russia; Basil, Ivan's successor, was acknowledged to have a despotic power over his subjects greater than that of any other Christian rulers over theirs.

EUROPE TURNS TO THE OCEANS

Much of Europe's future seems already discernible by 1500. A great process of definition and realization had been going on for centuries. Europe's land limits were now filled up; in the East further advance was blocked by the consolidation of Christian Russia, in the Balkans by the Ottoman Empire of Islam. The first, crusading, wave of overseas expansion was virtually spent by about 1250. With the onset of the Ottoman threat in the fifteenth century, Europe was again forced on the defensive in the eastern Mediterranean and Balkans. Those unhappy states with exposed territories in the East, such as Venice, had to look after them as best they could. Meanwhile, others were taking a new look at their oceanic horizons. A new phase of western Europe's relations with the rest of the world was about to open.

In 1400 it had still seemed sensible to see Jerusalem as the centre of the world. Though the Vikings had crossed the Atlantic, Europeans could still think of a world which, though spherical, was made up of three continents, Europe, Asia and Africa, around the shores of one land-locked sea, the Mediterranean. A huge revolution lay just ahead which for ever swept away such views, and the route to it lay across the oceans, because elsewhere advance was blocked. Europe's first direct contacts with the East had been on land rather than on water. The caravan routes of Central Asia were their main channel and brought goods west to be shipped from Black Sea or Levant ports. Elsewhere, ships rarely ventured far south of Morocco until the fifteenth century. Then, a mounting wave of maritime enterprise becomes noticeable. With it, the age of true world history was beginning.

ADVANCES IN MARITIME TECHNOLOGY

One explanation of the boom in maritime enterprise was the acquisition of new tools and skills. Different ships and new techniques of long-range navigation were needed for oceanic sailing and they became available from the fourteenth century onwards, thus making possible the great effort of exploration which has led to the fifteenth century being called "the Age of Reconnaissance". In ship design there were two crucial changes. One was specific, the adoption of the sternpost rudder; though we do not know exactly when this happened, some ships had it by 1300. The other was a more gradual and complex process of improving rigging. This went with a growth in the size of ships. A more complex maritime trade no doubt spurred such developments. By 1500 the tubby medieval "cog" of northern Europe, square-rigged with a single sail and mast, had

The Portuguese galleons and caravels represented in this manuscript were in use during the late 16th century.

developed into a ship carrying up to three masts, with mixed sails. The main-mast still carried square-rigging, but more than one sail; the mizzen-mast had a big lateen sail borrowed from the Mediterranean tradition; a fore-mast might carry more square-rigged sails, but also newly invented fore-and-aft jib sails attached to a bowsprit. Together with the lateen sail aft, these head-sails made vessels much more manoeuvrable; they could be sailed much closer to the wind.

Once these innovations were absorbed, the design of ships which resulted was to remain essentially unchanged (though refined) until the coming of steam propulsion. Though he would have found them small and cramped, Columbus' ships would have been perfectly comprehensible machines to a nineteenth-century clipper captain. Since they carried guns, though tiny ones by comparison with what was to come, they would also have been comprehensible to Nelson.

Prince Henry of Portugal (1394–1460), portrayed in this detail from a triptych panel, was known as "the Navigator". One of his main contributions to navigation was his establishment at Sagres of a settlement where he gathered together mathematicians, shipbuilders and cartographers. At this nautical think-tank, the combination of classical and Arabic knowledge produced significant advances in ship design.

NAVIGATIONAL INNOVATIONS

By 1500 some crucial navigational developments had also taken place. The Vikings had first shown how to sail an oceanic course. They had better ships and navigational skill than anything previously available in the West. Using the Pole Star and the sun, whose height above the horizon in northern latitudes at midday had been computed in tables by a tenth-century Irish astronomer, they had crossed the Atlantic by running along a line of latitude. Then, with the thirteenth century, there is evidence of two great innovations. At that time the compass came to be commonly used in the Mediterranean (it already existed in China, but it is not certain that it was transmitted from Asia to the West), and in 1270 there appears the first reference to a chart, one used in a ship engaged on a crusading venture. The next two centuries gave birth to modern geography and exploration. Spurred by the thought of commercial prizes, by missionary zeal and diplomatic possibilities, some princes began to subsidize research. In the fifteenth century they came to employ their own cartographers and hydrographers. Foremost among these princes was the brother of the King of Portugal, Henry, "the Navigator" as English-speaking scholars were later to call him (unsuitably, for he never navigated anything).

PORTUGUESE EXPLORATION

The Portuguese had a long Atlantic coast. They were land-locked by Spain, and virtually barred from the Mediterranean trade by the experience and armed force with which the Italians guarded it. Almost inevitably, it seems, they were bound to push out into the Atlantic and they had already started to familiarize themselves with northern waters

Spanish cartographer Juan de Cosa drew up this first general map of the New World around 1500.

when Prince Henry began to equip and launch a series of maritime expeditions. His initiative was decisive. From a mixture of motives, he turned his countrymen southwards. Gold and pepper, it was known, were to be found in the Sahara; perhaps the Portuguese could discover where. Perhaps, too, there was a possibility of finding an ally here to take the Turk in the flank, the legendary Prester John. Certainly there were converts, glory and land to be won for the Cross. Henry, for all that he did so much to launch Europe on the great expansion which transformed the globe and created one world, was a medieval man to the soles of his boots. He cautiously sought papal authority and approval for his expeditions. He had gone crusading in North Africa, taking with him a fragment of the True Cross. This was the beginning of the age of discovery, and at its heart was systematic, government-subsidized research, but it was rooted in the world of chivalry and crusade which had shaped Henry's thinking. He is an outstanding example of a man who wrought much more than he knew.

The Portuguese pushed steadily south. They began by hugging the African coast, but some of the bolder among them reached the Madeiras and had begun to settle there already in the 1420s. In 1434 one of their captains passed Cape Bojador, an important psychological obstacle whose overcoming was Henry's first great triumph; ten years later they rounded Cape Verde and established themselves in the Azores. By then they had perfected the caravel, a ship which used new rigging to tackle head winds and contrary currents on the home voyage by going right out into the Atlantic and sailing a long semicircular course home. In 1445 they reached Senegal. Their first fort was built soon after. Henry died in 1460, but by then his countrymen were ready to continue further south. In 1473 they crossed the Equator and in 1487 they were at the Cape of Good Hope. Ahead lay the Indian Ocean; Arabs had long traded across it and pilots were available. Beyond it lay even richer sources of spices. In 1498 Vasco da Gama dropped anchor at last in Indian waters.

COLUMBUS AND THE NEW WORLD

By the time Vasco da Gama ventured into the Indian Ocean, another sailor, the Genoese Columbus, had crossed the Atlantic to look for Asia, confident in the light of Ptolemaic geography that he would soon come to it. He failed. Instead he discovered the Americas for the Catholic Monarchs of Spain. In the name of the "West Indies" the modern map commemorates his continuing belief that he had accomplished the discovery of islands off Asia by his astonishing venture, so different from the cautious, though brave, progress of the Portuguese towards the East round Africa. Unlike them, but unwittingly, he had in fact discovered an entire continent, though even on the much better-equipped second voyage which he made in 1493 he explored only its islands. The Portuguese had reached a known continent by a new route. Soon (though to his dying day Columbus refused to admit it, even after two more voyages and experience of the mainland) it began to be realized that what he had discovered might not be Asia after all. In 1494 the historic name "New World" was first applied to what had been found in the western hemisphere. (Not until 1726, though, was it to be realized that Asia and America were not joined together in the region of the Bering Straits.)

THE IMPORTANCE OF THE ATLANTIC

The two enterprising Atlantic nations tried to come to understandings about their respective interests in a world of widening horizons. The first European treaty about trade outside European waters was made by Portugal and Spain in 1479; now they went on to delimit spheres of influence. The pope made a temporary award, based on a division of the world between them along a line a hundred leagues west of the Azores, but this was overtaken by the treaty of Tordesillas in 1494 which gave to Portugal all the lands east of a line of longitude running 370 leagues west of Cape Verde and to Spain those west of it. In 1500 a Portuguese squadron on the way to the Indian Ocean ran out into the Atlantic to

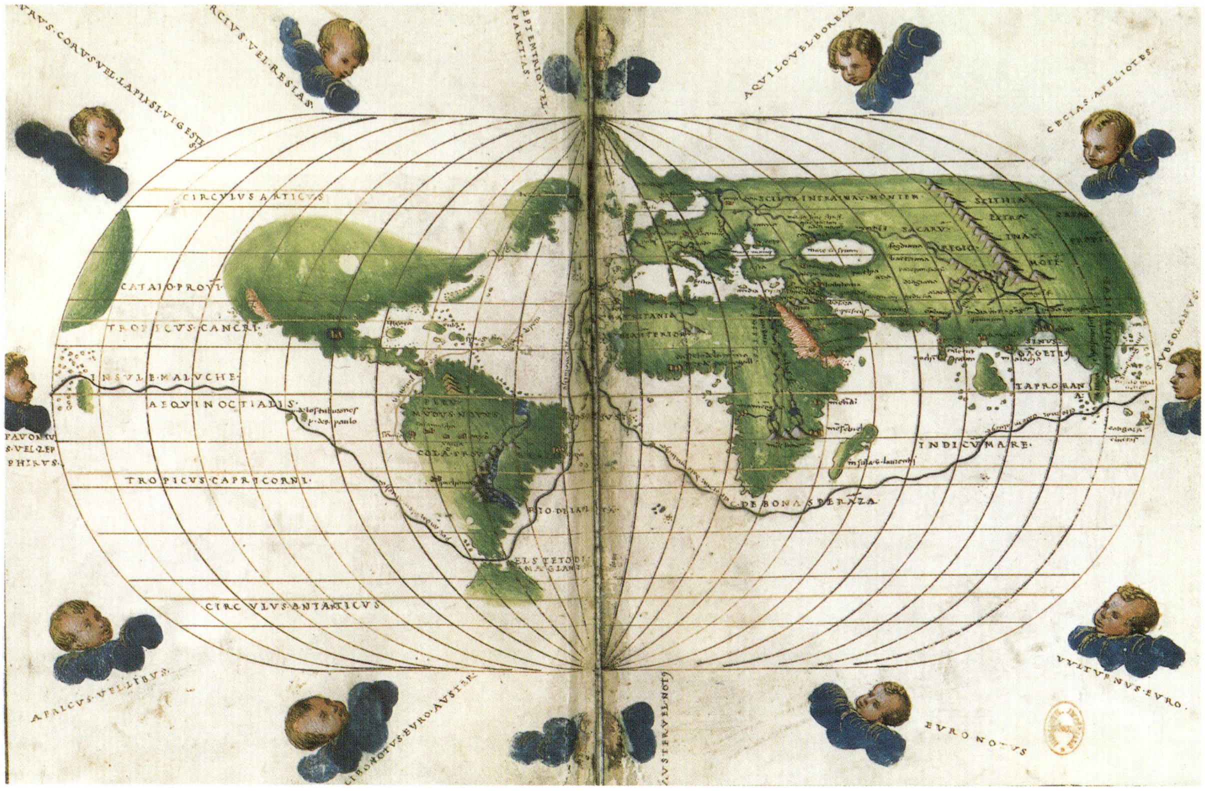

This map of the world, drawn up by Battista Agnese in 1540, shows the route Magellan followed in the first circumnavigation of the globe.

avoid adverse winds and to its surprise struck land which lay east of the treaty line and was not Africa. It was Brazil. Henceforth Portugal had an Atlantic as well as an Asian destiny. Though the main Portuguese effort still lay to the east, an Italian in Portuguese service, Amerigo Vespucci, soon afterwards ran far enough to the south to show that not merely islands but a whole new continent lay between Europe and Asia by a western route. Before long it was named after him, America, the name of the southern continent later being extended to the northern, too.

THE FIRST CIRCUMNAVIGATION OF THE GLOBE

In 1522, thirty years after Columbus' landfall in the Bahamas, a ship in the Spanish service completed the first voyage round the world. Its commander had been Magellan, a Portuguese, who got as far as the Philippines, where he was killed, having discovered and sailed through the straits named after him. With this voyage and its demonstration that all the great oceans were interconnected, the prologue to the European age can be considered over. Just about a century of discovery and exploration had changed the shape of the world and the course of history. From this time the nations with access to the Atlantic would have opportunities denied to the land-locked powers of central Europe and the Mediterranean. In the first place this meant Spain and Portugal, but they would be joined and surpassed by France, Holland and, above all, England, a collection of harbours incomparably placed at the centre of the newly enlarged hemisphere, all of them easily accessible from their shallow hinterland, and within easy striking distance of all the great European sea routes of the next two hundred years.

The voyages undertaken by Italian, Portuguese and Spanish sailors during the 15th century brought about great improvements in map-making. This "Mappamundi" (Map of the World) by Fra Mauro dates from 1459.

PROGRESS IN CARTOGRAPHY

The enterprise behind these changes had only been possible because of a growing substratum of maritime skill and geographical knowledge. The new and characteristic figure of this movement was the professional explorer and navigator. Many of the earliest among them were, like Columbus himself, Italian. New knowledge, too, underlay not only the conception of these voyages and their successful technical performance, but also allowed Europeans to see their relationship with the world in a new way. To sum the matter up, Jerusalem ceased to be centre of the world; the maps men began to draw, for all their crudity, are maps which show the basic structure of the real globe.

In 1400 a Florentine had brought back from Constantinople a copy of Ptolemy's *Geography*. The view of the world it contained had been virtually forgotten for a thousand years. In the second century CE Ptolemy's world already included the Canaries, Iceland and Ceylon, all of which found a place on his maps, along with the misapprehension that the Indian Ocean was totally enclosed by land. Translation of his text, misleading as it was, and the multiplication of copies first in manuscript and then in print (there were six editions between 1477, when it was first printed, and 1500) was a great stimulus to better map-making. The atlas – a collection of engraved and printed maps bound in a book – was invented in the sixteenth century; more Europeans than ever could now buy or consult a picture of their world. With better projections, navigation was simpler, too. Here the great figure was a Dutchman, Gerhard Kremer, who is remembered as Mercator. He was the first man to print on a map the word "America" and he invented the projection which is still today the most familiar – a map of the world devised as if it were an unrolled cylinder, with Europe at its centre. This solved the problem of providing a flat surface on which to read direction and courses without distortion, even if it posed problems in the calculation of distances. The Greeks of the fourth century BCE had known the world was a globe and the making of terrestrial and celestial globes was another important branch of the geographical revolution (Mercator made his first globe in 1541).

An allegory of Amerigo Vespucci's famous voyage, carried out in the service of the Portuguese monarchy. Vespucci first discovered the bay of Rio de Janeiro, then, on reaching the south of Patagonia, he realized that he was not sailing along the coastline of southern Asia, as he had thought, but along the shores of a new continent – America.

A NEW CONFIDENCE

The most striking thing about this progression is its cumulative and systematic nature. European expansion in the next phase of world history would be conscious and directed as it had never been before. Europeans had long wanted land and gold; the greed which lay at the heart of enterprise was not new. Nor was the religious zeal which sometimes inspired them and sometimes cloaked their springs of action even from the actors themselves. What was new was a growing confidence derived from knowledge and success. Europeans stood in 1500 at the beginning of an age in which their energy and confidence would grow seemingly without limit. The world did not come to them, they went out to it and took it.

The scale of such a break with the past was not to be seen at once. In the Mediterranean and Balkans, Europeans still felt threatened and defensive. Navigation and seamanship still had far to go – not until the eighteenth century, for example, would there be available a timekeeper accurate enough for exact sailing. But the way was opening to new relationships between Europe and the rest of the world, and between European countries themselves. Discovery would be followed by conquest. A world revolution was beginning. An equilibrium which had lasted a thousand years was dissolving. As the next two centuries unrolled, thousands of ships would put out year after year, day after day, from Lisbon, Seville, London, Bristol, Nantes,

This imaginary portrait of the Graeco-Egyptian astronomer and geographer Ptolemy was painted in the 15th century by Justus of Ghent.

This 16th-century portrait depicts Francisco de Almeida (1450–1510), who was a soldier and explorer and the first viceroy of Portuguese India.

Antwerp and many other European ports, in search of trade and profit in other continents. They would sail to Calicut, Canton, Nagasaki. In time, they would be joined by ships from places where Europeans had established themselves overseas – from Boston and Philadelphia, Batavia and Macao. And during all that time, not one Arab dhow was to find its way to Europe; it was 1848 before a Chinese junk was brought to the Thames. Only in 1867 would a Japanese vessel cross the Pacific to San Francisco, long after the great sea-lanes had been established by Europeans.

THE EUROPEAN MIND

In 1500 Europe is clearly recognizable as the centre of a new civilization; before long that civilization was to spread to other lands, too. Its heart was still religion. The institutional implications of this have already been touched upon; the Church was a great force of social regulation and government, whatever vicissitudes its central institution had suffered. But it was also the custodian of culture and the teacher of all, the vehicle and vessel of civilization itself.

THE FIRST EUROPEAN UNIVERSITIES

Since the thirteenth century the burden of recording, teaching and study so long borne by the monks had been shared by friars and, more important still, by a new institution, in which friars sometimes played a big part – the university. Bologna, Paris and Oxford were the first universities; by 1400 there were fifty-three more. They were new devices both for concentrating and directing intellectual activity and for education. One result was the revivifying of the training of the clergy. Already in the middle of the fourteenth century half the English bishops were graduates. But this was not the only reason why universities had been set up. The Emperor Frederick II founded the University of Naples to supply administrators for his south Italian kingdom; and when in 1264 Walter de Merton, an English bishop and royal servant, founded the first college at Oxford, among his purposes was that of providing future servants for the crown.

The universities' importance for the future of Europe, though, was greater than this, yet it could not have been foreseen and proved in one respect incalculable. Their existence

Students are portrayed attending a class at the Sorbonne in this 16th-century illustration. The Maison de la Sorbonne was founded in 1257 by Robert de Sorbon as a theological college, and soon became the central institution of the University of Paris.

Medieval universities

This map indicates medieval Europe's major universities and the dates when they were founded.

assured that when laymen came to be educated in substantial numbers, they, too, would be formed by an institution under the control of the Church and suffused with religion. Furthermore, universities would be a great uniting, cosmopolitan force. Their lectures were given in Latin, the language of the Church and the lingua franca of educated people until the twentieth century. Its former pre-eminence is still commemorated in the vestigial Latin of university ceremonies and the names of degrees.

THE CLASSICAL HERITAGE

Law, medicine, theology and philosophy all benefited from the new institution. Philosophy had all but disappeared into theology in the early medieval period. Only one important figure stands out, John Scotus Erigena, an Irish thinker and scholar of the ninth century. Then, as direct translation from Greek to Latin began in the twelfth century, European scholars could read for themselves works of classical philosophy. The texts became available from Islamic sources. As the works of Aristotle and Hippocrates were turned into Latin they were at first regarded with suspicion. This persisted until well into the thirteenth century, but gradually a search for reconciliation between the classical and Christian accounts of the world got under way and it became clear – above all because of the work of two Dominicans, Albertus Magnus and his pupil Thomas Aquinas – that reconciliation and synthesis were indeed possible. So it came about that the classical heritage was recaptured and rechristened in western Europe. Instead of providing a contrasting and critical approach to the theocentric culture of Christendom, it was incorporated within it. The classical world began to be seen as the forerunner of the Christian. For centuries men and women would turn for authority in matters intellectual to religion or to the classics. Of the latter it was Aristotle who enjoyed unique prestige. If it could not make him a saint, the Church at least treated him as a kind of prophet.

The immediate evidence was the remarkable systematic and rationalist achievement of medieval scholasticism, the name given to the intellectual effort to penetrate the meaning of Christian teaching. Its strength lay in its embracing sweep, displayed nowhere more brilliantly than in the *Summa Theologica* of Aquinas which has been judged, contrastingly, both its crowning achievement and a brittle synthesis. It strove to account for all phenomena. Its weakness lay in its unwillingness to address itself to observation and experiment. Christianity gave the medieval mind a powerful training in logical thinking, but only a few people, isolated and untypical, could dimly see the possibility of breaking through authority to a truly experimental method.

St Thomas Aquinas

The teacher and theologian Thomas Aquinas was born into a noble family in Roccasecca, near Aquino, in around 1225. At the age of six he was sent as an oblate to the well-known monastery of Monte Cassino. He went on to study at the University of Naples and was admitted, against his family's wishes, to the Dominican order of mendicants in 1243. Aquinas obtained his Master's degree in Paris in 1257, at which point he began to have his work published; the most notable product of his early years was Book I of *Summa contra gentiles*. It was in the Vatican in Italy, however, that Aquinas began work in 1266 on the treatise which would eventually make him famous: his *Summa Theologica*. This influential work was still incomplete when Aquinas died in 1274.

The aim of all of Aquinas' work, which is collectively known as "Thomism", was to adapt and reconcile Aristotle's writings to Christian thinking, using arguments based on reasoning as well as faith. *Summa Theologica* includes the "five ways", which claim to offer proof of God's existence. Although his writing caused divisions within the Church – the Dominicans supported his theories, while the Franciscans opposed them – in time, the philosophy of Thomas Aquinas was to become the official doctrine of the Catholic Church.

This 14th-century fresco, from the church of St Maria Novella in Florence, represents the triumph of St Thomas Aquinas.

ISLAM AND EUROPE

Nevertheless, within the Christian culture the first signs of liberation from the enclosed world of the early Middle Ages can be seen. Paradoxically, Christendom owed them to Islam, though for a long time there was deep suspicion and fear in the attitudes of ordinary people towards Arab civilization. There was also ignorance (before 1100, one medievalist has pointed out, there is no evidence that anyone in northern Europe had ever heard the name of Muhammad). Not until 1143 was a Latin translation of the Koran available. Easy and tolerant relationships between the Faithful and the Infidel (both sides thought in the same terms) were possible only in a few places. In Sicily and Spain, above all, the two cultures could meet. There the great work of translation of the twelfth and thirteenth centuries took place. The Emperor Frederick II was regarded with the deepest suspicion because, although he persecuted heretics, he was known to welcome Jews and Saracens to his court at Palermo. Toledo, the old Visigothic capital, was another especially important centre. In such places scribes copied and recopied the Latin texts of the bestsellers of the next six centuries. Euclid's works began a career of being copied, recopied and then printed, which may well have meant that in the end they surpassed the success of any book except the Bible – at least until the twentieth century – and became the foundation of mathematics teaching in western Europe until the nineteenth century. In such ways the Hellenistic world began again to irrigate the thought of the West.

During the reign of Alfonso X, the Iberian peninsula enjoyed a time of fruitful cooperation between the Christian, Muslim and Jewish cultures which coexisted there. From a manuscript entitled *The Book of Chess, Dice and Boards*, written by the king himself, this illustration represents a Christian and a Muslim playing chess.

NEW LINKS WITH ANTIQUITY

Roughly speaking, the Islamic transmission of antiquity began with astrology, astronomy and mathematics, subjects closely linked to one another. Ptolemy's astronomy reached the West by this route and was found a satisfactory basis for cosmology and navigation until the sixteenth century. Islamic cartography was in fact more advanced than European for most of the Middle Ages, and Arab sailors used the magnet for navigation well before their European counterparts (yet it was the latter who were to carry through the great oceanic discoveries). The astrolabe had been a Greek invention, but its use was spread in the West by Arab writings. When Chaucer wrote his treatise on its use, he took as his model an earlier Arab one. The arrival from Arab sources of a new numeration and the decimal point (both of Indian origin) was perhaps most important of all; the latter's usefulness in simplifying calculation can be easily tested by trying to write sums in Roman numerals.

Of the sciences of observation other than astronomy, the most important to come to the West from Islam was medicine. Besides providing access to the medical works of Aristotle, Galen, and Hippocrates (direct translation from the Greek was not begun until after 1100), Arabic sources and teachers also brought into European practice a huge body of therapeutic, anatomical and pharmacological knowledge built up by Arab physicians. The prestige of Arab learning and science made easier the acceptance of more subtly dangerous and subversive ideas; Arab philosophy and theology, too, began to be studied in the West. In the end, even European art seems to have been affected by Islam, for the invention of perspective, which was to transform painting, is said to have come from thirteenth-century Arab Spain. Europe offered little in exchange except the technology of gunnery.

To no other civilization did Europe owe so much in the Middle Ages as to Islam. For all their dramatic and exotic interest, the travels of a Marco Polo or the missionary wanderings of friars in Central Asia did little to change the West. The quantity of goods exchanged with other parts of the world was still tiny, even in 1500. Technically, Europe owed for certain to the Far East only the art of making silk (which had reached her from the Eastern Empire) and paper which, though made in China in the second century CE, took until the thirteenth to reach Europe and then did so again by way of Arab Spain. Nor did ideas reach Europe from nearer Asia, unless like Indian mathematics they had undergone refinement in the Arabic crucible. Given the permeability of Islamic culture, it seems less likely that this was because in some sense Islam insulated Europe from the Orient by imposing a barrier between them, than because China and India could not make their impact felt across such huge distances. They had hardly done so, after all, in pre-Christian antiquity, when communications had been no more difficult.

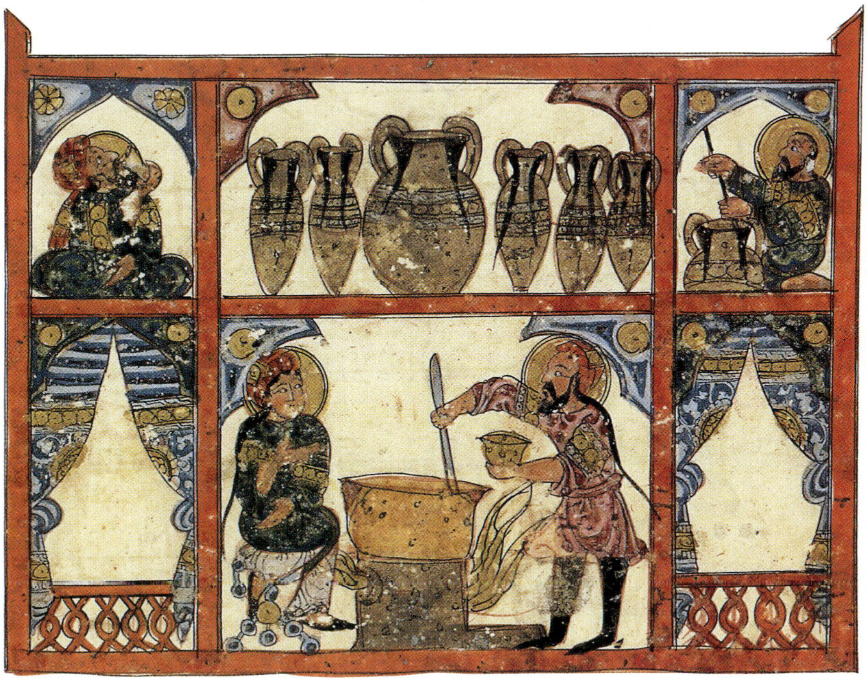

Great advances were made in the fields of astronomy and medicine in medieval times, largely thanks to knowledge that came from the Islamic world. This 13th-century illustration shows a scene in an Arab pharmacy.

DANTE AND ERASMUS

The reintegration of classical and Christian, though manifested in work like that of Aquinas, was an answer, ten centuries late, to Tertullian's jibing question about what Athens had to do with Jerusalem. In one of the supreme works of art of the Middle Ages – some would judge *the* supreme – the *Divine Comedy* of Dante, the importance of the re-attachment of the world of Christendom to its predecessor is already to be seen. Dante describes his journey through Hell, Purgatory and Paradise, the universe of Christian truth. Yet his guide is not a Christian, but a pagan, the classical poet Virgil. This role is much more than decorative; Virgil is an authoritative guide to truth, for before Christ, he foretold Him. The classical poet has become a prophet to stand beside those of the Old

Erasmus of Rotterdam

"Such practices of princes have long been zealously adopted by supreme pontiffs, cardinals, and bishops, and indeed, have almost been surpassed. Yet if any of these were to reflect on the meaning of his linen vestment, snow-white in colour to indicate a pure and spotless life; ... of his crozier, a reminder of his watchful care of the flock entrusted to his keeping ... . But as things are, they think they do well when they're looking after themselves, and responsibility for their sheep they either trust to Christ himself or delegate to their vicars and those they call brothers. They don't even remember that the name 'Bishop', which means 'overseer', indicates work, care, and concern. Yet when it comes to netting their revenues into the bag they can play the overseer well enough – no 'careless look-out' there.

"Similarly, the cardinals might consider how they are the successors of the apostles and are expected to follow the example of their predecessors, and that they are not the lords but the stewards of the spiritual riches for every penny of which they will soon have to render an exact account."

An extract from *Praise of Folly* (1511) by Desiderius Erasmus (1466–1536), translated by Betty Radice.

Testament. Though the notion of a link with antiquity had never quite disappeared (as attempts by enthusiastic chroniclers to link the Franks or the Britons to the descendants of the Trojans had shown) there is in Dante's attitude something marking an epoch. It is an acceptance of the classical world by Christendom, and this, for all the scholastic clutter of its surroundings, was decisive in making possible a change which has usually been seen as more radical: the great revival of humanistic letters of the fifteenth and sixteenth centuries.

One central figure of that moment of cultural history was Erasmus of Rotterdam, a sometime monk and later, as the foremost exponent of classical studies of his day, the correspondent of most of the great humanists. Yet he still saw his classics as the entrance to the supreme study of scripture and his most important book was an edition of the Greek New Testament. The effects of printing a good text of the Bible were, indeed, to be revolutionary, but Erasmus had no intention of overthrowing religious order, for all the vigour and wit with which he had mocked and teased puffed-up churchmen, and for all the provocation to independent thought which his books and letters provided. His roots lay in the piety of a fifteenth-century mystical movement in the Low Countries called the *devotio moderna*, not in pagan antiquity.

THE RENAISSANCE IN EUROPE

SOME OF THOSE WHO BEGAN to cultivate the study of classical authors, and to invoke explicitly pagan classical ideals, invented the notion of the Middle Ages to emphasize their sense of novelty. They in their turn were spoken of as the agents of a "rebirth" of a lost tradition, a "Renaissance" of classical antiquity. Yet they were formed in the culture which the great changes in Christian civilization from the twelfth century onwards had made possible. To speak of Renaissance may be helpful if we keep in mind the limitations of the context in which we use the word, but it falsifies history if we take it to imply a transformation of culture marking a radical break with medieval Christian civilization. The Renaissance is and was a useful myth, one of those ideas which help human beings to master their own bearings and therefore to act more effectively. Whatever the Renaissance may be, there is no clear line in European history which separates it from the Middle Ages – however we like to define them.

What can be noticed almost everywhere, though, is a change of emphasis. It shows especially in the relation of the age to the past. Artists of the thirteenth century, like those of the sixteenth, portrayed the great figures of antiquity in the garb of their own day. Alexander the Great at one time looks like a medieval king; later, Shakespeare's Caesar wears not a toga but doublet and hose. There is, that is to say, no real historical sense in either of these pictures of the past, no awareness of the immense differences between past and present human beings. Instead, history was seen at best as a school of examples. The difference between the two attitudes is that in the medieval view antiquity could also be scrutinized for the signs of a divine plan, evidence of whose existence once more triumphantly vindicated the teachings of the Church. This was St Augustine's legacy and what Dante accepted. But by 1500 something else was also being discerned in the past, equally unhistorical, but, some felt, more helpful to their age and predicament. Some saw a classical inspiration, possibly even pagan, distinct from the Christian, and a new attention to classical writings was one result.

RENAISSANCE ART AND LITERATURE

The idea of Renaissance is especially linked to innovation in art. Medieval Europe had seen much of this; it seems more vigorous and creative than any of the other great centres of

One of the most representative and best-known works of the Renaissance era is *The Birth of Venus*, by Sandro Botticelli (1444–1510). The model for the figure of Venus was Giulio de' Medici's beautiful mistress, Simonetta Cattaneo.

civilized tradition from the twelfth century onwards. In music, drama and poetry new forms and styles were created which move us still. By the fifteenth century, though, it is already clear that they can in no sense be confined to the service of God. Art is becoming autonomous. The eventual consummation of this change was the major aesthetic expression of the Renaissance, transcending by far its stylistic innovations, revolutionary though these were. It is the clearest sign that the Christian synthesis and the ecclesiastical monopoly of culture are breaking up. The slow divergence of classical and Christian mythology was one expression of it; others were the appearance of the Romance and Provençal love poetry (which owed much to Arabic influence), the deployment of the Gothic style in secular building such as the great guildhalls of the new cities, or the rise of a vernacular literature for educated laymen of which perhaps the supreme example is Chaucer's *Canterbury Tales*.

Workers at a medieval printing house, including the proofing corrector and, beside him, the printer.

Such changes are not easily dated, because acceptance did not always follow rapidly on innovation. In literature, there was a particularly severe physical restriction on what could be done because of a long-enduring shortage of texts. It was not until well into the sixteenth century that the first edition of Chaucer's complete works was printed and published. By then a revolution in thinking was undoubtedly under way, of which all the tendencies so far touched on form parts, but which was something much more than the sum of them and it owes almost everything to the coming of the printed book. Even a vernacular text such as the *Canterbury Tales* could not reach a wide public until printing made large numbers of copies easily available. When this happened, the impact of books was vastly magnified. This was true of all classes of book: poetry, history, philosophy, technology and, above all, the Bible itself. The effect was the most profound change in the diffusion of knowledge and ideas since the invention of writing; it was the greatest cultural revolution of these centuries.

THE PRINTING REVOLUTION

The new technique owed nothing to stimulus from China, where it was already practised in a different form, except very indirectly, through the availability of paper. From the fourteenth century, rags were used in Europe to make paper of good quality and this was one of the elements which contributed to the printing revolution. Others were the principle of printing itself (the impressing of images on textiles had been practised in twelfth-century Italy), the use of cast metal for typefaces instead of wood (already used to provide blocks for playing-cards, calendars and religious images), the availability of oil-based ink, and, above all, the use of movable metal type. It was the last invention which was crucial. Although the details are obscure, and experiments with wood letters were going on at the beginning of the fifteenth century in Haarlem, there seems to be no good reason not to credit it to the man whose name has traditionally been associated with it, Johannes Gutenberg, the diamond polisher of Mainz. In about 1450 he and his colleagues brought the elements of modern printing together, and in 1455 there appeared what is agreed to be the first true book printed in Europe, the Gutenberg Bible.

Gutenberg's own business career was by then a failure; something prophetic of a new age of commerce appears in the fact that he was probably under-capitalized. The accumulation of equipment and type was an expensive business and a colleague from whom he borrowed money took him to court for his debts. Judgment went against Gutenberg, who lost his press, so that the Bible, when it appeared, was not his property. (Happily, the story does not end there; Gutenberg was in the end ennobled by the archbishop of Mainz, in recognition of what he had done.) But he had launched a revolution. By 1500, it has been calculated, some thirty-five thousand separate editions of books – *incunabula*, as they were called – had been published. This probably means between fifteen and twenty million copies; there may well have been already at that date fewer copies of books in manuscript in the whole world. In the following century there were between a hundred and fifty and two hundred thousand separate editions and perhaps ten times as many copies printed. Such a quantitative change merges into one which is qualitative; the culture which resulted from the coming of printing with movable type was as different from any earlier one as it is from one which takes radio and television for granted. The modern age was the age of print.

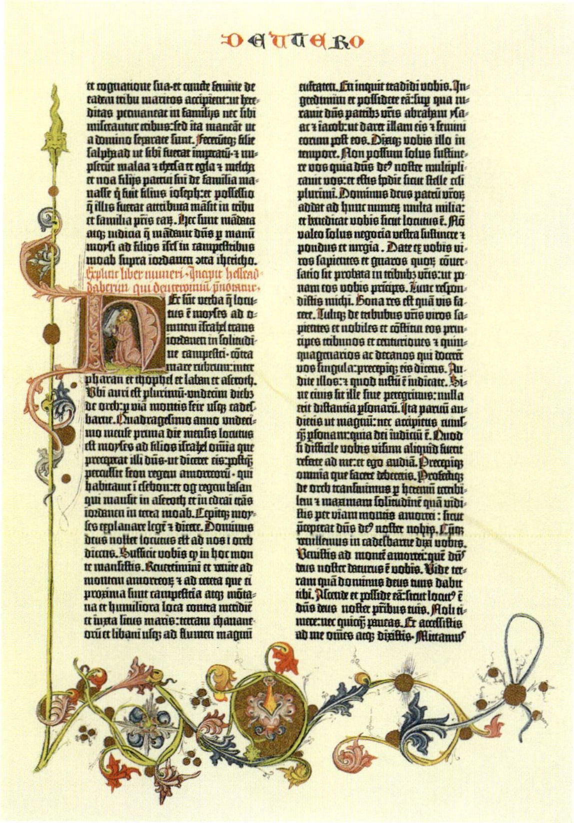

Only 300 copies of the first edition of the Gutenberg Bible were printed. Around 50 copies of the book survive today – a page from one of them is shown here.

THE DIFFUSION OF PRINTED BIBLES

It is interesting, but natural, that the first printed European book should have been the Bible, the sacred text at the heart of medieval civilization. Through the printing press, knowledge of it was to be diffused as never before and with incalculable results. In 1450 it would have been very unusual for a parish priest to own a Bible, or even to have easy access to one. A century later, it was becoming likely that he had one, and in 1650 it would have been remarkable if he had not. The first German Bible was printed in 1466; Italian and French translations followed before the end of the century, but the English had to wait for a New Testament printed in their language until 1526. Into the diffusion of sacred texts – of which the Bible was only the most important – pious laymen and churchmen alike poured resources for fifty to sixty years; presses were even set up in monastic houses. Meanwhile, grammars, histories, and, above all, the classical authors now edited by the humanists also appeared in increasing numbers. Another innovation from Italy was the introduction of simpler, clearer typefaces modelled upon the manuscript of Florentine scholars who were themselves copying Carolingian minuscule.

From the end of the 14th century, science entered an era of increased specialization. Technological advances, however, did not mean that religion became less omnipresent: the great clock being inaugurated in this 14th-century manuscript illustration is crowned with a crucifix.

The impact could not be contained. The domination of the European consciousness by printed media would be the outcome. With some prescience the pope suggested to bishops in 1501 that the control of printing might be the key to preserving the purity of the faith. But more was involved than any specific threat to doctrine, important as that might be. The nature of the book itself began to change. Once a rare work of art, whose mysterious knowledge was accessible only to a few, it became a tool and artifact for the many. Print was to provide new channels of communication for governments and a new medium for artists (the diffusion of pictorial and architectural style in the sixteenth century was much more rapid and widespread than ever before because of the growing availability of the engraved print) and would give a new impetus to the diffusion of technology. A huge demand for literacy and therefore education would be stimulated by it. No single change marks so clearly the ending of one era and the beginning of another.

A DAWNING MODERNITY

It is very hard to say exactly how such changes affected Europe's role in the coming era of world history. By 1500 there was certainly much to give confidence to the few Europeans who were likely to think at all about these things. The roots of their civilization lay in a religion which taught them they were a people voyaging in time, their eyes on a future made a little more comprehensible and perhaps a little less frightening by contemplation of past perils navigated and awareness of a common goal. As a result Europe was to be the first civilization aware of time not as endless (though perhaps cyclical) pressure, but as continuing change in a certain direction, as progress. The chosen people of the Bible, after all, were going somewhere; they were not simply a people to whom inexplicable things happened which had to be passively endured. From the simple acceptance of change was, before long, to spring the will to live in change – which was to be the peculiarity of modern human beings. Secularized and far away from their origins, such ideas could be very important; the advance of science soon provided an example. In another sense, too, the Christian heritage was decisive for, after the fall of Byzantium, Europeans believed that they alone possessed it (or in effect alone, for there was little sense among ordinary folk of what Slav, Nestorian or Coptic Christianity might be). It was an encouraging idea for those who stood at the threshold of centuries of unfolding power, discovery and conquest. Even with the Ottomans to face, Europe in 1500 was no longer just the beleaguered fortress of the Dark Ages, but a stronghold from which men were beginning to sally forth in counter-attack. Jerusalem had been abandoned to the infidel, Byzantium had fallen. Where should be the new centre of the world?

The men of the Dark Ages who had somehow persevered in adversity and had built a Christian world from the debris of the past and the gifts of the barbarians had thus wrought infinitely more than they could have known. Yet such implications required time for their development; in 1500 there was still little to show that the future belonged to the Europeans. Such contacts as they had with other peoples by no means demonstrated the clear superiority of their own way. Portuguese in West Africa might manipulate black people to their own ends and relieve them of their gold dust and slaves, but in Persia or India they stood in the presence of great empires whose spectacle often dazzled them. The Europeans of 1500 were thus, and in many other ways, far from modern. We cannot without an effort understand them, even when they speak Latin, for their Latin had overtones and associations we are bound to miss; it was not only the language of educated men (and a few women), but the language of religion.

THE OMNIPRESENCE OF RELIGION

In the half-light of a dawning modernity the weight of religion remains the best clue to the reality of Europe's first civilization. Religion was one of the most impressive reinforcements of the stability of a culture which has been considered in this book almost entirely from an important but fundamentally

Written in Galician-Portuguese, the "Songs of the Virgin Mary" are attributed to Alfonso X, who is thought to have based them on various manuscripts sent to him by Louis XI of France. Here, a musician is shown performing one of the songs, accompanied by a lady playing two idiophones (a type of castanet).

anachronistic perspective, that of change. Except in the shortest term, change was not something most Europeans would have been aware of in the fifteenth century. The deepest determinant of the lives of all of them was still the slow but ever-repeated passage of the seasons, a rhythm which set the pattern of work and leisure, poverty and prosperity, of the routines of home, workshop and study. English judges and university teachers still work to a year originally divided by the need to get in the harvest. On this rhythm were imposed those of religion itself. When the harvest was in, the Church blessed it and the calendar of the Christian year provided the more detailed timetable to which life was lived. Some of it was very old, even pre-Christian; it had been going on for centuries and could hardly be imagined otherwise. It even regulated many people's days, for every three hours the religious were called to worship and prayer in thousands of monasteries and convents by the bell of their house. When it could be heard outside the walls, laymen set the pattern of their day by it, too. Before there were striking clocks, only the bell of the parish church, cathedral or monastery supplemented the sun or the burning of a candle as a record of passing time, and it did so by announcing the hour of another act of worship.

CHRISTIANITY'S DUALISM

It is only in a very special, long perspective that we can rightly speak of centuries during which this went on and on as ones of "revolutionary" changes. Truly revolutionary as some changes were, even the most obvious of them – the growth of a town, an onset of plague, the displacement of one noble family by another, the building of a cathedral or the collapse of a castle – all took place in a remarkably unchanged setting. The shapes of the fields tilled by English peasants in 1500 were often still those visited by the men who wrote them down in Domesday Book, over four hundred years before, and when men went to visit the nuns of Lacock in order to wind up their house in the 1530s, they found, to their amazement, these aristocratic ladies still speaking among themselves the Norman-French commonly used in noble families three centuries earlier.

Such immense inertia must never be forgotten; it was made all the more impressive and powerful by the fleeting lives of most men and women of the Middle Ages. Only very deep in the humus of this society did there lie a future. Perhaps the key to that future's relationship with the past can be located in the fundamental Christian dualism of this life and the world to come, the earthly and the heavenly. This was to prove an irritant of great value, secularized in the end as a new critical instrument, the contrast of what is and what might be, of ideal and actual. In it, Christianity secreted an essence to be utilized against itself, for in the end it would make possible the independent critical stance, a complete break with the world Aquinas and Erasmus both knew. The idea of autonomous criticism would only be born very gradually, though; it can be traced in many individual adumbrations between 1300 and 1700, but they only go to show that, once again, sharp dividing lines between medieval and modern are matters of expository convenience, not of historical reality.

In this painting by Bonifacio de' Pitati (1487–1553) God as the "Eternal Father" appears to be protecting the city of Venice from the advance of a mass of threatening black storm clouds.

Time chart (625 BCE–1725 CE)

Siddhartha Gautama, who became known as the Buddha, or "enlightened one", lived from c.563 to c.483 BCE. This 6th-century bronze statue of him was made during the later Gupta period.

Bronze Buddha

The emergence of the Nox culture in northern Nigeria

600 BCE

500 BCE

551–478 BCE
Life of Confucius, Chinese philosopher

All China's feudal kingdoms were united under the Ch'in Dynasty in 221–206 BCE. These infantrymen are part of the terracotta army which guarded the tomb of the First Emperor Shih-Huang-ti.

Terracotta army figures

200 BCE

100 BCE

c.150 BCE
Buddhism introduced into China

c.110 BCE
The Silk Route is opened

220 CE
The end of the Later Han Dynasty

265–316 CE
Western Ch'in Dynasty

320–c.550 CE
The Gupta Dynasty in India

200 CE

300 CE

Teotihuacán civilization

The Maya civilization in Mesoamerica was at its height between 600 and 900 CE. This detail from the Madrid Codex shows a number of Maya gods, priests and nobles.

Detail from a Maya codex

618–907 CE
T'ang Dynasty

This illustration depicts the 7th-century T'ang emperor Yen Li-Pen. The T'ang Dynasty's capital in Shensi province was one of the world's most cosmopolitan cities.

Portrait of a T'ang emperor

711–1492 CE
The Spanish Reconquest

600 CE

700 CE

The Investiture Contest lasted from 1073 until 1122. This manuscript illustration suggests a solution: God gives St Peter's keys, the symbol of spiritual power, to the pope and a sword, the symbol of secular power, to the emperor.

Manuscript illustration

960–1126 CE
Sung Dynasty in China

1000–1300 CE
The first European universities are founded

1122 CE
Concordat of Worms

1000 CE

1100 CE

1095 CE
Pope Urban II advocates the First Crusade

This 15th-century sculpture, which is known as the "Sun Stone", represents the solar calendar of the Aztec people of Mexico. In the central circle is the face of the Sun God.

Aztec "Sun Stone"

1498 CE
Vasco da Gama reaches India

1400 CE

1500 CE

1368–1644 CE
Ming Dynasty in China

1453 CE
Constantinople falls to the Turks

1492 CE
Columbus discovers the New World

1526–1858 CE
Moghul Empire in India

447–438 BCE
The Parthenon is built in ancient Greece

315 BCE
Megasthenes visits the Maurya court

268–232 BCE
The reign of Asoka

400 BCE — 300 BCE

The decline of the Olmec civilization

326 BCE
Alexander the Great reaches the Indus

25 CE
Foundation of the Later Han Dynasty

0 — 100 CE

43 CE
The Romans conquer Britain

This stucco head of the Buddha dates from India's Kushana period (c.50–240 CE), during which representations of the Buddha became common and Hellenistic influences gave way to a more recognizably Indian style.

Kushana Buddha

400 CE — 500 CE

The arrival of Buddhism in Japan resulted in the introduction of the Chinese T'ang culture. The architecture of the Nara period (710–784) imitated T'ang models, as seen in the Buddha Hall of the mid-8th-century Todaiji shrine in Nara, which was largely rebuilt in 1709.

Todaiji shrine in Japan

909 CE
The end of the T'ang Dynasty in China

800 CE — 900 CE

794–1185 CE
The Heian period in Japan

The Hausa settle in the Daura Kingdom in northern Nigeria

Statue of Yorimoto

Yorimoto was the head of the Japanese Minamoto clan. In 1192 he was made lifelong, hereditary chief of all the armies, which signified the beginning of the shogunate era.

1206–1227 CE
Chingis Khan is Mongol emperor

1274 and 1281 CE
Mongol attempts to invade Japan

1309–1377 CE
The Avignon papacy

1338–1573 CE
The Ashikaga shogunate in Japan

1200 CE — 1300 CE

1185–1333 CE
Kamakura period of military feudalism in Japan

1197 CE
The Inca Empire is founded

The Maya Empire begins to decline

1337–1558 CE
The Hundred Years' War

The Taj Mahal – one of the world's most beautiful buildings – was constructed by the grief-stricken Shah Jahan as a memorial to his wife Mumtaz Mahal (meaning "Jewel of the Palace").

Taj Mahal, India

1600 CE — 1700 CE

1644–1912 CE
Ch'ing Dynasty in China

The bronzes made in Benin in North Africa were a "royal art": only the *oba* (king) could own them. This 16th-century Benin bronze bust portrays Idia, the mother of Oba Esigie. Her hair is covered by a beaded coral cap.

Benin bronze bust

VOLUME 5 *Chapters and contents*

Chapter 1

India

Chapter 2

Imperial China

Chapter 3

Japan

Chapter 4

Worlds Apart

Chapter 5

Europe: the First Revolution

Chapter 6

New Limits, New Horizons

SERIES CONTENTS

Volume 6

THE MAKING OF THE EUROPEAN AGE

Volume 7

THE AGE OF REVOLUTION

Volume 8

THE EUROPEAN EMPIRES

Volume 9

EMERGING POWERS

Volume 10

THE NEW GLOBAL ERA

INDEX

Page references to main text in roman, to box text in **bold** and to captions in *italic*.

A

B

C

D

E

ACKNOWLEDGMENTS

The publishers wish to thank the following for their kind permission to reproduce the illustrations in this book:

KEY

b bottom; c centre; t top; l left; r right
AAA: Ancient Art & Architecture Collection Ltd
AGE: A.G.E. Fotostock
AISA: Archivo Iconografico SA
AKG: AKG London
BAL: Bridgeman Art Library
BL: British Library, London
BM: British Museum, London
BN: Bibliothèque Nationale, Paris
BNM: Biblioteca Nacional, Madrid
ET: e.t. Archive
MAN: Museo Arqueológico Nacional, Madrid
NMI: National Museum of India, New Delhi
RHPL: Robert Harding Picture Library
RMN: Réunion des Musées Nationaux, Paris
SMPK: Staatliche Museen zu Berlin-Preussischer Kulturbesitz
V&A: By courtesy of the board of trustees of the Victoria & Albert Museum, London
WFA: Werner Forman Archive

Front cover: BAL / BN
3 FotoBox / Rafael Samano
7 Oronoz / Archivo Municipal, Burgos
8 Corbis / Charles and Janette Lenars
9 MAN
11 Oronoz
12 AISA
13 AAA / Ronald Sheridan
14 MAN
15 V&A
16 BAL / NMI
17 Angelo Hornak / NMI
18 Sam Fogg
19 WFA / Philip Goldman Collection
21 BAL / NMI
22 Museum für Indische Kunst, SMPK, Berlin / Jürgen Liepe (I10198)
23 Museum für Indische Kunst, SMPK, Berlin / Iris Papadollos (I10148)
24 AISA
25 BAL / BL (Add. 22703, f.52v)
26 V&A
27 BAL / V&A
28 V&A
29 V&A
31 Mary Evans Picture Library
33 ET / V&A
34 AISA
35 BL (J.2.2)
36 BN (Fr.2810, f.84)
37 Index / H.A. Rayner-TCL
38 Metropolitan Museum of Art, New York
39 Index / Freston-TPS
40 Museum für Völkerkunde, SMPK, Berlin
42 RHPL / FL Kennett
43 National Palace Museum, Taipei
44 Museum für Völkerkunde, SMPK, Berlin
45 CM Dixon
46 AISA / BM
47tl Index / C Milne-Masterfile
47b Museo Oriental, Valladolid
49 ET / Musée Guimet, Paris
50 AISA / Golestan Palace, Teheran
51 University of California, Berkeley Art Museum / Benjamin Blackwell
53 Museum of Fine Arts, Boston / Denman Waldo Ross Collection
54 AISA
55 BL (Or8210 / P2)
56 National Palace Museum, Taipei
58 BN (Fr.2810, f.54)
59 BN (Fr. 2810, f.69)
60 WFA
61 BAL / BL
62 ET / BN
64 Gutenberg-Museum, Mainz / Studio Popp
65t BAL / Fitzwilliam Museum, University of Cambridge
65b Herzog August Bibliothek, Wolfenbüttell (1.2.2. Geogr. 2°)
67 WFA / Christies's
68 Japanese Gallery, London
69 Japanese Gallery, London
70t AGE
70b Michael Holford
71 Index / Massonori
72 Index / PA Thompson
73 Tokyo National Museum
74 Museum of Imperial Collections, Sannomaru Shozokan / International Society for Education and Information, Tokyo
75 Tokyo Fuji Art Museum
76 AISA / Museo d'Arte Orientale, Eduardo Chissone, Genoa
77 Idetmitsu Museum of Arts, Tokyo
78 WFA / MH de Young Memorial Museum, San Francisco
79 WFA / Kuroda Collection, Japan
80 AISA / Museo dos Reis, Porto
81 AAA
83 BAL/ Private Collection
84 Giraudon / Musée Condé, Chantilly
85 BM
86 Index
87 Giraudon / Musée Historique des Tissus, Lyons
88 BN (Esp. 30, f.5v)
89 National Museum of Denmark / Kitt Wess
90 WFA / BM
91 BM
93 AISA
94 Museo de América, Madrid
95 Museo de América, Madrid
96 BN (Mex. 59–64, f.1)
97 Index / Museo Nácional de Antropología, Mexico
98 Museo de América, Madrid
99 AISA
100 AISA / BNM
101 RMN / Louvre, Paris
102 Biblioteca Centrale della Regione Siciliana, Palermo (Ms. I.E.8, c.8r)
103 BN (Latin 17716, f. 91)
104 AISA / Biblioteca Apostolica Vaticana, Rome
105 Thüringer Universitäts und Landesbibliotek, Jena (Ms. Boc. q6, f.79r)
106 BN (Ms. Latin 3893, f.1)
107 BL (Harl.5102, f.32)
108 Firo-Foto / R de Seynes
109 Museo de Navarra, Pamplona / Luis Prieto Saenz de Tejada
110 Scala / Santa Croce, Florence
111 Museo del Prado, Madrid
112 AKG / Erich Lessing
114 Lauros-Giraudon
115 Firo-Foto
117 AISA / Národní knihovna, Prague
118 Rheinisches Bildarchiv / Wallraf-Richartz-Museum, Cologne
120 Oronoz / Coleccion Duques de Alba, Madrid
121 ET / Honourable Society of Inner Temple
122 Scala / Biblioteca Nazionale Centrale, Florence
123 Index / BAL / BL
124 Public Record Office, London
125 BN (Fr.5054, f.71)
127 BN (Fr 87, f.117)
128 FotoBox / Rafael Sámano
130 BL (Add.27695, f.8)
131 ET
132 Index / Fabbri
134 AAA
135 AISA / Biblioteca Medicea-Laurenziana, Florence
137t The Bodleian Library, Oxford (Ms. Douce 208, f. 120v)
137b Oronoz / BNM
138 Oronoz / Museo de la Catedral, Avila
139 BL (Add.27695, f.8)
140 Bibliothèque Royale Albert 1e, Brussels (Ms 13076-77, f.24v)
141 AKG / Bibliothèque Royale Albert 1e, Brussels
142 AKG / Erich Lessing / Kunsthistorisches Museum, Vienna
143 AISA
144 S. Fiore-Firo Foto / Biblioteca Nazionale Universitaria, Turin
146 Scala / Galleria degli Uffizi, Florence
147 Rheinisches Landesmuseum, Bonn
148 Lauros-Giraudon / Galleria Regionale della Sicilia, Palermo
149 National Gallery, London
150 BN (Fr. 2829, f.39v)
151 BL (Egerton 1500, f.45v)
153 AISA
154 BL (Royal 16b vi, fol.404v)
155 Oronoz
156 AKG / Stadtmuseum, Sterzing
158 AAA
159 ET / Academia das Ciências, Lisbon
160 Giraudon / Museu Nacional de Arte Antiga, Lisbon (Inv. 1361)
161 Museo Naval, Madrid
162 BN (Pl.12)
163 Oronoz / Biblioteca Nazionale Marciana, Venice
164 Oronoz / Museo Naval, Madrid
165 RMN / Louvre, Paris / Arnaudet
166 ET / Museu Etnográfico da Sociedade de Geografia, Lisbon
167 ET / BN
169 Scala / S Maria Novella, Florence
170 Oronoz / Biblioteca del Monasterio de El Escorial
171 The Metropolitan Museum of Art, New York. Cora Timken Burnett Collection of Persian Miniatures and other Persian art objects, bequest of Cora Timken Burnett, 1956 / Schecter Lee
173 Scala / Galleria degli Uffizi, Florence
174 BN (Fr.1537, f.29v)
175 Staatsbibliotek zu Berlin – Preussischer Kulturbesitz, Abteilung, Jahr und Urheber (Inc. 1511 Bd 1, c.84r)
176 BN (Fr. 455, f. 9)
177 Oronoz / Biblioteca del Monasterio de El Escorial
179 Scala / Accademia, Venice

MAPS

Maps copyright © 1998 Debate pages 20, 92, 119, 136, 145
Maps copyright © 1998 Helicon/Debate pages 10, 30, 129, 152, 168

TEXT CREDITS

The publishers wish to thank the following for their kind permission to reproduce the translations and copyright material in this book. Every effort has been made to trace copyright owners, but if anyone has been omitted we apologize and will, if informed, make corrections in any future edition.

p.123 extract from *The Canterbury Tales* by Geoffrey Chaucer, edited by A.C. Spearing (Cambridge University Press 1995) copyright © 1966. Reproduced by permission of Cambridge University Press; p.172 extract from *Praise of Folly* by Desiderius Erasmus, translated by Betty Radice (Penguin Classics 1971, revised edition 1993) translation copyright © Betty Radice, 1971. Reproduced by permission of Penguin Books Ltd.